"What is the shape of Christian discipleship fitted to the watershed moment Earth now faces? It's radical, creative, and practical. But let diverse young peace and justice activists and visionaries instruct you. Their fresh biblical exegesis, interlaced with the experience of coming home to their bioregions and its waters of life, will inspire you from front to back in this remarkable volume. I wholly commend *Watershed Discipleship*."

—LARRY RASMUSSEN
Reinhold Niebuhr Professor Emeritus of Social Ethics, Union Theological Seminary;
Author, *Earth-Honoring Faith: Religious Ethics in a New Key*

"Myers brings a much-needed prophetic voice to the church with his call to watershed discipleship. The way he frames the issues—along with hopeful actions—and then engages an array of younger voices makes this anthology poignant. The book helps the church rediscover that the bioregional lens is critical to practicing the good news of the gospel. This material will be required reading in the collegiate courses I teach and with congregations seeking a new paradigm for living out their faith."

—LUKE GASCHO
Executive Director, Merry Lea Environmental Learning Center, Goshen College;
Leader, Mennonite Creation Care Network

"Read and emulate these fierce young farmers, organizers, artists, and engineers. They are challenging racist systems of colonial ecocide with empowered and humble relationships to land, water, creature, and neighbor. This book is important not because it offers some shred of hope for the future of the church but because it shows Christians who are relevant allies in the struggle for the planet."

—LAUREL DYKSTRA
Salal + Cedar Watershed Discipleship Community, Coast Salish Territory

"Ched Myers and the team of young authors he has assembled offer in this volume a Spirit-inspired, theologically grounded call to action that is filled with passionate hope. They summon readers into a spiritual and deeply reverent relationship with water and with other people through engagement with water. And they bid us draw upon the Spirit to transform seemingly intractable situations in which watersheds are abused and people are exploited in the process. These authors teach watershed discipleship as a path of resistance to ways of living that breed social and ecological disaster and illuminate a path toward transformation and renewal. They wed prescient critique with faith-rooted hope and practical, constructive proposals for change. The result is a remarkable paradigm for doing theology and theological ethics, a practical vision for bioregionally reoriented societies, and a prophetic witness to God's life-giving love for this splendid creation. People in the church, academy, and activist communities will be wise to drink from the wellspring of this extraordinary proposal for what it means to be people of faith in the early twenty-first century."

—CYNTHIA MOE-LOBEDA
Professor of Theological Ethics,
Pacific Lutheran Theological Seminary and the Graduate Theological Union

Watershed Discipleship

Watershed Discipleship

Reinhabiting Bioregional Faith and Practice

Edited by
CHED MYERS

Foreword by
Denise M. Nadeau

CASCADE *Books* • Eugene, Oregon

WATERSHED DISCIPLESHIP
Reinhabiting Bioregional Faith and Practice

Cascade Books
An Imprint of Wipf and Stock Publishers
199 W. 8th Ave., Suite 3
Eugene, OR 97401

www.wipfandstock.com

PAPERBACK ISBN: 978-1-4982-8076-1
HARDCOVER ISBN: 978-1-4982-8078-5
EBOOK ISBN: 978-1-4982-8077-8

Cataloguing-in-Publication data:

Names: Myers, Ched, ed.

Watershed discipleship : reinhabiting bioregional faith and practice. / Ched Myers, ed.

Eugene, OR: Cascade Publications, 2016 | Includes bibliographical references and index.

Identifiers: ISBN 978-1-4982-8076-1 (paperback) | ISBN 978-1-4982-8078-5 (hardcover) | ISBN 978-1-4982-8077-8 (ebook)

Subjects: LCSH: 1. Watershed management. | 2. Ecology Religious aspects Christianity. | 3. Political theology. | 4. Title.

Classification: BT 695.5 .W37 2016 | CALL NUMBER (ebook)

Manufactured in the U.S.A.   10/20/16

To those gone before, in gratitude:
Jim Corbett and Charity Hicks;

To those battling still, with respect:
Fred Vigil and Julie Tumamait;

To those coming up, in hope:
Willem, Isaac, Gabe, and their generation.

Prophecies from the Watershed Confederacy

Rose Marie Berger

In those days, when *the crown*
o'er the earth melted and humans
were thick upon the land
a sigh rose up and weeping
from rocks, rivers, hills and streams:
abandon your house,
abandon what you possess,
build a boat instead.
Bless your *curach* with pine boughs
and singing. Kiss the runnels and rills,
estuaries and arroyos who bear you up.
Be born again
into water and living spirit.
*

Then from the heavens
sky-brothers fought;
the stars in their orbits did battle.
Moon and water rose as one,
rode roughshod over culvert,
subaltern sewer, corrugated pipe.
The pretty petals of the rich fell
slick, opaque against the muddy bank.
The stream Kishon swept
those lordly enemies away;
that ancient river, Kishon.
And Ha-Shem kept his word to the fish.
To sleek, trinitarian salmon
who out-braved the Lords of profit,
Ha-Shem said, 'Swim swiftly now.
Come hide in my headwaters
where the brothers will give you
strength, where against your enemies

the mothers will make ceremony,
even if they die, as the Maidu
warrior-women died defending
the River of Sorrows.'
And so they ran   up ladders, ledges,
fords, dams. From pool to resting pool,
flashing, slashing tails, lithe and pinked
with power, a fish-rush headlong
up the ancient river, cold as
silver, flecked and cut with broken
stars. Empty-stomached Chum, Chinook,
Coho, blessed with hunger for Ha-Shem
and the Maidu-mother songs.

*

To the human remnant Ha-Shem said:
'If you cannot see the water,
you will not see the Water Walker.
If you misconceive bread,
you will not conceive water.
Seek life instead of riches.'

Notes

the crown / o'er the earth melted: Shakespeare, *Antony and Cleopatra.*

The stream Kishon . . .that ancient river, Kishon: Judges 5:21.

And Ha-Shem kept his word / to the fish: From Rashi's commentary on Judges 5.

abandon your house, abandon what you possess, build a boat instead: David Ferry. 1993. "from Gilgamesh: Tablet 11." In *Gilgamesh: A New Rendering in English Verse.* New York: Farrar, Straus and Giroux.

Maidu warrior-women / died defending the River of Sorrows': See Peter J. Hayes. 2005. *The Lower American River: Prehistory to Parkway.* Carmichael, CA: The American River Natural History Association.

Water Walker: See Mark 6:30–52 and Denise Nadeau's Foreword.

Seek life instead of riches: David Ferry, "from Gilgamesh: Tablet 11."

Contents

Foreword

Listening to Water Walkers

Denise M. Nadeau

"Water is spirit and a relative." This is a teaching I have learned from many Indigenous women over the years. There are several dimensions to it: water is alive; it is sacred; it is part of a holistic system, a greater interconnected whole; and we have obligations to water as a relative with whom we are in relationship. How can these teachings inform how we engage with Watershed Discipleship?

The difficulty for me has been to internalize what these teachings mean in order to change my practice. I am constantly struggling to free myself from Euro-Western objectifications of water. Water as a commodity, as a human right, as a resource—these conceptions all conjure up the notion of water's utility for humans. Underlying them is a deep disconnection from water. The crisis of water depletion, destruction, and pollution, as well as lack of access to clean and affordable water in much of the world, is a spiritual crisis as much as a political, social, and economic one. However, much of our organizing around water justice on Vancouver Island has centered humans in the struggle, rather than seeing the deep interconnections that define an embodied relationship with water. I have often found myself drained by and even resentful of activism for watershed protection that does not emanate from spiritual principles.

My journey to unlearn this objectification of water, and to experience water as a living relative, continues to be a long one. My colleague Alannah Young Leon first taught me that in her Anishinabe tradition women carry

[handwritten margin note:] Similar to Xns committed to environment bt still seeing earth as humans "garden" to be managed as "stewardship"

the responsibility to uphold the sanctity of water, to honor and protect it. I began to understand the scope of these responsibilities when I attended, with Alannah, the Three Fires *Midewiwin* initiation ceremonies in Bad River, Wisconsin in 2004. There I first observed a women's ceremony of honoring water which involved songs, stories, and sharing of water. And there I was introduced to the work of the Mother Earth Water Walkers.

In 2003, Josephine Mandamin and other Anishinabe women associated with the Three Fires Lodge began what was to become the annual Mother Earth Water Walk. The Anishinabe live around the Great Lakes, and the first ceremonial walk circled Lake Superior. Each subsequent year, Water Walkers have walked around the other Great Lakes, then some of their tributary rivers, and beyond. Drawing on Anishinabe teachings, the goal of the Walkers has been to change the popular perception of water from that of a resource to that of a sacred being that must be treated as such, and to strengthen actions to protect water for future generations. The Walkers begin and end each day with a water ceremony; the walk is then led by a woman carrying a copper vessel of water, usually accompanied by a man carrying an eagle staff. Water Walkers routinely cover distances from five hundred to more than one thousand kilometers.

In the past decade, the influence of Water Walkers has spread, informing many similar projects. Indigenous women all over Turtle Island have been drawing on their respective water teachings to inspire and inform diverse actions to protect water and watersheds:

- The Tar Sands Healing Walk in Northern Alberta, where oil extraction is polluting the Athabasca and Mackenzie River watersheds, has embodied a ceremonial call for what Asian Canadian Rita Wong calls "ethical water" (2013).

- Idle No More, a women-initiated Indigenous movement, arose out of the need to stop a Canadian federal omnibus bill that has removed environmental protections of most of our rivers and waterways.

- The anti-fracking Mi'kmaq women warriors of Elsipogtog credit Water Walkers for informing their activism.

These are just a few examples of how women are taking the lead in spiritually-grounded water activism. Across Turtle Island, women are using educational workshops, ceremonial actions, and social media to promote Indigenous water teachings. All nations and nationalities are welcome to participate or support these walks. Mother Earth Water Walk (http://www.

motherearthwaterwalk.com) and Water Walkers United (http://www.wa-terwalkersunited.com) are two expressions of this Indigenous grassroots activism.

A few years ago I invited the late Violet Caibaiosai, a Mother Earth Water Walker, to speak at an interfaith panel of women addressing the sacredness of water. Soon after she arrived in Vancouver, Violet and I went down to the ocean so she could acknowledge and honor the water in this traditional territory of the *Tsleil-Waututh* (Burrard), *XwMuthkwium* (Musqueam), and *Skwxuwu-7mesh* (Squamish) Nations. I learned from her how to offer tobacco to the water, and have maintained this practice since. I have learned that in order to bring the spiritual dimension into our relationship with water, one must practice that relationship by embodying reverence and reciprocity, the primary principles inherent in ceremony.

The Anishinabe way of life is centered on relationships, each of which carry responsibilities. The function of ceremony is to remind us about and to restore those relationships. This is why ceremony is critical to the work of protecting water and watersheds. If people feel a relational connection to the watershed in which they live, it is easier for them to act in an embodied way upon their responsibilities. Moreover, there is power in ritual and ceremony to effect change; one can draw on the energy of Spirit/spirits to transform seemingly intractable situations in which water and watersheds are being abused.

Another way I have learned to shift my relationship with water has been by articulating my relationship to specific watersheds. My French ancestors came to what is now called Quebec twelve generations ago, intermarrying with the Mi'gmaq on the *Gespeg* (Gaspé) peninsula but also colonizing their land. They drew maps that ignored watershed boundaries that had long been observed by people deeply connected to the life of the rivers and ocean. Cognizant of this history, I have worked to develop commitments to the *Gesgapegiag* (Cascapedia) River and Port Daniel River watersheds in *Gespe'gawa'gi*, the traditional territory of the seventh district of the Mi'qmaq Nation.

Besides these ancestral responsibilities I am slowly learning how to be a relative and visitor in the lands and waterways of the territory of the K'omoks Nation on Vancouver Island, where I live between the Trent and Puntledge River watersheds. By identifying myself in terms of the traditional territory and watersheds in which I reside, I encourage people to cultivate a "watershed mind," as Peter Marshall puts it. It requires a cultural shift to acknowledge how intimately we are connected to water, both in our bodies (which are 75 percent water) and as bodies in place. Like our ancestors, we live in relationship to specific bodies of water for sustenance. My colleagues Dorothy Christian, from the Secwepemc (Splat'sin)/Syilx Nations, and Rita Wong challenge us to reimagine ourselves "past our skin" as a living part of a watershed, with which we are both interdependent and dependent (2013: 245).

Water, of which there is only a finite amount in the world, is the ultimate connector. It joins us to our ancestors and to the generations ahead, as Mi'kmaq anti-fracking activist Suzanne Patles has asserted (2014). It connects us to specific places, people and creatures we have not seen, life that is far away from us and life that came long before us. The work of protecting watersheds is thus not just for human beings; it is for all Creation, and for the past and the future.

I have learned from Alannah Young Leon that it is important to use song in honoring water. While many Indigenous nations have songs to honor water bodies with which they have a relationship, these are often private. Anishinabe activist Doreen Day has created a *Nibi* (water) song that is available on line, and she encourages all to sing it (song and story at http://www.motherearthwaterwalk.com/?attachment_id=2244). In workshops on water that Alannah and I facilitate we teach this song to model addressing water as spirit and relative. We invite all to say the words, "We thank you, we love you and we respect you" whenever they engage with the waterway nearest to them.

Nuu-chah-nulth activist Chaw-win-nis, at a recent workshop for Indigenous youth, reminded us that listening involves more than having an open mind and an open heart. In listening we take on the responsibility of being a witness and, in Coastal traditions, the call to act in response to what we have heard. I asked Musqueam elder Larry Grant to explain the meaning of listening in his Coast Salish language. He told me that the word xʷəy̓əne:mət ɬeʔ (in halq̓eméylem) is "Listen!" I looked up the word in my Mi'gmaq dictionary and found that *eulistuatl* means "listen to someone carefully."

What does it mean for Christians to listen to Indigenous women who are walking this walk? We are being invited to integrate respectfully Indigenous ways of knowing into our lives, and to how we relate to water and watersheds. Drawing from our Christian tradition, we can think in terms of the language of consecration, and draw from the deep wells of the

Spirit within to guide and nourish us on this journey. The concept of watershed discipleship overcomes the artificial separation of humans from the natural world, grounding the work in deep commitment to all of creation. In listening to the voices of Indigenous women we engage in an interfaith relationship where we share a common conviction concerning the unity of creation. We are as well acknowledging the fact we are visitors, settlers on occupied but unceded territories, invited to follow the protocols of the nations in whose territories we live and work.

I am honored to contribute to this collection on watershed discipleship, a call to action by young writers who approach watershed reinhabitation from the dimension of the sacred. Ched Myers and I first met in Hawai'i twenty-five years ago at a conference of faith-rooted activists joining to support Indigenous self-determination movements throughout Oceania. Our respective journeys have had many parallels since, resonating again strongly in this project. I invite us all, as we walk our walk, to *listen* to the Indigenous voices in the communities in which we are doing our work. We can learn the original names of the waters in our regions, raise awareness about water walks in our areas, or even become a Water Walker, and educate about the sacredness of water. Let us involve youth in all our efforts, and practice both physical and spiritual engagement with water, approaching the water bodies in our bioregions with humility, reverence and respect.

Whenever we observe ceremony with water—from thanking the first drink of water we take in the day to acknowledging it in whatever ritual way is appropriate for our community—we affirm our interconnection, our oneness, with water and the watersheds of which we are part. We are also thereby joining as allies to support what Cherokee scholar Jeff Corntassel calls "everyday acts of Indigenous resurgence," living out our relational, place-based responsibilities to land and waterways (2012).

I close with excerpts from Rita Wong's poem "Declaration of Intent," which I offer as a prayerful invocation to this anthology:

> Let the colonial borders be seen for the pretensions they are
> i hereby honour what the flow of water teaches us
> the beauty of enough, the path of peace to be savoured
> before the extremes of drought and flood overwhelm the careless
>
> . . .
>
> I hereby invoke fluid wisdom to guide us through the muck
> I will apprentice myself to creeks and tributaries, groundwater and glaciers
> Listen for the salty pulse within, the blood that recognizes marine ancestry

In its chemical composition and intuitive pull
I will learn through immersion, flotation and transformation
As water expands and contracts, I will fit myself into its ever changing
    dimensions
Molecular and spectacular water will return what we give it, be that
Arrogance and poison, reverence and light, ambivalence and respect
Let our societies be revived as watersheds (2015:14).

References

Christian, Dorothy and Rita Wong. 2013. "Untapping Watershed Mind." Pp. 232–253 in *Thinking with Water*, edited Cecilia Chen, Janine MacLeod and Astrida Neimanis. Montreal: McGill-Queen's University Press.

Corntassel, Jeff. 2012. "Re-envisioning Resurgence: Indigenous Pathways to Decolonization and Sustainable Self-Determination." *Decolonization: Indigeneity, Education and Society* 1(1):86–101.

Patles, Suzanne. 2014. "Talk given at a strategy session co-sponsored by First Nations Studies and the English Department at Simon Fraser University (downtown Harbour Centre campus)," January 24th, 2014; available at https://www.youtube.com/watch?v=lkN1Yz88VDU.

Wong, Rita. 2015. *undercurrent*. Gibsons, B.C.: Nightwood Editions.

———. 2013. "Ethical Waters: Reflections on the Healing Walk in the Tar Sands." *Feminist Review* (103):133–139.

Acknowledgments

THIS ANTHOLOGY IS THE culmination to date of my long journey into a bioregionalist Christian faith and practice (see my Introduction for some of the autobiographical back story). It is, more specifically, the fruit of the last five years of reflection, organizing, and education around the theme of "Watershed Discipleship." I introduced this phrase (inspired by the work of Gary Snyder and Brock Dolman) in 2010 at one of our Bartimaeus Institutes (http://www.bcm-net.org/BI) as part of my ongoing search for how to promote bioregionalism in North American churches. Since then we have been intensively workshopping and developing this theme in colloquia, lectures, trainings, networking, and conversation around North America.

This book is the product of a Bartimaeus Cooperative Ministries (BCM) mentoring project during 2014–15, in which I worked with the contributors on theological reflection and writing. Most of the chapters in this collection were presented by their authors in draft form at the BCM Festival of Radical Discipleship in Oak View in February 2014, after which they underwent intensive review. While the editing process with these young, mostly unpublished writers has often been challenging, their ideas and perspectives speak strongly for themselves. We look forward to continuing our collaboration with these colleagues in the work of building capacity for the Watershed Discipleship movement in the coming years.

This project was made possible with support from a Research Grant from the Louisville Institute (http://www.louisville-institute.org/) and a Mentoring for Young Adults Grant from the Forum for Theological Exploration (http://fteleaders.org/); we thank both organizations. Parts of this collection are being translated into Spanish, and will be published and distributed among Spanish speaking communities engaging in this conversation. This aspect of the project is made possible by a grant from the Bob

H. Johnson Family Foundation of Tulsa, Oklahoma, and we thank Steven Johnson for his facilitation of this support.

I am grateful to longtime friends and collaborators Denise Nadeau and Rose Marie Berger for their respective original contributions that open this volume, lending it the "spiritual covering" of seasoned elders. For more than a month, my partner in life and work Elaine Enns lent her considerable copyediting skills and attention to detail to help prepare the final manuscript for publication; without her help I would have been shipwrecked. BCM office manager Chris Wight also gave timely and cheerful technical support. Thanks to Rodney Clapp and Ian Creeger for shepherding this manuscript through the Wipf & Stock system, and to Adella Barret for doing most of the indexing. Above all, I am grateful to my younger colleagues for their contributions to this volume, valuable ideas which broaden and deepen our understanding of Watershed Discipleship, and most importantly, which they each strive to incarnate in the varying contexts of their respective work.

A word about those to whom this collection is dedicated. Jim Corbett is truly the spiritual grandfather of this project; Quaker rancher, borderlands human rights pioneer, and goatwalker, he demonstrated how Settlers might caretake and re-covenant with beloved land, and I am honored to have known him. Water warrior Charity Hicks died too soon, but is still the spiritual grandmother of the Detroit water struggle, which you will read about in Chapters Four and Five. *¡Presente!* Fred Vigil is a veteran water rights activist in northern New Mexico who first taught me the political, social and spiritual meaning of watersheds; I have deep respect for him as a keeper of intergenerational wisdom. So too Julie Tumamait, a local Chumash elder who consistently extends hospitality and instruction to those of us who live in the traditional territory of her people here in the Ventura River Watershed. And Willem, Isaac, and Gabriel are the firstborn of three different young families (including two contributors) to whom we are close; they were each birthed during the season in which this book was being curated. We name them on behalf of their generation, which will carry on this movement—*if* we carry out our responsibilities as Watershed Disciples faithfully enough to secure their future.

Contributors

(in order of their appearance in this volume)

Rose Marie Berger, a Catholic poet and peace activist, is a senior associate editor, columnist, and poetry editor for *Sojourners* magazine. Author of *Who Killed Donte Manning?: The Story of an American Neighborhood*, she frequently speaks, leads retreats, and preaches in churches, seminaries, and on college campuses. Rose is a native of the American River watershed in northern California, and for 30 years has lived in the Anacostia River watershed in Columbia Heights, Washington, D.C.

Denise M. Nadeau is a theologian, somatic psychotherapist, spiritual companion, and educator of mixed European heritage. She grew up in Quebec and still spends time in Gespe'gawa'gi and Montreal, where she is an Affiliate Assistant Professor in Religion at Concordia University. She resides in the traditional homelands of the K'omoks Nation on Vancouver Island, where she teaches and writes about Indigenous-Settler relations, decolonization of the body, and the deconstruction of whiteness and colonialism in Christianity.

Ched Myers is an activist theologian who has worked in social change movements for forty years. With a Masters degree in New Testament Studies, he is a popular educator who animates Scripture and issues of faith-based peace and justice. He has published over 100 articles and more than a half-dozen books, most of which can be found at www.ChedMyers.org. He and his partner Elaine Enns, who helped edit this volume, codirect Bartimaeus Cooperative Ministries (www.bcm-net.org) in the Ventura River watershed of southern California.

Contributors

Katerina Friesen lives in Elkhart, Indiana, part of the St. Joseph River watershed, where she recently completed a M.Div. degree in theology and peace studies at Anabaptist Mennonite Biblical Seminary. Prior to this she worked as a community garden organizer in Oxnard, California and was a member of the Abundant Table farm community. Her interests and writing revolve around climate change, agriculture, and indigenous justice in relation to the kindom of God.

David Pritchett grew up running barefoot around the foothills of Mt. Kenya, and now lives in Portland, Oregon, where he is a collaborator with the Wilderness Way Community and EcoFaith Recovery. As an associate medical director for a detoxification center and as a permaculture teacher and designer, he works for the health and recovery of both people and landscapes.

Jonathan McRay is a farmer, permaculture designer, writer, and community peacebuilder who works with with Vine and Fig, a neighborhood collective that cultivates works of mercy, social justice, and ecological sustainability as the foundation for a nonviolent way of life. He has an M.A. in Conflict Transformation with emphasis in restorative justice, community development, agroecology, and rural watershed restoration. He has worked in Palestine-Israel and Mozambique, done action research on rural watershed restoration, and currently lives in the Shenandoah Valley.

Lydia Wylie-Kellermann is a mother, writer, and activist in the Detroit River Watershed. She co-edits wwww.radicaldiscipleship.net and *On the Edge*, a Detroit Catholic Worker Paper, and works for Word and World: A People's School, which endeavors to bridge the gap between seminary, sanctuary, street, and soil (http://www.wordandworld.org/).

Erinn Fahey focuses on hydrologic and hydraulic analysis and design and water resources at a civil engineering consulting firm. Rooted in southwest Detroit, she is a part of a neighborhood that values community, urban agriculture, local economy, and spiritual reflection. She straddles the worlds of activism and engineering and strives to integrate them.

Sarah Thompson is a scholar-activist from Elkhart, Indiana (Potawatomi traditional lands) whose ancestral streams of African-American intellectuals and European-American Mennonite preachers manifest in a passion for justice. A Fulbright scholar with a B.A. from Spelman College in

Comparative Women's and International Studies, she completed an M.Div. from Anabaptist Mennonite Biblical Seminary in 2011, and currently serves as Executive Director of Christian Peacemaker Teams (http://www.cpt.org/).

Matthew Humphrey works to integrate the life of faith with practices of caring for Creation with his partner Roxy and their three children. Since earning his M.A. in Theological Studies from Regent College in Vancouver, B.C., he has worked with A Rocha Canada, a Christian environmental stewardship organization (www.arocha.ca), as an educator and practitioner. Alongside overseeing experiments in sustainable agriculture, Humphrey teaches geography and environmental theology through partnerships with churches, colleges, and community groups.

Sarah Nolan is co-founder and Director of Programs and Community Partnerships at The Abundant Table, and works closely with the Episcopal Church locally and nationally to grow faith, food and farming initiatives. She is also a worker/owner of the South Central Farmers' Cooperative and runs their Community Supported Agriculture Program, which provides organic vegetables to families throughout Los Angeles County. Sarah recently completed an M.A. in ministry, leadership, and service at Claremont School of Theology.

Erynn Smith was born, raised, and still works in the Calleguas Creek Watershed in Ventura County, CA. After earning her bilingual teaching credential for Spanish from California State University Channel Islands, she joined The Abundant Table as an intern. Over the past six years she has developed their farm education program, which she now directs, providing agricultural and nutrition education to youth in classrooms and on the farm, to promote growing healthy food, farm systems, and community.

Reyna Ortega is from the Districto Federal in Mexico; her paternal grandfather cultivated maize and watermelon before her family moved to the capital city. Reyna immigrated to the United States when she was fourteen, where she found work as a harvester in celery and strawberry fields. A mother of four young girls, she joined The Abundant Table in 2011, and now manages their five-acre farm with her partner Guadalupe. She is a trained lay preacher and an outspoken advocate for farmworker rights and dignity.

Sasha Adkins is an environmental health researcher with strong interests in ecological justice and endocrine disruption. Sasha holds a Master's degree in international public health and is a doctoral candidate in environmental studies. Sasha has lived on a sailboat, in an eco-village, and in over forty other places, and is currently based in Providence, RI.

Victoria Machado is a third generation South Floridian. When starting her Masters program in Religion and Nature at the University of Florida, she became a live-in community member with the Gainesville Catholic Worker. She is currently active in the Eco-Stewards Program, a grassroots community that shapes young adult leaders through place-based experiences that connect faith and the environment, and works on water issues in Florida.

Tevyn East integrates her artistic gifts with faith-led resistance through her production company Holy Fool Arts. She produced and performed a one-woman show entitled "Leaps and Bounds" that critiques the growth-oriented economy and its impact on the earth, and which toured to more than 150 communities around North America and was made into a film in 2011. She is the Director of the Carnival de Resistance, a traveling carnival, village, and school that focuses on ecological justice and radical theology.

Jay Beck is a percussionist, vocalist, drum-maker, and educator who has been performing, teaching, touring and recording professionally for many years, including as a member of the band Psalters. He seeks to aid resistance movements and develop reconciliation through studying the art forms and spirituality of oppressed nomadic and indigenous communities. He is a core organizer for the Carnival de Resistance and collaborates with his partner Tevyn East in Philadelphia to present theater that emphasizes the voice of the divine inside creation.

Introduction

A Critical, Contextual, and Constructive Approach to Ecological Theology and Practice

CHED MYERS

THIS ANTHOLOGY INTRODUCES AND explores Watershed Discipleship, a new (and ancient) paradigm for ecological theology and practice that I and my fellow contributors believe is key to addressing the new (and ancient) crisis confronting human civilization. This collection seeks to accomplish two objectives. First, it hopes to engage the current field of ecological theology with an approach we believe is more radical in its critique of prevailing paradigms; more contextual in its praxis; and more constructive in its alternative proposals. Second, it introduces to the conversation more than a dozen colleagues under the age of forty, representing the first generation to have grown up fully under the shadow of climate crisis. They are faith-rooted activists, educators, and practitioners who do theology with appropriate urgency and passion, though none are professional theologians, and their voices deserve our attention.

These essays reflect a cross-section of a small but growing movement of faith and practice across North America that is embracing Watershed

Discipleship as an expression of both resistance and renewal. This framing discourse is an intentional "triple entendre":

1. It recognizes that we are in a *watershed historical moment of crisis*, which demands that environmental and social justice and sustainability be integral to everything we do as Christians and citizen inhabitants of specific places;

2. It acknowledges the bioregional locus of an incarnational following of Jesus: our individual discipleship and the life and witness of the local church take place inescapably *in a watershed context*;

3. And it implies that we need to be *disciples of our watersheds*.[1]

This Introduction explores each of these talking points briefly, since they represent the basic elements of our approach in this volume, offering bibliographic notes for those wishing to go deeper into any of the many related issues.[2]

I. Watershed Moment: The Endgame of the Anthropocene

It is impossible to overstate the depth and breadth of the social and ecological crises that have been stalking human civilization for centuries, and now arrived in the Anthropocene epoch.[3] These interlocking catastrophes

1. In workshopping these talking points, Todd Wynward (2015) pointed out the third entendre: that New Testament discipleship is a journey of learning from, following, and coming to trust the "rabbi"—which in this case is the "Book of Creation." St. Bonaventure was one of many throughout church history who spoke of nature as a kind of Scripture: "Throughout the entire creation, the wisdom of God shines forth. . . .Truly, whoever reads this book will find life and will draw salvation" (cited at www.bookofnature.org/library/ngb.html).

2. Parts of this Introduction (and of the Afterword to this volume) were originally presented in a paper to the Mennonite Scholars and Friends Forum of the American Academy of Religion on Nov. 23, 2013 in Baltimore, Maryland and later published in Myers (2014a).

3. This term, popularized by Nobel Prize-winning atmospheric chemist Paul Crutzen, has become shorthand for humans' over-determining impact on nature. For an overview and introductory videos, see www.anthropocene.info/en/home; for "maps" of this new reality see http://thebreakthrough.org/index.php/programs/conservation-and-development/mapping-the-anthropocene. Throughout this essay I use the term "crisis" not only in its conventional contemporary meaning, but also in the New Testament sense: the Greek *krisis* connotes a crucial decision, most often connoting apocalyptic "judgement" in which human beings reap the consequences of bad behavior (e.g. Rev

that are backing us into an historical cul-de-sac include on the social side: intensifying economic disparity, wealth concentration, and racialized poverty; entrenched racial, ethnic, and religious balkanization and enmity; and the globalization of militarized politics. On the environmental side they include: climate catastrophe and carbon addiction; habitat destruction and species extinction; and resource exhaustion (so-called "peak everything"). Scientific assessments of this matrix of violence, injustice, and unsustainability have converged in a grim consensus that the human project is well down the road of what Derrick Jensen calls an "Endgame" (2006)—whether or not those of us insulated by race, class, or national or geographic privilege feel it yet existentially. As Worldwatch Institute's Ed Ayres poignantly put it at the turn of the millennium, we face an historical ultimatum that represents "God's Last Offer" (1999).

Elements of this sobering diagnosis are finally dawning on world leaders, from popes to presidents, particularly in the wake of the recent 2015 United Nations climate summit in Paris. I will not, therefore, belabor the problem statement here; longtime environmental analyst James Speth's terse summary will suffice:

> How serious is the threat to the environment? Here is one measure of the problem: all we have to do to destroy the planet's climate and biota and leave a ruined world to our children and grandchildren is to keep doing exactly what we are doing today, with no growth in the human population or the world economy. Just continue to release greenhouse gases at the current rates, just continue to impoverish ecosystems and release toxic chemicals at current rates, and the world in the latter part of the century won't be fit to live in (2008:x).

This dark horizon has generated a spectrum of cultural moods, from pessimistic brooding to slow-burn despair, and from narcissistic resignation to determined technocratic optimism. In many activist circles, assessments of dwindling prospects are taking on a decidedly apocalyptic tenor.

Under the shadow of an earlier (and equally foreboding) apocalyptic moment (the 1962 Cuban Missile Crisis), the incisive contemplative Thomas Merton reflected on the "disorder," "absurdity," and "emptiness of 'the end.'" "Christian hope," he asserted, "*begins* where every other hope stands frozen stiff before the face of the Unspeakable" (1966:5). Merton's dictum poses an evangelical challenge to our churches in this hour. But whether or

---

18:10).

3

not he is right depends upon whether we Christians choose *discipleship* or *denial* (see Myers 1994:3ff). Our faith and practice from now on will unfold either in *light* of or in *spite* of these social and ecological crises. This anthology explores the former trajectory, in hopes of dissuading co-religionists from perpetuating the latter one.

Over the last quarter century, "creation care" and "earth spirituality" movements have gained widespread traction among Christians. Environmental stewardship is arguably the fastest growing expression of public concern in North American churches, initially among mainstream Catholics and Protestants but increasingly among evangelicals as well.[4] But while the creation care trend has been necessary to help recalibrate our faith and practice; it is not yet sufficient in its responses to the creation crisis we now face everywhere. On one hand, prescriptive suggestions commended to congregations are too often merely cosmetic. "Going green" by recycling or light bulb changes—but avoiding political controversies such as Tar Sands extraction or mountain top removal mining—does not lead toward the deep paradigm shifts with which churches need to wrestle.[5] On the other hand, environmental theologies tend still to be either overly abstract, insufficiently radical in diagnosis, and/or not practically constructive.[6] The church will embody a moral equivalent to these times neither by advocating for minor reforms nor by offering a new rhetorical lexicon. Rather, it needs to promote pastoral and theological disciplines that are on the one

---

4. The contemporary literature on ecotheology is too voluminous to cite, but see comprehensive bibliographies online at http://fore.research.yale.edu/religion/christian-ity/bibliography/ and http://www.cep.unt.edu/ecotheo.html. A proliferation of websites reflect these ecclesial efforts, including www.webofcreation.org; http://earthministry.org; www.creationcare.org; www.blessedearth.org, and that of my own denomination, http://www.mennocreationcare.org/. A good recent evangelical ecotheology primer is Brunner et al. (2014). The inevitable counter-reaction is also underway among conservatives who are either unashamed climate deniers (e.g. http://standupforthetruth.com/hot-topics/environmental-movement/) or duplicitous "greenwashers" (e.g. www.cornwallalliance.org).

5. For example, a day of briefings and "dialogue" for a hundred faith leaders from across the political and religious spectrum at the White House and co-hosted by the Environmental Protection Agency on February 25, 2014, focused on pragmatic initiatives only; the controversial Keystone XL pipeline project was never broached (see http://clbsj.org/?page_id=8).

6. There are of course notable exceptions, including Northcott (2013), Rasmussen (2012), Jenkins (2008), Gebara (1999), McKibben (1994), McFague (1993), Reuther (1992), and the earliest of all, written originally in 1971 by the venerable (and still battling) John Cobb (1995).

hand *radical,* diagnosing the root pathologies within and around us while also drawing deeply on the roots of our faith traditions, yet which on the other hand are *practical,* empowering deliberate steps toward significant change. Our task as Christians is nothing less than working to help turn our history around—which is, as it happens, the meaning of the biblical discourse of repentance.[7]

To do this we must critically examine and overturn core paradigms and presumptions that have nurtured the crisis of the Anthropocene. In very broad brush strokes, I contend that most symptoms of our Endgame can be traced to three interrelated philosophical errors, which slowly but surely prevailed in Western Christendom, and eventually underwrote a half-millennium of increasingly global domination:

1. Since the time of Constantine, a *functional docetism* has numbed Christians to the escalating horrors of both social and ecological violence, because spiritual or doctrinal matters always trump terrestrial or somatic ones. If it is assumed that salvation occurs outside of or beyond creation, it will be pillaged accordingly.

2. Since the late medieval Doctrine of Discovery, a theology and/or politics of *entitlement* to land and resources—both in the colonizing and extractive senses—gave *carte blanche* first to imperial expansion and conquest, then to capitalist production and consumption without limits.[8] Moreover, it has relieved both colonial and industrial protagonists of any responsibility to restore degraded land and biotic (including human) communities, past and present.

---

7. For a model of this radical yet practical dialectic we might well look to the preaching of John the Baptist (see Luke 3:7–18). See my comments on this passage at http:// radicaldiscipleship.net/2015/12/11/the-baptists-radical-critique-of-entitlement-repentance-as-radical-discontinuity/, and longer exploration of the Baptist's message and the contemporary approach of addiction and recovery (Myers, 2001).

8. In 1452 the Papal bull *Dum Diversas* authorized the King of Portugal "to invade, search out, capture, vanquish, and subdue all. . . pagans whatsoever. . . wheresoever placed, and the kingdoms' . . . possessions, and all movable and immovable goods whatsoever held and possessed by them, and to reduce their persons to perpetual slavery, and to apply and appropriate to himself and his successors the . . . possessions, and goods, and to convert them to his and their use and profit . . ." See http://www.doctrineofdiscovery. org/dumdiversas.htm. Since Katerina Friesen's essay (Chapter One) focuses in part on the Doctrine of Discovery, I refer the reader there for more context and detail—particularly her discussion of the "principle of contiguity" as it relates to watersheds.

3. Since the dawn of the Enlightenment and Industrial Revolution, the *anthropological presumption* that humans rule over creation—shared with equal ferocity by religious traditionalists and secular modernists—has endorsed how technological development exploits and re-engineers nature to benefit human settlement alone (and increasingly only the elite).

These three errors are embraced as articles of faith by the modernist project—and by the various versions of Christian faith that have ridden shotgun with it. What all three have in common is a fantasy of human autonomy that refuses an identity of creatureliness, which requires that we live within the limits *of* the earth. This despite the unequivocal claim of the Genesis account that we were birthed *from* the earth.[9] Docetic disembodiment has engendered a culture of displaced and displacing European mobility, facilitating the historic conquest and colonization of the homelands and habitats of others, while rationalizing slavery and genocide. Ideologies of entitlement, with their assertions of ownership, have justified expropriation of land and resources, bankrupting of natural fertility, privatizing of the commonwealth, and consolidation of power among elites. And presumptive androcentrism has allowed the earth and her lifeforms to be turned into commodities to be extracted, traded, consumed, and disposed.

Critical eco-theology, then, must journey upstream to the headwaters of the pathological culture that has brought us to this point—a sort of "vision quest" to find out where we have gone wrong (see Myers 1993, 2013). But we must critique and combat these errors constructively and practically (not just deconstructively and ideologically, as is so often the case in the postmodern academy). This requires an approach that is robustly incarnational rather than docetic, symbiotic rather than Promethean, and sustainable rather than selfish. If the roots of the Anthropocene crisis lie in our alienation from the earth, then it is to the earth we must return (to paraphrase the warning in Genesis 3:19). But not in theory, nor rhetorically, nor as a romantic ideal. Rather, discipleship must be restored to the center of ecological theology, and practices of genuinely sustainable reinhabitation restored to the center of discipleship.

In 2017, Christians will commemorate the quincentenary of the Protestant Reformation, launched when Martin Luther famously proclaimed:

---

9. Lynn White's famous essay, "The Historical Roots of Our Ecological Crisis" (1967), was correct in its indictment of Christendom's culpability in the modern ecological crisis, but largely wrong in tracing the origins of these ideas to the Judeo-Christian scriptural tradition; on this see the Afterword, as well as Myers (2004) and Jenkins (2009).

"Here I stand, I can do no other." Given the crisis outlined above, it is past time for a "new Reformation" in which our churches stand *against* ecocide and *for* a just and sustainable future. Such a groundswell has not developed to date in North America, however, because industrial culture has rendered most Christians unable to answer the question: "Where is the *here* upon which we take our stand?" We have been socialized to be more loyal to abstractions and superstructures than literate in the actual biosphere that sustains us; more adept at mobility than grounded in the bioregions in which we reside (but do not truly *inhabit*). In this Kairos moment, then, churches must therefore confront the question—to paraphrase that classic and annoying refrain from the back of the station wagon on the family road trip—"Are we *here* yet?"

II. Watershed Context: The Journey of Bioregional Re-place-ment

The most hopeful current public discourse for deconstructing denial of, and awakening citizens to "response-ability" for, the inconvenient truths of the Anthropocene is being developed by the "Transition" movement. Scarcely a decade old, it is a "grassroots network of local communities that are working to build ecological resilience in response to peak oil, climate destruction, and economic instability."[10] A small circle of us are trying to adopt this movement into churches, including British theologians Timothy Gorringe and Rosie Beckham, who believe the Transition approach "tries to steer between the apocalyptic (social chaos, local warlordism) and the starry eyed (hi tech, zero carbon)" versions of an energy-descending future. They urge us to "highlight how consonant the emphases of Transition are with the Christian narrative" (2013:9, 13).

The contributors to the present anthology concur that every aspect of Christian faith and practice must now be reevaluated in terms of a Transition ethos. We share the conviction that the church's urgent vocation must be—as Catholic Worker cofounder Dorothy Day (and others who embrace "prefigurative politics") put it—to help "build a new world in the shell of the old." The Transition ethos, focusing on the contextual and practical, urges

---

10. Citation from www.transitionnetwork.org; see also www.transitionus.org. The contemporary manifesto is permaculture designer Rob Hoskins's *The Transition Handbook* (2008); a pioneering work was John William Bennett's *The Ecological Transition: Cultural Anthropology and Human Adaptation* (1976).

communities to use the skills and resources we have to do what we can—against our culture's grain of paralysis and exoneration. But it also exhorts us to start *where we are*—and as noted, that is the rub for the placeless.

Kentucky farmer Wendell Berry has for a half century been the foremost critic of placelessness in North America. In a 1989 essay entitled "The Futility of Global Thinking," he asserted: "No place on the earth can be completely healthy until all places are . . . The question that must be addressed is not how to care for the planet, but how to care for each of the planet's millions of human and natural neighborhoods . . . which is in some precious way different from all the others" (1989:16).[11] Around the same time Gary Snyder, celebrated poet of the modern ecology movement, sounded a similar note in a seminal essay entitled "Coming into the Watershed."

> The usual focus of attention for most Americans is the human society itself with its problems and its successes, its icons and symbols . . . the land we all live on is simply taken for granted—and proper relation to it is not taken as part of "citizenship." But . . . people are beginning to wake up and notice that the United States is located on a landscape with a severe, spectacular, spacey, wildly demanding, and ecstatic narrative to be learned. Its natural communities are each unique, and each of us, whether we like it or not—in the city or countryside—live in one of them . . . When enough people get that picture, our political life will begin to change, and it will be the beginning of the next phase of American life (1992:65f).[12]

When I encountered both these texts in the early 1990s they "spoke to my condition," as Quakers say.

The first Gulf War had enraged me anew as a citizen of empire; Indigenous responses to the Columbus quincentenary had uncovered afresh the deep wounds of colonization's long and bitter legacy; and Los Angeles (my hometown) had just been torched by massive riots for the second time in my life because of endemic social and racial disparity. I was worn out from organizing responses to all three issues, and desperately wanted to be able to say "Yes" to some alternative vision of what is possible. Amidst it all, my father died suddenly, my last link to five generations of family roots in California. On top of my deepening political despair about "empire as a way

11. In this, of course, Berry was resonating with Martin Luther King, Jr.'s famous assertion from Birmingham City Jail that "we are caught in an inescapable network of mutuality, tied in a single garment of destiny" (1986:290).

12. See also Snyder (1990). For a fascinating record of the long-running correspondence between these two prophets of place, see Snyder and Berry (2015).

of life" (Williams 1980), I began to experience personal symptoms of what (I later learned) eco-psychologists call "solastalgia." This is the condition of being homesick in a home place that has been degraded or destroyed (Albrecht 2005).

Throughout my life I have seen the fragile chaparral and oak savannah landscapes of southern California bulldozed and paved over relentlessly by manic, unregulated "development": suburban tracts and trophy homes; resorts and boutique wineries; golf courses and shopping malls; military complexes and industrial agriculture. This ruination has been sponsored primarily by transplanted opportunists pursuing lifestyle fantasies or corporate exploiters seeking quick profit. As Wendell Berry laments, the functionaries of global capitalism "have no local allegiances; they must not have a local point of view . . . in order to be able to desecrate, endanger, or destroy a *place*" (1987:51). Shaken by war, Indigenous truthtelling, urban uprising, and personal loss, a fierce desire arose in me to defend what little was left of the native landscapes that had been profoundly imprinted upon my soul.

Years of solidarity work in the 1980s with Indigenous communities struggling for self-determination throughout the Pacific Basin had taught me that it is those who are most deeply rooted in their place who are most likely to sustain fierce, long-term resistance, even against great odds (see Myers 1990). This is because rooted people are ultimately fighting *for* a way of life, not just *against* one. Conversely, it is difficult for the placeless to stand for or against anything of lasting significance.[13] I thus commenced what I came to call a journey of "re-place-ment," which has demanded both outward (political, social, ecological) and inward (psychic, spiritual,

13. Elaine Enns (2015) and I suggest three phases of Settler placelessness in the historical process of colonization: 1) the displacing conquests of the eighteenth century (and before); 2) the dis-placed extractive development of the nineteenth century (which continues); and 3) the placeless alienation of the twentieth century. According to Maori activist Donna Awatere, "for European immigrants, original trauma lay in the dis-connection from their roots. Only a people severed from their own land and culture could . . . so systematically disinherit indigenous peoples from theirs" (Myers, 1994:133). Recently, Mark Van Steenwyk drew to my attention the remarkable diagnosis along these very lines from Simone Weil's 1947 *The Need for Roots*: "Uprootedness is by far the most dangerous malady to which human societies are exposed, for it is a self-propagating one. For people who are really uprooted there remain only two possible sorts of behaviour: either to fall into a spiritual lethargy resembling death, like the majority of the slaves in the days of the Roman Empire, or to hurl themselves into some form of activity necessarily designed to uproot, often by the most violent methods, those who are not yet uprooted, or only partly so . . . Whoever is uprooted himself uproots others. Whoever is rooted himself doesn't uproot others" (1952:47–48).

theological) transformation. And it began by exploring the ecological and social terrain of southern California in earnest, determined to reinhabit the place I was living *on* but not, in Snyder's sense, *in*. During this process, my effort to articulate a First World theology and practice of discipleship concluded by "coming out" as a bioregionalist (Myers, 1994:336ff).[14]

Bioregionalism is a contemporary movement with spiritual and intellectual roots first in the lifeways of traditional indigenous cultures, and second in Henry David Thoreau's mid-nineteenth century experiments at Walden Pond and Lewis Mumford's early twentieth-century critique of industrial "super-congestion" and alternative proposal of "ecoregionalism" (McGinnis 1999:3).[15] Kirkpatrick Sale's 1985 primer provides a helpful definition: "*Bio* is from the Greek word for forms of life . . . and *region* is from the Latin *regere*, territory to be ruled . . . They convey together a life-territory, a place defined by its life forms, its topography and its biota, rather than by human dictates; a region governed by nature, not legislature. And if the concept initially strikes us as strange, that may perhaps only be a measure of how distant we have become from the wisdom it conveys" (1985:43).

More recently, many bioregionalists (myself included) have emphasized an even more specific locus for reinhabitory literacy and engagement, focusing on what is most basic to life: water (see Myers 2014b). John Wesley Powell, in the 1860s the first non-native person to raft successfully down the Colorado River and later a government geographer, gave the first modern definition of a watershed: "It is that area of land, a bounded hydrologic

14. This is, in brief, the autobiographical backstory of this volume. While the response to my early advocacy for bioregionalism was underwhelming, over the following decade I was encouraged to see a similar interest in a theology of place begin to emerge (see e.g., Inge 2003, Bartholomew 2011, and Sheldrake 2001).

15. According to Doug Aberly, a movement pioneer and chronicler, "Bioregionalism is a body of thought and related practice that has evolved in response to the challenge of reconnecting socially-just human cultures in a sustainable manner to the region-scale ecosystems in which they are irrevocably embedded. Over nearly twenty-five years this ambitious project of 'reinhabitation' has carefully evolved far outside of the usual political or intellectual epicenters" (in McGinnis 1999:14f). See further Aberly's *Boundaries of Home* (1993) and *Futures by Design* (1994). For an influential manifesto, see Dodge (1981); other notable early works include Cheney (1989), Andrus et al. (1990); and Thayer (2003), who provide a comprehensive bibliography of bioregionalist writing prior to 1999 at http://bioregion.ucdavis.edu/who/biblio.html. For current bioregionalist organizing see websites for Canada (www.ibspei.ca/index.htm), the U.S. (http://wp.bioregionalcongress.net/), and the U.K. (www.bioregional.com/). Pritchett (Chapter Two), McRay (Chapter Three), Humphrey (Chapter Seven) and Machado (Chapter Ten) also discuss various aspects of bioregional theory.

system, within which all living things are inextricably linked by their common water course and where, as humans settled, simple logic demanded that they become part of the community."[16] Wherever we reside—city, suburb, or rural area—our lives are intertwined within such a "bounded hydrologic system," no matter how ignorant we may be about it (which most of us are). *All* human life is watershed-placed, without exception—and the same is therefore true of every expression of Christian discipleship.

A watershed is the area covered in water's journey from its origination in the hydrological cycle, to how it drains from the ridges and high points of a given geography, to an end point in a pond, lake, or ocean. Each watershed comprises a unique mix of habitats that influence each other, including forests, wetlands, fields and meadows, rivers and lakes, farms and towns. The 2,110 watersheds in the continental U.S. come in all sizes: the Mississippi Basin is the third largest watershed in the world, draining 41 percent of the lower forty eight states into the Gulf of Mexico, while my Ventura River watershed is a scant 227 square miles.

Brock Dolman, a permaculturist and founder of the Occidental Art and Ecology Center in Northern California (www.oaecwater.org), likes to use the watershed metaphor of a cradle, a "Basin of Relations," in which every living organism is interconnected and dependent on the health of the whole (2008). He argues that watersheds "underlie all human endeavors and form the foundation for all future aspirations and survival." This form of "social, local, intentional community with other life forms and inanimate processes, like the fire cycle and the hydrological cycle" represents "the geographic scale of applied sustainability, which must be regenerative, because we desperately are in need of making up for lost time" (Prandoni 2015).

Watershed consciousness is not just an ecological orientation, but a way of looking at the world. Pattern literacy shapes our imagination. Below are two radically contrasting aerial images of earth. The first is the San Rafael desert near Hanksville, Utah, which shows clearly that even in the most arid climate on the continent, the Colorado Plateau, the single most defining feature from the air is the way water flows. A theological reading of this, a universal geographical characteristic, would have to conclude that fluvial geomorphology is the chief design feature of creation that has not been

---

16. Powell (1961); his definition is still used by the U.S. Environmental Protection Agency, through which one can locate one's watershed in the U.S. (go to http://cfpub.epa. gov/surf/locate/index.cfm).

re-engineered by human society.[17] The second image below, on the other hand, an aerial view of nearby Las Vegas, Nevada, exhibits patterns typical of modern urban sprawl throughout North America.[18] What is most evident here is not how the water flows—this is invisible—but how the automobile traffic and housing tracts flow (see Gorringe 2011). This landscape has been completely redesigned according to human artifice. The profound differences between the design patterns of nature and modern metropolis express an essential aspect of what is unsustainable about industrial civilization. If the design orthodoxies of our built environment have brought us to the brink of ecological and social collapse, then a radical response must advocate a return to the art, science, *and theology* of "biomimicry" (see e.g. http://biomimicry.org/). We have lost our way as creatures of God's biosphere, and only the map that is woven into Creation can lead us home. And that map is defined by watersheds.

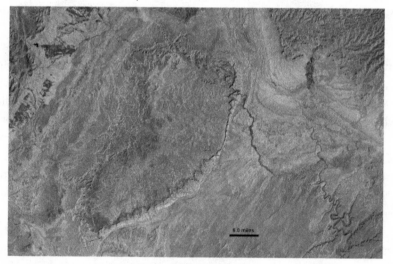

San Rafael Desert, Utah.

17. Photograph at: httpe//plantsandrocks.blogspot.com/2012/04/field-trip-plans-swell-surprise.html.

18. Photograph at: http://www.hdtimelapse.net/details.php?movie_id=149. In 2011 artist Joy Charbonneau created aerial images based on hydrological maps of Canada (see http://www.theglobeandmail.com/news/national/water-map-test/article27565222/). John Allemang (2015) writes of these beautiful and poignant images: "We see a vast land stripped of imposed borders, latitudinal hierarchies and self-important markings of human settlement, where the interconnected tracery of creeks, brooks, streams, rivers, basins and lakes is allowed to reclaim its quiet, rippling dominance. All those tiny, sinuous lines and expansive, irregular white shapes ramify and multiply to capture the constant, cyclical flow in a single image of astonishing abundance."

Aerial View Las Vegas, NV.

A watershed re-orientation also represents, in my opinion, the kind of radical political paradigm shift called for by the crisis of the Anthropocene. In Western culture, our social imaginations and worldviews have been profoundly shaped by two-dimensional political maps. The problem is, these are social reproductions that enshrine problematic historical legacies of colonization and exploitation, while rendering nature secondary or invisible altogether. Below is a recent watershed map of the United States imagined by John Lavey.[19]

19. Lavey (2013); see also Wilson (2013). Lavey's map is based on John Wesley Powell's 1879 proposal that new states in the American West being brought into the union be formed around watersheds, rather than arbitrary political boundaries. He believed, presciently, that because of an arid climate, state organization decided by any other factor would lead to water conflict. But powerful forces (most prominently the rail companies) were pressing that borders be aligned to facilitate commercial agriculture. The West, Powell argued, was too dry and its soils too poor to support agriculture at a scale common in the East. so he produced a map depicting what "watershed states" might look like. The rail lobby prevailed in Congress, with profound and continuing consequences. This "watershed moment" in U.S. history is also noted by Pritchett (Chapter Two); for a recent exploration of Powell's legacy, see Loeffler and Loeffler (2012).

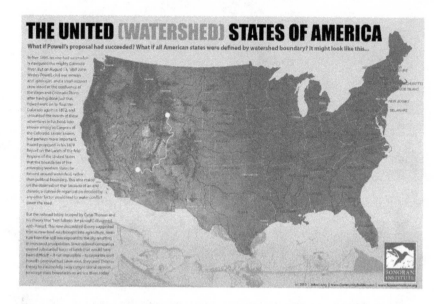

To take an example from my bioregion, below is a map of the bound-aries of Ventura and Los Angeles Counties, overlaid onto those of the local watersheds (my Ventura River Watershed is highlighted).[20] The per-ceptual and adjudicatory disconnect is apparent. Political boundaries are often straight—no continental U.S. state is without one—while watershed boundaries never are. But straight lines are the first order of abstraction, alienating us from the topographical and hydrological realities that actu-ally sustain life. As Arundhati Roy (2015) recently put it: "An old-growth forest, a mountain range or a river valley is more important and certainly more lovable than any country will ever be." How might our political cul-ture change if basic units of governance were determined by "nature rather than legislature"?

20. Map found at www.waterboards.ca.gov/losangeles/water_issues/programs/re-gional_program/Water_Quality_and_Watersheds/ventura_river_watershed/summary.shtml. Nolan, Smith and Ortega (Chapter Eight) refer to their efforts to farm in the various watersheds of Ventura County.

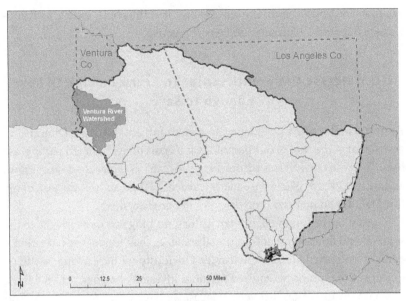

County vs. Watershed boundaries, Ventura and Los Angeles.

It is both theologically sound and politically radical to propose, therefore, that we Christians ought to recenter our citizen-identity in the *topography of creation* rather than in the *political geography of dominant cultural ideation,* in order to ground our discipleship practices in the watershed where we embody our faith. Such a political theology rehabilitates the Anabaptist (and Christian anarchist) conviction that God cannot be identified with the State and its abstractions (see more on this in the Afterword). Consequently, our loyalty to God's good creation trumps *all* human ideological and hegemonic claims (Myers 1994:358ff; Taylor 2000). This approach portends a final repudiation of Constantinianism (see also McRay's reflections in Chapter Three), and makes way for contemporary experiments in bioregional self-determination and confederation, including traditional Indigenous tribal polities, as suggested below.

Bioregional thought and practice have been largely ignored by Christian theology and ethics, but this volume hopefully heralds a sea-change.[21] Watershed Discipleship roots Creation Care in place, and offers a radical-

21. Exceptions include Thomas Berry (1999:103–10; Dalton 1999:98ff) and Diarmu O'Murchu (2008) from the New Cosmology movement. Non-professional theologians Wendell Berry and Wes Jackson operate within the spirit of bioregionalism, but do not use its discourse, as did the late Jim Corbett (1991, 2005), one of the persons to whom this volume is dedicated.

yet-practical approach to Transition faith. It is thus both critical and contextual; but above all, it seeks to be constructive.

III. Watershed Apprenticeship: To Learn Enough to Love Enough to Save

Almost a half century ago, Senegalese environmentalist Baba Dioum suggested that at the root of our pathology is a crisis of *affection*. To paraphrase him: "We won't save places we don't love, we can't love places we don't know, and we don't know places we haven't learned."[22] This captures the task of my third talking point: becoming disciples *of* our watersheds.

From the beginning of human history, nothing was more crucial to the survival and flourishing of traditional societies than a symbiotic, relational ethos of watershed literacy and loyalty. Obviously, we have a long way to go to recover the intimacy required to know, love, and save our places. Living as we do on top of or "between" places, we have little idea where to find basic things like water, or food, or shelter, as our ancestors did, much less an understanding of what the watershed asks of us to maintain equilibrium. The ecological Endgame has revealed this ignorance as perhaps our costliest form of docetism.

Watershed mapping and ecoliteracy are practical tools for apprenticing to a place. Our learning curve will be steep: geological features, soil types, climate zones, flora and fauna, as well as built environments and their social history, the peopled stories, and histories of flourishing, oppression and displacement.[23] This curriculum needs to impact our personal spiritual disciplines, ecclesial expressions, education systems and public policies (see some of my suggestions in the Afterword). To take a modest local example, after years of lobbying, activists recently persuaded the Ventura County-wide Stormwater Program to install road signs around our valley reading "Entering the Ventura River Watershed." This "sign of the times" may seem

---

22. I first encountered this formulation from a local chaparral ecologist; Tim Nafziger later traced it to Dioum's 1968 speech in India (see http://everything2.com/title/Baba+Dioum).

23. On watershed mapping see http://education.nationalgeographic.com/education/activity/mapping-watersheds/?ar_a=1; and www.nativemaps.org. Resources abound for building ecoliteracy (see e.g. http://www.ecoliteracy.org/); a popular beginning point is Peter Warshall and Kevin Kelly's questionnaire called "The Big Here" (online at http://www.sustainablefutures.org/?page_id=1029).

a minor victory, but if maps are a battleground for shaping consciousness, how much more the public signage that directs us around a landscape!

It is important to emphasize here that apprenticing to our watershed neither implies, nor should it tolerate, a provincialist escape from wider issues of society or politics, as has too often been true of middle-class conservationist agendas. As Snyder reminds us, "Watershed consciousness and bioregionalism is not just environmentalism . . . but a move toward resolving both nature and society with the practice of a profound citizenship in both the natural and the social worlds" (2008:235). Each of the contributors to this volume are steeped in peace and justice activism and education, and understand that most watersheds on the planet bear the marks of modern human oppression and degradation. Social disparity, exclusion, and violence—historic and current—can and should be mapped and engaged at the watershed level. And true bioregionalism requires a constructive reimagining of economic, political and social lifeways.

With the globalized capitalist system driving us deeper into the Anthropocene Endgame, a watershed focus compels us to re-engage what Wendell Berry (1987) calls the "Great Economy" of nature. Molly Scott Cato's recent work (2013) signals that the discipline of bioregional economics has arrived.[24] This new (and ancient!) economic orientation has been popularized by the local food movement, which asks what can be harvested, produced, and consumed sustainably in a given bioregion. The same logic should be extended to every aspect of economic life, from resource extraction to waste management. A regenerative local economy requires the sustainable development of indigenous (or naturalized) assets, while weaning ourselves off the exotic and the outsourced, including labor and capital.[25] Local ecological capacity, not markets or profit margins, should be the final arbiter of economic planning and decision making.

Montana politician Daniel Kemmis, an important progenitor of contemporary bioregionalism, argues that "reinhabitory politics" arises from

24. See economic metrics applied to watersheds in Rhode Island (www.watershedcounts.org/economic.html) and Washington (www.eartheconomics.org/FileLibrary/file/Reports/Puget%20Sound%20and%20Watersheds/Puyallup/Puyallup_Watershed_Report_Online_Version.pdf). Ecological economist Paul Hawken suggests that an economy functions *like* a watershed (http://urbanhabitat.org/node/511). An early expression of bioregional economics was Lietaer and Warmoth (1999); see also http://www.reliableprosperity.net/bioregional_economies.html.

25. See, e.g., www.zerowaste.org/; www.financialpermaculture.org/. Mark Boyle promotes "the convergence of permaculture principles with gift economics" (www.permaculture.co.uk/articles/wild-economics-interview-mark-boyle).

"the efforts of unlike people to live well in specific places" (1990:82; 2001). Our political culture would be healthier if it mirrored the "hetarchy" of nature, privileging local self-determination and bioregional confederation over the centralized state, a model of self-determination that in fact characterized most of pre-modern history (see Carr 2004, Eckersley 1992, Whitaker 2005). Sale argues that tendencies toward fragmentation would be constrained by the fact that watershed citizens "share the same configurations of life ... social and economic constraints ... environmental problems and opportunities, and so there is every reason to expect contact and co-operation among them" (1985:94f). The temptation toward provincialism or "NIMBYism" should be constrained by the fact that the ecological and social health of all watersheds are interrelated. As Sarah Thompson points out (Chapter Six), all local struggles have global correlates, and like the biosphere itself, are interconnected. Snyder calls for confederated "watershed councils" to be the locus of bioregional governance (2008:229). Many such bodies have already formed across North America—some advisory, some adjudicatory—suggesting that new practices of citizenship are already being built in the shell of unsustainable political systems.[26]

Central to a watershed ethos should be a commitment to restorative justice for all those displaced in the past and marginalized in the present. The land itself is an historic subject whose story must be learned.[27] The current health of a place must be assessed from the perspective of both land and people who have experienced degradation: poisoned agricultural fields and farmworkers; paved over strip malls and low-wage workers; threatened riparian habitat and homeless people. In particular, we must learn the legacy of Indigenous communities—whether disappeared, displaced, or "inconveniently" present (King 2013). Though many traditional lifeways were casualties of conquest and colonization, our collective survival depends upon learning how First Nations lived sustainably long before Settlers ar-

26. Our local Ventura River Watershed Council exemplifies how grassroots, governmental, and business interests can cooperate in regional mapping, planning, management, and restoration (http://venturawatershed.org/). The Watershed Management Group is a pioneering non-profit organization in Arizona (http://watershedmg.org/). See also Foster (1984) and Woolley et al. (2002).

27. A magnificent example of this approach is Will Campbell's *Providence* (2002), narrating Southern history from the perspective of a one square-mile plot of land in Mississippi; see also Lang (2002) and Pepper (1993). I have had the pleasure of working with Jim Bear Jacobs, a Mohican living in Minneapolis who has crafted a brilliant local tour of native history that emphasizes that one can only truly access the stories *through* the places that hold them (Boyd 2012).

rived. The fact that Native peoples have survived genocidal policies testifies to their remarkable ability to resist assimilation and retain traditional skills—as Nadeau's profile of the extraordinary Waterwalking movement in the Foreword shows. It is also important to learn from other traditional people of the land, both at home (e.g., immigrant Mexican *vaqueros* or Hispanic *acequia* stewards) and abroad (e.g., Palestinian olive farmers or Basque sheep herders), for they too are living repositories of the wisdom and practical competencies arising from a placed way of life.[28]

Indeed, the full restoration of any watershed in North America must include the demanding process of "truth and reconciliation," about which Canada's experiment concerning its Indian Residential Schools legacy has much to teach us (see www.trc.ca; Enns 2015). Restorative justice commitments should also extend to non-human inhabitants of the watershed.[29] (Might not the Jesus of Matthew 25 also ask, "I was an endangered Steelhead Trout, and you did not restore my habitat"?). Katherine McCabe's notion of "Just Sustainability" represents "an approach that recognizes the inseparable nature of social and environmental justice and sustainability, and pushes for organizations and governmental institutions to become more aware of the relationships that exist between inequality, injustice and environmentally unsustainable practices" (McCabe 2009). Such integration is intrinsic to a constructive discipleship that seeks to reinhabit a watershed fully.

Through a mix of social and ecological analysis, Scripture study, and theological imagination, and personal narratives and interviews, the essays in this collection by my younger colleagues around North America reflect the critical, contextual, and constructive approach of Watershed Discipleship. Each contributor suggests ways to work on learning to know to love to save—and perhaps be saved by—one's bioregion:

1. Katerina Friesen contends that the Christian missionary vocation should be redirected to our home places, where we need to learn the contours of historic "watershed conquest" in order to be about the work of restorative justice;

---

28. Northern New Mexico *acequia* activist Fred Vigil, one of the persons to whom this volume is dedicated, was the first person to teach me about watersheds—without using that terminology, because the concept was so deeply integrated into his traditional Hispanic culture. For a brief overview, see Sandoval (2010).

29. The field of ecological restorative justice is just now developing; see, e.g. Weisman (2012), Preston (2011), and www.restorativejustice.org/press-room/07kindscrimes/ecological-crimes.

2. David Pritchett examines the urban grid and its long imperial history, how it has contradicted and compromised our watersheds, and how we can subvert it, taking inspiration from legends of the prophet Daniel;

3. Jonathan McRay argues that a political theology of the kingdom of God must be grounded in the biblical vision of a "transfigured earth," and explores stories of how rivers reconcile, including the tale of Elisha and Naaman;

4. Lydia Wylie-Kellermann connects her personal story of immersion into the Detroit watershed with current political struggles for water justice for the urban poor, and shows how one parish recovered water as a sacrament;

5. Erinn Fahey, a water engineer, explores her vocational contradictions and aspirations, the challenges of designing green infrastructure for everyone, and calls for "visionary engineering" that could even be informed by a biomimicry of beavers;

6. Sarah Thompson interviews a visionary community organizer in Atlanta who sees ecojustice struggles among poor people of color as the next stage of the civil rights movement, and connects this story with Christian Peacemaker Teams's violence reduction and anti-oppression work around the world;

7. Matthew Humphrey urges evangelicals to wean off theological abstraction and political exoneration by recovering the biblical call to creaturely covenant with place, and reads the current struggle against oil pipelines in British Columbia through the warning tale of Naboth's vineyard;

8. Sarah Nolan interviews Erynn Smith and Reyna Ortega of The Abundant Table project in Ventura County, tracing their parallel and contrasting journeys and chronicling their struggles as tenant organic farmers and food justice activists and educators across three different watersheds;

9. Sasha Adkins maps the disaster of plastics culture from a public health perspective, revealing how its toxic trail runs within our bodies, around our watersheds and across the globe, and calls for a spiritual examination of our relationship with disposability;

10. Victoria Machado draws parallels between bioregionalist orientation and the Catholic Worker movement as an expression of local and contextual service and advocacy, and suggests that Watershed Discipleship coheres with the Worker's continuing evolution;

11. Tevyn East and Jay Beck narrate the design, rationale and initial incarnations of the Carnival de Resistance, a traveling village demonstration project that integrates discipleship pedagogy, carnival arts, and environmental justice and sustainability, and which mimics "disturbance ecology" while reinvigorating the cultural commons.

My Afterword concludes this collection with some reflections on watershed hermeneutics, theology and ecclesiology.

This anthology argues that Watershed Discipleship can help us both forge a different human future that is sustainable, resilient, and just, *and* inspire the next great renewal of a church determined to live in light of, not in spite of, the looming ecological endgame. We are, says Dolman, "perched on the tipping point of a watershed moment . . . Now is the time to bring our communities together to set in motion plans and processes that ensure our watersheds will remain healthy in perpetuity. Your home basin of relations is your lifeboat" (2008).

Dolman's lifeboat metaphor recalls the story of Noah's ark, one of the great biblical metaphors for our covenantal duty to preserve terrestrial life. But it also conjures up that archetypal gospel moment when Jesus must force his disciples to get into their boat to cross to the "other side." This is a journey they are reluctant to embrace, having nearly drowned on a previous voyage, yet during their crossing, the great "I AM" is revealed to them at the heart of a lethal storm (Mark 6:45–52). This volume is offered with the prayer that the Spirit that hovers still over creation will summon people of faith to embark on the journey of solidarity *with, in,* and *among* our watershed arks. May we as disciples in this difficult hour follow Father Noah and Brother Jesus into the coming storm!

References

Aberly, Doug. 1993. *Boundaries of Home: Mapping for Local Empowerment*. Philadelphia: New Society.
———. 1994. *Futures by Design: The Practice of Ecological Planning*. Philadelphia: New Society.

Albrecht, Glenn. 2005. "Solastalgia: A New Concept in Human Health and Identity." *Philosophy Activism Nature* 3:41–44.

Allemang, John. 2015. "Vast, interconnected and stunningly beautiful: A view of Canada's waterways." *The Globe and Mail* online. December 2002. (http://www.theglobeandmail.com/news/national/water-map-test/article27565222/.)

Andrus, Van, Christopher Plant, Judith Plant, and Eleanor Wright, eds. 1990. *Home! A Bioregional Reader.* Philadelphia: New Society.

Ayres, Ed. 1999. *God's Last Offer: Negotiating for a Sustainable Future.* New York: Four Walls Eight Windows.

Bartholomew, Craig. 2011. *Where Mortals Dwell: A Christian View of Place for Today.* Grand Rapids: Baker Academic.

Bennett, John William. 1976. *The Ecological Transition: Cultural Anthropology and Human Adaptation.* Piscataway, NJ: Transaction.

Berry, Thomas. 1999. "The Hudson River Valley: A Bioregional Story." In *At Home on the Earth: Becoming Native to Our Place,* edited by David Landis Barnhill, 103–10. Berkeley, CA: University of California Press.

Berry, Wendell. 1987. *Home Economics.* San Francisco: North Point.

———. 1989. "The Futility of Global Thinking." *Harper's Magazine.* September, 16–22.

———. 1990. *What Are People For?* Berkeley: Counterpoint.

Boyd, Cynthia. 2012. "Using the Dakota War to talk about racism, stereotypes and violence." *Minnpost,* October 12. (https://www.minnpost.com/community-sketchbook/2012/10/using-dakota-war-talk-about-racism-stereotypes-and-violence).

Brunner, Daniel, Jennifer Butler and A.J. Swoboda. 2014. *Introducing Evangelical Ecotheology: Foundations in Scripture, Theology, History, and Praxis.* Grand Rapids: Baker Academic.

Campbell, Will. 2002. *Providence.* Waco, TX: Baylor University Press.

Carr, Mike. 2004. *Bioregionalism and Civil Society: Democratic Challenges to Corporate Globalism.* Vancouver: University of British Columbia Press.

Cato, Molly Scott. 2013. *The Bioregional Economy: Land, Liberty and the Pursuit of Happiness.* London: Routledge.

Cheney, Jim. 1989. "Postmodern Environmental Ethics: Ethics as Bioregional Narrative." *Environmental Ethics* 11(2):117–34.

Cobb, John C. 1995. *Is It Too Late? A Theology of Ecology.* Rev. ed. Denton, TX: Environmental Ethics.

Corbett, Jim. 1991. *Goatwalking: A Guide to Wildland Living, A Quest for the Peaceable Kingdom.* New York: Viking.

———. 2005. *A Sanctuary for All Life.* Englewood, CO: Howling Dog.

Dalton, Anne Marie. 1999. *A Theology for the Earth: The Contributions of Thomas Berry and Bernard Lonergan.* Ottawa: University of Ottawa Press.

Dodge, Jim. 1981. "Living by Life: Some Bioregional Thought and Practice." *Co-evolution Quarterly,* 32:6–12.

Dolman, Brock. 2008. *Basins of Relations: A Citizen's Guide to Protecting and Restoring Our Watershed.* Occidental, CA: Water Institute.

Eckersley, Robyn. 1992. *Environmentalism and Political Theory: Toward an Ecocentric Approach.* New York: State University of New York Press.

Enns, Elaine. 2015. "Settler 'Response-Ability.'" *Geez,* Fall 34, 34–37.

Foster, Charles. 1984. *Experiments in Bioregionalism: The New England River Basins Story.* Hanover, NH: University Press of New England.

Gebara, Ivone. 1999. *Longing for Running Water: Ecofeminism and Liberation*. Minneapolis: Fortress.

Gorringe, Timothy. 2011. *The Common Good and the Global Emergency: God and the Built Environment*. Cambridge: Cambridge University Press.

Gorringe, Timothy, and Rosie Beckham. 2013. *The Transition Movement for Churches: A Prophetic Imperative for Today*. Norwich, UK: Canterbury.

Hoskins, Rob. 2008. *The Transition Handbook: From Oil Dependency to Local Resilience*. White River Junction, VT: Chelsea Green.

Inge, John. 2003. *A Christian Theology of Place: Explorations in Practical, Pastoral, and Empirical Theology*. Aldershot, UK: Ashgate.

Jenkins, Willis. 2008. *Ecologies of Grace: Environmental Ethics and Christian Theology*. Oxford: Oxford University Press.

———. 2009. "After Lynn White: Religious Ethics and Environmental Problems." *Journal of Religious Ethics* 37 (2):283–309.

Jensen, Derrick. 2006. *Endgame, Volumes I and II*. New York: Seven Stories.

Kemmis, Daniel. 1990. *Community and the Politics of Place*. Norman, OK: University of Oklahoma Press.

———. 2001. *This Sovereign Land: A New Vision for Governing the West*. Washington, DC: Island.

King, Martin Luther Jr. 1986. "Letter from Birmingham City Jail." In *The Essential Writings and Speeches of Martin Luther King, Jr.*, edited by James Washington, 290–302. San Francisco: HarperSanFrancisco.

King, Thomas. 2013. *The Inconvenient Indian: A Curious Account of Native People in North America*. Minneapolis: University of Minnesota Press.

Lang, William. 2002. "Bioregionalism and the History of Place." *Oregon Historical Quarterly* 103 (4, Winter) 414–19.

Lavey, John. 2013. "The United (Watershed) States of America." Community Builders. (http://communitybuilders.net/the-united-watershed-states-of-america.)

Lietaer, Bernard and Art Warmoth. 1999. "Designing Bioregional Economies in Response to Globalization." Ausar Consulting, uploaded March 17, 2010. (http://ausar.com/Articles-EEconomy/Designing%20Bioregional%20Economies.pdf.)

Loeffler, Jack and Celestia, eds. 2012. *Thinking Like a Watershed: Voices from the West*. Albuquerque: University of New Mexico Press.

McCabe, Katherine. 2009. "The Environment on Our Doorsteps: Community Restorative Justice and the Roots of Sustainability." Master of Science thesis, University of Michigan. (http://deepblue.lib.umich.edu/handle/2027.42/64292.)

McFague, Sallie. 1993. *The Body of God: An Ecological Theology*. Minneapolis: Augsburg Fortress.

McGinnis, Michael Vincent. 1999. *Bioregionalism*. London: Routledge.

McKibben, Bill. 1994. *The Comforting Whirlwind: God, Job and the Scale of Creation*. Grand Rapids: Eerdmans.

Merton, Thomas. 1966. *Raids on the Unspeakable*. New York: New Directions.

Myers. Ched. 1993. "The Wilderness Temptations and the American Journey." In *Richard Rohr: Illuminations of His Life and Work*, edited by A. Ebert and P. Brockman, 143–57. New York: Crossroads.

———. 1994. *Who Will Roll Away the Stone? Discipleship Queries for First World Christians*. Maryknoll, NY: Orbis.

————. 2001. "Beyond the 'Addict's Excuse': Public Addiction and Ecclesial Recovery." In *The Other Side of Sin* edited by S. Nelson and A. Sung Park, 87–108. New York: SUNY.

————. 2004. "'To Serve and Preserve': The Genesis Commission to Earth Stewardship," *Sojourners*, March, 28–33.

————. 2013. "From Garden to Tower (Genesis 1–11): Re-Visioning Our Origins." In *Buffalo Shout, Salmon Cry: Conversations on Creation, Land Justice and Life Together*, edited by Steve Heinrichs, 109–26. Harrisburg, PA: Herald.

————. 2014b. "Reinhabiting the River of Life (Rev 22:1–2): Rehydration, Redemption, and Watershed Discipleship." *Missio Dei: A Journal of Missional Theology and Praxis* 5 (2). Online: http://missiodeijournal.com/article.php?issue=md-5-2&author=md-5-2-myers.

————. 2014a. "From 'Creation Care' to 'Watershed Discipleship': Re-Placing Ecological Theology and Practice." *The Conrad Grebel Review* 32 (3) 250–75.

Myers, Ched and Robert Aldridge. 1990. *Resisting the Serpent: Palau's Struggle for Self-Determination*. Baltimore: Fortkamp.

Northcott, Michael. 2013. *A Political Theology of Climate Change*. Grand Rapids: Eerdmans.

O'Murchu, Diarmu. 2008. *Ancestral Grace: Meeting God in Our Human Story*. Maryknoll, NY: Orbis.

Pepper, David. 1993. *Eco-Socialism: From Deep Ecology to Social Justice*. New York: Routledge.

Powell, John Wesley. 1961. *The Exploration of the Colorado River and Its Canyons*. New York, Dover Publications. Online at https://archive.org/details/explorationofcol1961powe (first published in 1895 as *Canyons of the Colorado*).

Prandoni, Marita. 2015. "Know Your Lifeboat: An Interview With Permaculturist Brock Dolman," uploaded June 1. (http://ecohearth.com/eco-zine/eco-heroes/1088-know-your-lifeboat-an-interview-with-permaculturist-brock-dolman.html.)

Preston, Brian. 2011. "The Use of Restorative Justice for Environmental Crime." *Criminal Law Journal*. 35(3) 136–53.

Rasmussen, Larry. 2012. *Earth-honoring Faith: Religious Ethics in a New Key*. Oxford: Oxford University Press.

Reuther, Rosemary Radford. 1992. *Gaia and God: An Ecofeminist Theology of Earth Healing*. San Francisco: HarperSanFrancisco.

Roy, Arundhati. 2015. "Edward Snowden Meets Arundhati Roy." *The Guardian*, November 28. (http://www.theguardian.com/lifeandstyle/2015/nov/28/conversation-edward-snowden-arundhati-roy-john-cusack-interview.)

Sale, Kirkpatrick. 1985. *Dwellers in the Land: The Bioregional Vision*. San Francisco: Sierra Club.

Sandoval, Arturo. 2010. "Ancient Traditions Keep Desert Waters Flowing." *YES! Magazine*. May 13. (http://www.yesmagazine.org/issues/water-solutions/ancient-traditions-keep-desert-waters-flowing).

Sheldrake, Philip. 2001. *Spaces for the Sacred: Place, Memory, and Identity*. Baltimore, MD: Johns Hopkins University Press.

Snyder, Gary. 1990. *The Practice of the Wild*. Berkeley, CA: Counterpoint.

2008. *A Place in Space: Ethics, Aesthetics, and Watersheds*. Rev. ed. San Francisco: Counterpoint.

————. 1992. *Wild Earth*. Canton, NY: Cenozoic Society.

Snyder, Gary, and Wendell Berry. 2015. *Distant Neighbors: The Selected Letters of Wendell Berry and Gary Snyder*. San Francisco: Counterpoint.

Speth, James. 2008. *The Bridge at the Edge of the World: Capitalism, the Environment, and Crossing from Crisis to Sustainability*. New Haven, CT: Yale University Press.

Taylor, Bron. 2000. "Bioregionalism: An Ethics of Loyalty to Place." *Landscape Journal* 19(1&2) 50–72.

Thayer, Robert, ed. 2003. *Lifeplace: Bioregional Thought and Practice*. Berkeley, CA: University of California Press.

Weil, Simon. 1952. *The Need for Roots: Prelude to a Declaration of Duties towards Mankind*. London: Routledge & Kegan Paul. Translated by Arthur Wills.

Weisman, Tama. 2012. "Restorative Environmental Justice as a Way of Life: Learning from Ubuntu." *Dialogue and Universalism* 3(1) 92–109.

Whitaker, Mark. 2005. *Toward a Bioregional State: A Series of Letters About Political Theory and Formal Institutional Design in the Era of Sustainability*. E-book, iUniverse, Inc.

White, Lynn. 1967. "The Historical Roots of Our Ecological Crisis." *Science* 155:1203–7).

Williams, William Appleman. 1980. *Empire as a Way of Life*. New York: Oxford University Press.

Wilson, Reid. 2013. "Map: The United States of Watersheds." *The Washington Post online*, November 19. (https://www.washingtonpost.com/blogs/govbeat/wp/2013/11/19/map-the-united-states-of-watersheds/.)

Woolley, John, Michael Vincent Mcginnis and Julie Kellner. 2002. "The California Watershed Movement: Science and the Politics of Place." *Natural Resources Journal*. 42:133–82.

Wynward, Todd. 2015. *Rewilding the Way*. Harrisonburg, VA: Herald.

Chapter One

The Great Commission
Watershed Conquest or Watershed Discipleship?

KATERINA FRIESEN

Summary: This essay extends a commissioning home into our watersheds as a way of re-place-ment and repentance from the rootlessness affecting North American Christians today. I trace this rootlessness to Christendom and theologies that sanctioned colonialism. Watershed Discipleship offers a constructive framework for mission as a paradigm of repentance for the "Watershed Conquest" supported by colonial theologies and practices.[1]

DURING A COLLEGE INTERNSHIP program I lived with an Ikalahan host family in Imugan, a town in the Sierra Madre Mountains of northern Luzon, the Philippines. I often accompanied my host mother, Auntie Noemi, to tend her family's subsistence farm, where she grew many varieties of sweet potatoes, peanuts, beans, squash, garlic, and ginger. My host father worked as a pastor and community forester, maintaining the dipterocarp,

---

1. A version of this essay was previously published in *Missio Dei: A Journal of Missional Theology and Praxis*, Vol. 5:2 (August 2014), online at http://missiodeijournal.com/article.php?issue=md-5-2&author=md-5-2-friesen.

pine, and cloud forests and protecting the people's traditional "Ancestral Domain" against illegal loggers and other intrusions.

Auntie Noemi.

Rampant resource extraction in the form of mining and logging, both legal and illegal, has profoundly impacted Indigenous communities in the Philippines. Community-Based Forest Management (CBFM) is a promising response to the failure of state governance to protect the forests. CBFM puts forest management in the hands of local communities like the upland peoples with whom I stayed, and draws from their traditional knowledge to regulate sustainable forest use (see Guiang, Borlagdan, and Pulhi 2001). Legal recognition of the Ikalahan-Kalanguya Ancestral Domain, also called the Kalahan Forest Reserve, was the result of a secure land tenure agreement between the government of the Philippines and the Ikalahan people in the 1970s, the very first of its kind (Roxas 2006). A watershed centrally defines the 36,000 acre Domain; draining into the Magat River, it serves as a sanctuary to more than 150 endangered species of plants and animals. The people have decided collectively to protect their watershed; thus, those who live near sources of water cannot expand their farms, raise livestock intensively, or use chemical pesticides on the land. As a local community, they have limited their own potential growth for the sake of the well-being of the whole watershed, including the lowland peoples who live downstream.

Auntie Noemi told me that when her parent's generation converted to Christianity in the 1960s, they decided to expand their faith instead of their gardens. She contrasted their decision with communities outside of the Ancestral Domain who have denuded their once-forested slopes to make room for mono-crop agriculture that grow produce for distant markets. This kind of farming has created drastic erosion, and local people attribute an increase in cancer in those areas to the heavy use of synthetic chemical inputs. For the Ikalahan, Christian faith and care for their watershed go hand-in-hand.

Pastor Delbert Rice dancing the traditional tayaw.

The holistic mission strategies of Pastor Delbert Rice significantly strengthened the Ikalahan's commitments. Rice (*left in the photo*) was a missionary with the United Church of Christ in the Philippines (UCCP), and lived in Imugan from 1965 until his death in 2014. In contrast with other Protestant missionaries who had made evangelistic visits to the area starting in the 1930s, Rice did not preach against traditional practices like the *kanyaw* and the *baki* ritual feasts. Instead, he let the people decide which traditions to continue, which to reject, and which to adapt in light of their Christian conversion (Lee 2014). In his later years, Rice came to see learning, teaching, and promoting upland forest ecology as integral to his work as a missionary. The Christian gospel resonated with certain Ikalahan concepts, such as *li-teng*, which forms the basis for the people's care for their watershed. *Li-teng is* a deeply ecological word signifying abundant life for all, which Rice analogized to the Hebrew *shalom* (Native American theologian Randy Woodley has made similar analogies to the "Harmony Way" common among many Indigenous peoples, 2012). With their Christian faith strengthening certain traditional cultural and ecological practices, the Ikalahan have become a model throughout Southeast Asia for their CBFM practices, Indigenous educational programs, and ongoing expressions of restorative justice through the *tongtongan*, or council of elders.

Historically, Spain, the U.S. and Japan have all colonized or occupied the Philippines. The Ikalahan people have a long record of resistance. They have organized against: illegal logging; a "Marcos City" resort planned in the 1970s under the dictatorship; cell phone satellite towers; and most recently, Australian mining companies (Dumlao 2014). Love for the *naduntog nakayang*, "the high mountain forest where the clouds settle in mist around the trees," has compelled their struggle.[2] Their home is worth defending with their lives. During my six months living with the Ikalahan, however, I became increasingly aware of a significant gap in my own life. I began to ask myself: Was there a place for which I would put *my* life on the line? I did not know.

I grew up in a missionary family that then remained highly mobile. By age twenty-one I had moved ten times. I became accustomed to an ambivalent intermingling of emotions—the pain of leaving friends and place, but also the tingle of excitement associated with traveling somewhere new.

---

2. This phrase comes from the opening lines of an Ikalahan love song for place, the school anthem for the Indigenous Kalahan Academy, entitled "*Di naduntog nakayang, babalaw na ko-lapan*" ("In the high mountain forests, the clouds come down").

I envisioned myself working overseas, living the exhilarating life of a global nomad. No place held any claim over me, and I had no desire to limit my life to one place—until I lived within the Ikalahan Ancestral Domain. There the people's love for their home opened my eyes, and exposed the placeless dreams that were scripting my life goals.

Before I left the Philippines, my host family held a prayer service attended by local elders and friends. The pastor stood to give me a commission, and prayed that I would return home to the U.S. to apply what I had learned with them. This simple and profound commissioning changed my life, initiating a journey of repentance that turned me toward home.

Commissioning ceremony in the Philippines.

I. Commissioned Toward Home

Returning from the Philippines I felt disturbed by the fact that my own sense of home seemed as distant as a foreign land. This condition, I believe, is not unique, but reflects a widespread social-spiritual malady facing North American Christians today which, among other problems, poses a threat to the church's cross-cultural witness and mission. Without a sense of home, missionaries run the risk of sharing a gospel disinterested in place, abstracted from the geography of the watershed. As Jonathan McRay writes in Chapter Three of this volume, modern white Christians often forget that "land is not a commodity but a community of soil, water, air, plants, animals, and humans." Land is home and life.

Mission has been understood historically in terms of leaving home for the sake of spreading the gospel *elsewhere*. Perhaps no biblical verb has been as significant to the history of mission as the first one in Matthew's Great Commission: "*Go* therefore and make disciples of all nations, baptizing . . . and teaching them . . . " (Matt 28:19–20a). This exhortation does not *inherently* imply rootlessness or estrangement from the land—after all, it was delivered by and to Palestinian Jews who were deeply grounded in place. Yet the partnership of missionaries and imperialism beginning in the fifteenth century with the "Age of Discovery" meant that the Great Commission began to be understood in terms of conquest, through a theological anthropology that separated people's souls from their bodies and their lives from the land.

In their introduction to *Teaching All Nations: Interrogating the Great Commission*, Mitzi Smith and Jayachitra Lalitha summarize this approach:

> The violent evangelizing conquest method that dominated foreign missions proposed to gain control over native populations by any means necessary in order to facilitate their conversion to Christianity, and, by extension, the speedy and less complicated dominance and enculturation of colonized lands and peoples. Consequently, people who refused evangelistic strategies were forced under threat of death to convert to Christianity. European imperialism (and later American colonialism) in partnership with Christian evangelism spread their own tables with the resources of foreign lands, rendering the native people oppressed and impoverished. As Bishop Desmond Tutu has asserted, "They [the missionaries] said, 'let us close our eyes and pray.' When we opened them, we had the Bible and they had the land" (2014:2).

The long and oppressive legacy of colonizing mission has been increasingly problematized in contemporary Christianity, though it is by no means obsolete. However, contemporary apologists contend that cross-cultural mission can be the "life-blood of the church," and is necessary for its ongoing transformation (Walls 1996:1–25). Alan and Eleanor Kreider write, "After Christendom, missionary sending no longer follows imperial patterns; it no longer goes from Christendom to heathendom; it is, as Samuel Escobar has put it, from everywhere to everyone" (2011:51). This understanding of mission can, it is argued, radically de-couple Christianity from colonizing Christendom, preventing one cultural or social group from imposing a totalizing gospel on everyone else, as so often happened historically (Escobar 2003:73). But this paradigm poses a different dilemma: if the missionary has no sense of belonging to any particular place, mission from *everywhere* becomes mission from *nowhere*. Rootlessness cannot sustain cross-cultural mission after Christendom.

Indeed, rootlessness defined not only historically colonizing Christian mission, but secular cross-cultural projects as well, from political conquest to early anthropology to contemporary international commerce. Indigenous activists and scholars have theorized that what drives the Western colonizing compulsion, both for the nineteenth-century missionary and the twenty-first-century businessperson, is the "original trauma" of European displacement and alienation. Maori sovereignty advocate Donna Awatere (1984), for example, argues that European explorers, conquistadors, and Settlers, having been displaced (often involuntarily) from their *own* homelands in the Old World, would inevitably displace Indigenous peoples from lands the Europeans coveted in the New (see Myers 1994:342).

This pattern of "repetition-compulsion" was reenacted again and again. Even if European immigrants did not *intentionally* displace Indigenous peoples, they were often part of the colonizing strategy of the state. Scotch-Irish immigrants, for example, displaced by Highland clearances and rent-racking by wealthy landholders, were then used by colonial authorities to displace (or act as a "buffer class" against) Indigenous peoples in Western Pennsylvania and elsewhere during the seventeenth century (Leyburn 1962). Similarly, Elaine Enns (2015) has shown how Mennonites, fleeing hardship in the Ukrainian steppes, were recruited as agricultural colonists and given land on the Canadian prairies that had been taken away by the Crown from Cree tribes in the late 1800s.

Today, missionaries with no sense of home will be unable to understand and unwilling to stand with other people's struggles to defend and protect their homes. Unless we have learned how to *inhabit* deeply our own place, how will we be able to share and embody a gospel of *incarnation* elsewhere? To be confessional, it often takes a significant cross-cultural experience for middle-class North Americans like me to recognize our alienation. It was people rooted in their watershed in the cloud forests of the Philippines who led me to question my spiritual pathology of placelessness—and it was they who commissioned me to a "mission home." Ideally, however, we North Americans should face our rootlessness *before* journeying abroad, so we do not inflict it on people of place. The work of recognizing and repenting of placelessness, therefore, is as important as cross-cultural competence for contemporary missionary practitioners.

What if all mission, whether domestic or international, urban or rural, first required "reconciliation with our home place" as a foundation for proclaiming the gospel? Traditionally, Christians have understood reconciliation to God in Christ to concern primarily the human sphere. Yet God's reconciliation extends to *all* of creation, not just to humans: "For in Christ all the fullness of God was pleased to dwell, and through him God was pleased to reconcile to Godself all things, whether on earth or in heaven, by making peace through the blood of his cross" (Col 1:19–20). This biblical vision necessarily entails facing our own need for reconciliation with and in our ecological home places, understood in this volume as the watershed to which we belong and where our discipleship is grounded. This geographic specificity provides a helpful context for a commitment to "mission home," because we all were born in a watershed and live in one now, whether in North America or abroad. Becoming reconciled to our watershed requires learning to know and love it deeply. Before a missionary *goes*, in other words, she should know how to *stay*.

II. The Doctrine of Discovery and Watershed Conquest

Unfortunately, for North American Christians of European descent, this path to holistic reconciliation has been blocked by theologies of mission from which we must repent. Ched Myers points out in the Introduction to this volume that Western Christendom has actively underwritten three theological errors at the root of our crisis of placelessness:

1. A docetism that privileges spiritual matters over social and ecological ones;

2. The presumption of human domination over creation;

3. A theology and politics of "divinely granted" entitlement to land and resources.

Each of these historically have undergirded missionary and colonialist—and more recently, anthropological and economically driven—projects of exploitation of both people and land. In light of this, mission as reconciliation must begin with repentance. Because *metanoia* connotes a change of both mind and action, we must recognize the consequences of these errors and actively change historical direction from the theologies of placelessness that persist today. Here I will explore the destructive outcomes of the third error: the entitlement expressed (and embodied) in the "Doctrine of Discovery."

Almost from the beginning of Christendom, mission and colonialism have been interdependent forces; in modernity they have been "historically linked indissolubly with the colonial era and with the idea of a magisterial commissioning" (Bosch 1991:228). The integration of political and religious dominion between church and empire was preeminently articulated in the fifteenth century Doctrine of Discovery, known as the "law of Christendom." It "endowed European conquerors with self-assumed divine title over all 'discovered' land and peoples" (Grande 2008:208), legitimating the subjugation of land, people, and resources to serve church and crown.

Even prior to Columbus's first voyage westward, the Holy See began issuing a series of papal bulls, official religious decrees that document the "genesis of competing claims by Christian monarchies and states in Europe to a right of conquest, sovereignty, and dominance over non-Christian peoples, along with their lands, territories, and resources during the so-called Age of Discovery" (Frichner 2010:7–8). The Great Commission (Matt 28:19–20) was deployed as a central biblical rationale for the European conquest of new worlds. *Dum diversas* (1452) and *Romanus pontifex* (1455) provided the initial legal and religious justification for the subjugation of Indigenous peoples and their lands in the name of spreading Christianity "to all nations." In fact, *Dum diversas* explicitly declared the need to convert not only peoples but also *the land itself* (Newcomb 2012).

This Doctrine has legitimated the destruction of land and peoples by European powers worldwide. Law professor Robert J. Miller has shown how it provided justification for the very establishment of the United States, where its theological rationale continued in secular constructs such as Manifest Destiny, the providential mission of America to expand and occupy the continent (2008). Of particular importance is the Doctrine's "principle of contiguity," which "held that the discovery of a mouth of a river gave the discovering country claim over all the lands drained by that river; even if that was thousands of miles of territory" (Miller 2008:4). Tragically, the geographic scope of watersheds was used to expand the scope of conquest through which the U.S. claimed large territories as if they were unoccupied or undefended by the Indigenous peoples who lived there.

Contiguity figured in the definition and appropriation of the Louisiana Territory, the western drainage system of the Mississippi, and explains why Lewis and Clark raced to discover the mouth of the Columbia River. This was not a heroic, morally neutral expedition as I learned in public education; rather, it was a race to take the entire Pacific Northwest. The discovery of the mouth of that river created a claim over not only Oregon country (the drainage system of the Columbia River), but also *any adjacent coast* (Miller 2008:99–108). At the heart of the Doctrine of Discovery's ideology of entitlement, then, was "Watershed Conquest," which as my Anabaptist Mennonite Biblical Seminary professor David Miller points out, represents the great colonial antithesis to our contemporary visions of Watershed Discipleship.

Moreover, the Doctrine was preserved and enshrined in early international law, through which it continues today. In the pivotal 1823 Supreme Court Case *Johnson v. M'Intosh*, the U.S. Senate cited the 1493 papal bull *Inter caetera* as justification for its dominion (King 2013:466). Appeals to the Doctrine appear in government documents that assert a legal basis for the annexation of Texas, Colorado, Arizona, Florida, New Mexico and other states by the U.S. (Miller 2008:67–88). It undergirds the U.S. government's repeated denial of full title to land for Native Americans, resulting in historic displacement and impoverishment. As recently as 2005, the U.S. Supreme Court case *City of Sherrill v. Oneida Nation of Indians* drew from the Doctrine to limit the sovereignty of the Oneida Nation in New York (see: http://www.law.cornell.edu/supct/html/03–855.ZS.html).

The Doctrine of Discovery, though the product of late medieval ecclesial presumption and Age of Discovery politics, has been grafted into our identity today as Christians because of how it has shaped church history, and as U.S. citizens, since its doctrines have been encoded in our nation's laws. I believe that these theological and legal frameworks continue to hinder those of us who have benefitted historically from European conquest and settlement in our practice of mission, blinding us to the value of land and the primacy of home to Indigenous peoples. And they explain why so many U.S. missionaries unknowingly carry their culture of displacement abroad.

The legacy of entitlement theologies and conquest politics need not, however, have the last word in our national or ecclesial life. The history of

Watershed Conquest can be healed by Watershed Discipleship—a home mission of reinhabiting our bioregions and living out the gospel of reconciliation, marked by repentance and re-place-ment.

III. Repentance as Missional Paradigm Shift

Many Christian denominations and faith groups have publically issued statements repudiating the Doctrine of Discovery and have lamented its effects on Indigenous people and the land.[3] Such acknowledgments point the way forward for Christians to see how Christendom theologies of entitlement and conquest continue to hinder the good news of reconciliation, invite us to practice painful truth-telling, and help us to imagine a different way forward.

I am currently working with a group of Mennonites to educate Mennonite Church USA about the impacts of the Doctrine of Discovery. Rather than drafting a statement of repudiation, we began by making a documentary film for congregational education. It explores ways that Mennonite immigrants historically benefitted from the disenfranchisement of Indigenous peoples, and shows how colonizing logic continues to displace Indigenous people around the world through extractive industries like logging, mining, drilling, fracking, and plantation agriculture. This working group has helped me recognize and grieve the scope of destruction seeded by the Doctrine of Discovery. It has also led me to become more engaged in the tasks of repentance in my own watershed.

Ecclesial processes of addressing historic injustices are aided by an understanding of repentance as a paradigm for mission. Missiologist David Bosch, drawing from Hans Küng's study of theological paradigm shifts, describes significant transitions in the church's understanding of mission throughout Christian history (1991). In recent decades, the ancient paradigm of mission as reconciliation already noted above has gained significant traction as an alternative to the evangelistic strategies of expansion and conversion that prevailed during five centuries of European colonization. However, some missiologists recognize that the notion of reconciliation falls short without acknowledgement of the church's complicity in grievous

---

3. These include the Episcopal Church, the United Church of Christ, the United Methodist Church, the Unitarian Universalist Association, various Quaker groups, and the World Council of Churches. The Sisters of Loretto Community and other Catholic groups have pressured the Vatican to repeal the Doctrine (Gadoua 2014).

injustices during the Age of Conquest, including slavery and genocide. Matthew Lundberg writes that reconciliation is the "ultimate" call of the church-in-mission today, yet naïve and impossible without the "penultimate" practice of repentance (2010:201–217).

Repentance requires that the church practice not only confession of wrongdoing, but right relationship with the land and its peoples past and present. Learning about the Doctrine of Discovery led me to take leadership in helping plan a summer class at Anabaptist Mennonite Biblical Seminary entitled "The Trail of Death: A Pilgrimage of Remembrance, Lament and Transformation." This class traced the forced removal by the U.S. military of the Potawatomi people from northern Indiana to Kansas in 1838. Along the way, we met with Potawatomi descendants of those who survived the original Trail of Death. Our Mennonite histories are bound up with these legacies of displacement, as is the case in my present home in the St. Joseph River watershed. Mennonite and Amish Settlers, my ancestors by faith if not biology, bought land that was formerly inhabited by the Potawatomi. They drained the wetlands and "tamed the wilderness" with agriculture and its accompanying European civilization. By traveling the *via crucis* of the Potawatomi in this pilgrimage, we were better able to see what we formerly were blind to, open our hearts to mourn the dislocation of native cultures, and ask God to show what repentance requires of us today.

I see this Trail of Death pilgrimage as one step of repentance for Mennonites living in the St. Joseph River watershed, and hope it will lead to future steps. Ultimately, I believe that repentance entails a socio-political commitment to the kind of reconciliation that attends to reparations for what has been lost and stolen from Indigenous peoples. Myers writes, "To concede that we are part of the problem is a crucial hedge against both self-righteousness and escapism. But it is not enough: We must also imagine how we can be part of the resolution, the healing and the reconstruction" (1994:338).

Repentance involves not only a turning *away from* the ways of death promulgated by the Christendom of conquest, but also a turning *toward*. To paraphrase Kathleen Dean Moore, every time we say an emphatic *No!* to a way of destruction, we must say *Yes!* to something much more beautiful and life sustaining (DeMocker 2012:6). The *Yes!* proclaimed through the framework of Watershed Discipleship can help to shape a constructive paradigm of repentance.

IV. Watershed Discipleship and the Great Commission

Watershed Discipleship as "mission home" means that the good news of reconciliation begins in our own watersheds. Since the legacy of injustice under the Doctrine of Discovery was made possible by alienation from the land, our only hope for healing is to turn toward the land and learn what shape repentance may take there. Watershed Conquest used ecological boundaries to claim territory through Manifest Destiny, which was a secularized version of the Great Commission interpreted through a colonial hermeneutic. Watershed Discipleship, on the other hand, sees watershed boundaries as inscribed by the Creator to mark humble service to and love for a particular place. Rather than placeless expansionism and *dominion over*, Watershed Discipleship opens up a postcolonial interpretation of the Great Commission as reinhabitation and *submission to* the places where we reside.

In light of our context of placeless mobility and alienation, and the legacy of missionary transmission of a false gospel that denies rootedness and incarnation, I believe Watershed Discipleship offers the North American church an opportunity to interpret the "go" of the Great Commission differently. Can we not understand the three elements of Matthew 28:19–20 as: a) re-placing discipleship *in every watershed*; b) recovering baptism as a reinhabitory ritual of place; and c) embracing Jesus's teachings of restorative justice in each bioregion? This commission home calls us to be converted to and re-baptized in our watershed and the work of reconciliation *here*, before going elsewhere into the watersheds of others, so that we can be better ambassadors of reconciliation *there* (2 Cor 5:18–20). Just as Jesus was immersed into his own watershed in the Jordan River (submitting to John's "baptism of repentance)" we must first go deeper into our home place, to become disciples of Jesus through learning, knowing and loving our watershed. Only such an apprenticeship to our place can prepare us to work as missionaries (and apprentices) in the watershed homes of others, if we are so called.

I began with a personal story of a commission home that I received from Indigenous brothers and sisters in the Philippines. I had to answer the question, "What place would you give your life for/to?" which meant seeking a home in a watershed closer to my birthplace in California. A return to one's birthplace may not be the answer that others discern, of course. As I was writing this essay, I received word from Ikalahan friends that Pastor Delbert Rice had just passed away at his home in the Ancestral Domain.

Pastor Rice grew up near Corvallis, Oregon as a farm boy, and learned about ecology through spending his childhood working on the farm and playing in the forests. These early experiences in his home watershed influenced the mission work and creation care theology of his adult life (Lee 2014). He was an example of a faithful witness who poured out his life for the *li-teng*—the *shalom*—of the Ikalahan. He would often recall hikes with tribal elders during which he learned about the forests, wildlife, and the stories and songs of that place. These experiences of immersion in his adopted watershed shaped how he shared the gospel through his words and witness. His work with the elders in the 1970s led to the establishment of the Kalahan Educational Foundation (KEF), which successfully challenged land-grabbers in league with the Marcos dictatorship, and resulted in a secure land tenure agreement. Even in his last years, Rice worked passionately with the KEF to strengthen organic agriculture in the region and to resist foreign mining companies. Modeling Watershed Discipleship by re-placing himself deeply within the Ancestral Domain, we have everything to learn about mission from Rice and the people to whom he dedicated his life.

As I attempt to live out my own commissioning, I have begun to realize the shared roots between my own lack of home place and the larger historic uprooting theologies of Christendom. As church we need a framework whose transformative potential adequately counters the oppressive history of forced conversion of land and people, a resurrection way of liberation for all people and land more powerful than the death legacy of colonialism. As a people marred by placeless theologies, our challenge is to repent of Watershed Conquest through practicing Watershed Discipleship. We are being commissioned *home*, through the power of the One who will be with us "to the end of the age" (Matt 28:20b).

References

Awatere, Donna. 1984. *Maori Sovereignty*. Auckland: Broadsheet Magazine.

Bosch, David J. 1991. *Transforming Mission: Paradigm Shifts in Theology of Mission*. Maryknoll, N.Y.: Orbis.

DeMocker, Mary. 2012. "If your House is on Fire: Kathleen Dean Moore on the Moral Urgency of Climate Change." *The Sun* 444, December 2012, 4–15.

Dumlao, Artemio. 2013. "Report: Mining Harms Nueva Vizcaya's Resources." *The Philippine Star*. September 23. (http://www.philstar.com/nation/2013/09/23/1237254/report-mining-harms-nueva-vizcayas-resources.)

Enns, Elaine. 2015. "Facing History with Courage: Towards Restorative Solidarity." *Canadian Mennonite*. March 2, 4–8.

Escobar, Samuel. 2003. *The New Global Mission: The Gospel from Everywhere to Everyone.* Downers Grove, IL: InterVarsity.

Frichner, Tonya Gonnella. 2010. "Impact on Indigenous Peoples of the International Legal Construct Known as the Doctrine of Discovery, Which Has Served as the Foundation of the Violation of Their Human Rights." *A Preliminary Study Submitted by the Special Rapporteur to the UN Economic and Social Council,* UN Permanent Forum on Indigenous Issues, New York. February 3. (http://www.un.org/esa/socdev/unpfii/documents/E.C.19.2010.13%20EN.pdf.)

Gadoua, Renee. 2014. "Nuns Blast Catholic Church's 'Doctrine of Discovery' That Justified Indigenous Oppression." *The Huffington Post,* September 10. (http://www.huffingtonpost.com/2014/09/10/catholic-church-doctrine-of-discovery_n_5793840.html.)

Grande, Sandy. 2008. "Doctrine of Discovery." In *Encyclopedia of American Indian History,* Vol. 1, edited by B.E. Johansen and B.M. Pritzker, 208–10. Santa Barbara, CA: ABC-CLIO.

Guiang, Ernesto S., S.B. Borlagdan and J.M. Pulhin. 2001. *Community-Based Forest Management in the Philippines: A Preliminary Assessment.* Quezon City: Institute of Philippine Culture, Ateneo de Manila University, Quezon City.

King, Patti Jo. 2013. "Indian Sovereignty." In *Encyclopedia of American Indian Issues Today,* Vol. 2, edited by Russell M. Lawson, 464–75. Westport, CT: Greenwood.

Kreider, Alan, and Eleanor Kreider. 2011. *Worship and Mission after Christendom.* Waterloo, Ont.: Herald.

Lee, Eun Joo. 2014. *Arthur Delbert Rice, Jr.: Pursuit of Shalom, Encompassing Care of Creation in Mission in The Philippines.* PhD diss., Asbury Theological Seminary.

Leyburn, James G. 1962. *The Scotch-Irish: A Social History.* Chapel Hill, NC: The University of North Carolina Press.

Lundberg, Matthew D. 2010. "Repentance as a Paradigm for Christian Mission." *Journal of Ecumenical Studies* 45(2) 201–217.

Miller, Robert J. 2008. *Native America, Discovered and Conquered: Thomas Jefferson, Lewis & Clark, and Manifest Destiny.* Lincoln, NB: Bison.

Miller, Robert J., Jacinta Ruru, Larissa Behrendt, and Tracey Lindberg. 2012. *Discovering Indigenous Lands: the Doctrine of Discovery in the English Colonies.* Oxford: Oxford University Press.

Myers, Ched. 1994. *Who Will Roll Away the Stone? Discipleship Queries for First World Christians.* Maryknoll, NY: Orbis.

Newcomb, Steve. 2012. "The Doctrine of Discovery." *The Indigenous Peoples Forum on the Doctrine of Discovery,* The Arizona State Capitol House of Representatives, Phoenix, AZ, March 23. (https://www.youtube.com/watch?v=QZBKbNhfh-c.)

Roxas, Elizabeth. 2006. *Asia Good Education for Sustainable Development (ESD) Practice Project: The Ikalahan: Sustaining Lives, Sustaining Life.* The Philippines: Environmental Broadcast Circle Association, Inc. (http://www.agepp.net/files/agepp_philippines1_ikalahan_fullversion_en.pdf).

Smith, Mitzi J. and Jayachitra Lalitha, eds. 2014. *Teaching All Nations: Interrogating the Great Commission.* Minneapolis: Augsburg Fortress.

Walls, Andrews F. 1996. *The Missionary Movement in Christian History.* Maryknoll, NY: Orbis.

World Council of Churches. 2012. "Statement on the Doctrine of Discovery and its Enduring Impact on Indigenous Peoples." *WCC Executive Committee*. Bossey, Switzerland, February 17.

Woodley, Randy. 2012. *Shalom and the Community of Creation: An Indigenous Vision*. Grand Rapids: Eerdmans.

Chapter Two

Watershed Discipleship in Babylon
Resisting the Urban Grid

David Pritchett

Summary: This essay argues that the urban grid is an imperial construct that operates as an antithesis to the watershed. Ancient Mesopotamia was a stark example; scarce water was manipulated for the purpose of elites, who also imposed the grid on the landscape to control people. This architecture took its ultimate form in the gridiron plan used in the United States, which was imposed on much of the country as a way to settle the land and break up Indian governance. Ancient Babylon, born out of a long history of human manipulation of watersheds and people, was an example of how the grid operates as an imperial mechanism. Against the backdrop of this analysis, I read the biblical book of Daniel, set in the temporal and geographic heart of the Babylonian empire, as a handbook of resistance to the geometric hegemony of empire. As analogies to Daniel's defiance of the imperial system, I summarize a few contemporary examples of how people today are working against the grid.

THE URBAN GRID IS the antithesis of a watershed. The latter, as the fundamental unit of ecology, provides the basis for ecosystems to thrive. The former overlays an artificial geometry across the landscape, and provides the political infrastructure for the extraction and degradation of local ecosystems. A watershed connects all creatures within it by the common course of water. Species occupy different habitats based on microclimates within the watershed, yet all depend on the flow of water through the catchment area. In contrast, the urban grid isolates and divides: pavement acts as a barrier separating water from the dry soil; existing streams are often disrupted by or disappeared under built environment, buried by cement or piped into a sewer system; and streets disconnect people from their neighbors, often making spaces between houses dangerous due to automobile traffic flow.

Where watersheds follow the natural contour of the land, the urban grid levels it. As cities expand, the grid advances against native ecosystems, demolishing flora and fauna in its wake, and increasing the distance between healthy ecology and human communities. In the urban grid, the dense quartering of inhabitants creates a metropolitan metabolism that quickly outgrows the carrying capacity of the land on which it sits, requiring resources to be imported from external sources. In a watershed, energy is based on the harness of light by green plants bursting from the rain-soaked soil. These plants depend on the water cycle and local minerals available to them, and in turn form the energy basis for other creatures.

Above all, the urban grid is an entirely anthropogenic construct, and thus fraught with the contradictions of fallen humanity in concentrated ways. In contrast, watersheds are the chief design feature of Creation, honed by natural evolutionary processes over geologic time. Our preoccupation with and intensification of the former, and ignorance and destruction of the latter, has been disastrous.

I. The Urban Grid: A History of Hegemony

Urban grids date from ancient China to the pre-Columbian city of Tenochtitlan (Smith 2007). As a political mechanism, the urban grid operates under the "conviction that the anonymous masses were not entitled to a free environmental choice but were to be molded by a module that was determined by an intelligence higher than their own" (Moholy-Nagy 1968:172). The grid arrangement utilized for colonial designs can be seen in two famous examples of geometric planning: the Greek settlement of Miletus and the Roman military camp called a *castrum*, often used as a precursor to

Roman imperial colonies. This geometric configuration allowed for city planning that controlled the movement of goods in and out of the city, as well as managing the population. Straight streets allow military or police personnel a long line of sight and effective movement from one location to another. "The elective affinity between a strong state and a uniformly laid out city," asserted political scientist and anthropologist James C. Scott, "is obvious" (1998:55).

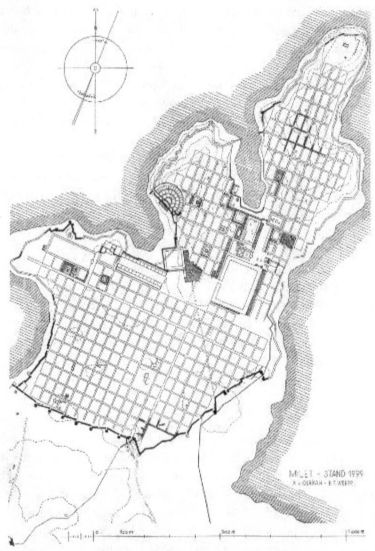

The Grid of Miletus (Source: http://www.uh.edu/engines/epi2542.htm)

City historian and sociologist Lewis Mumford elaborates how the grid plan functioned for imperial designs:

> The very weakness of the plan—its indifference to the contours of the land, to springs, rivers, shore lines, clumps of trees—only made it that much more admirable in providing a minimum basis of order on a site that colonists would not, for long, have the means to fully exploit. Within the shortest possible time, everything was brought under control (1961:192).

The grid was used throughout the centuries as a means of managing people and nature, but was expanded as a tool of colonization by the newly formed United States. The Land Ordinance of 1785 stipulates that the land of Ohio and westward be divided into a grid which could be subdivided from the level of county down to individual lots. City planning historian Sibyl Moholy-Nagy calls this act the "rebirth of Roman colonialism," which converted land into a speculative commodity (1968:172).

As Euro-Americans pushed west, the grid followed, allowing Settlers to stake out homestead claims. However, in the arid lands west of the 100th meridian—approximately halfway through Kansas—homesteading became increasingly difficult. Annual evaporation approached or surpassed annual rainfall, making traditional agriculture infeasible without irrigation. Geographer John Wesley Powell predicted this problem, and proposed an alternative to the grid. Instead of partitioning western lands according to the Land Ordinance of 1785, Powell suggested creating "watershed commonwealths," organized by a nested pattern of watersheds (deBuys 1999). These watershed commonwealths would ensure that residents would have decisive control over their own scarce water, and be able to mitigate their water conflicts. Further, because Settlers would have to fund and manage their own water resources, population of the western lands would remain low enough to be supported by the limited water supply. Powell's vision was unpopular: Congress wanted to retain rights to timber and mining resources; developers feared the commonwealth idea would slow expansion in the West; and homesteaders did not want to wait for the land to be properly surveyed and organized into watershed districts (Hutchinson 2000). The grid won out over the watershed.

Ultimately, three quarters of the U.S. came under the gridiron plan (Carstensen 1987:31). Geometric patterns—irrespective of land contours, climate aspects, and especially flow of water—were overlaid across an entire continent. Mumford complained that any person with a "triangle and a T square" could plan an entire metropolis without any training in sociology or architecture (1961:422). The gridiron paid no heed to the social needs of urban inhabitants, lacked planned space for public parks, and cost hilly cities like San Francisco untold amounts in energy used to transport goods directly up hills rather than on a contoured road systems (Mumford 1961:423). The gridiron was capitalism writ large onto the landscape, Mumford concluded: "On strictly commercial principles, the gridiron plan answered, as no other plans did, the shifting values, the accelerated expansion, the multiplying population, required by the capitalist regime" (1961:424).

Then, under the Dawes Act of 1887, the gridiron plan was extended into the reservations given to American Indian tribes. It called for the plotting and partition of tribally held lands (excluding a few Native American groups including the "Five Civilized Tribes" of the Cherokee, Chickasaw, Choctaw, Creek, and Seminole) into a grid plan similar to that established by the Land Ordinance of 1785. Bringing tribal territory under the gridiron plan commoditized Indian land into individual holdings, fragmented communal land tenure and effectively broke up tribal government. Dawes believed this would be ultimately helpful to Indian tribes. In a speech about the Cherokee he notes, "They have no selfishness, which is the bottom of civilization. Till this people will consent to give up their lands, and divide them among their citizens ... they will not make much more progress" (Otis 1973:10–11). The Dawes Act included stipulations that any Native person who wanted to be granted a parcel must register as an American Indian on the Dawes Rolls, which allowed them to be tracked by the nation-state (Scott 1998:65). The grid thus evolved into a hegemonic tool of imperial control and genocide.

II. Babylon and the Grid

Water and civilizations are inextricably linked. This is recognized in ancient Sumerian words for the cultivated countryside: "that which is fructified with water," or "the moistened ground" (Adams 1981:137). In Southern Mesopotamia, where annual rainfall was eight inches or less, all cities were located on the Tigris and Euphrates rivers (Pederson et al. 2010:118). The need to harness water for the agriculture necessary to support civilization was crucial to the growth of urbanization in the region. However, these urban attempts to control water ultimately failed for multiple reasons.

The practice of irrigation was a major contributing factor to the downfall of early Mesopotamian civilization. It took the form of many canals extending throughout the region, which over time drastically changed the landscape (Adams 1981:21–22). Irrigation precipitates salinization, particularly in arid regions; added water raises the water table, bringing underground minerals to the surface, and as water is used by plants or evaporates, it leaves behind salts. In Mesopotamia, there was not enough rainfall to leach the salts, and over time these minerals accumulated to increase soil salinity and damage crop yield. Ultimately, the process of desertification caused crop failure, as documented in the *Atrahasis*, a nineteenth-century BCE Akkadian epic: "The black fields became white, the broad plains choked with salt" (see Diamond 2005).

The natural meandering pattern of the rivers native to the geography of the Mesopotamian plain also caused settlement patterns to shift, and caused extensive problems for cities.[1] In Babylon, the Euphrates historically divided the heart of the city, but now cuts through the western half of the city. This change in course has been attributed by some to Nebuchadnezzar's palace, built so close to the riverbank as to modify the leeway of floods (Pedersen et al. 2010:137).

Sociologist and theologian Jacques Ellul noted that the first city in the Bible, built by Cain (Gen 4:17), was called "Enoch," meaning "to inaugurate" (1970:6). The Genesis tale is suggesting that the earth created by God was not "good" *enough* (see Gen 1) for rebellious humans, so a new world order had to be re-created. Indeed, ancient Babylon symbolized the triumph of the city over nature, with the grid impressed on the landscape as the epitome of exerting human will over natural processes.

The Neo-Babylonian Empire promoted urban society. Archaeologists have found that over half of the inhabitants in areas dated to this time lived in cities of 10,000 or more (Adams 1981:178). Robert Adams regards such a concentration of population as a "hypertrophic, 'unnatural' condition for an agricultural civilization with preindustrial transport technology" (1981:138). This is why Mesopotamian kingdoms depended on a politics of extraction. As archaeologist Hans Barstad remarks: "Having no natural

---

1. A classic example of this phenomenon can be seen in the Meander River in Turkey (from which we get our English word). The natural movement of the river was exacerbated by sedimentation due to deforestation further up the watershed; eventually the mouth of the Meander moved several miles from the port city of Priene (see map at https://en.wikipedia.org/wiki/B%C3%BCy%C3%BCk_Menderes_River#/media/File:Miletus_Bay_silting_evolution_map-en.svg).

resources of its own, the whole existence of the empire depended entirely upon the import of materials like metals, stone, and timber, and all sorts of food and luxury items" (1996:63–64).

Because of the line of sight down every street, the ziggurat—temple of Marduk, patron god of the city—could be seen from any vantage point in the city. A yearly procession led the statue of Marduk from the temple sanctuary through the streets and far outside city walls into the uncultivated steppe, in order to "turn the whole countryside into sacred landscape" (Van de Mieroop 2003:273). The Babylonian epic *Enuma Elish* records Marduk slaying Tiamat, primordial goddess of water and chaos, in order to fashion the world from her corpse, in which humans dwell to serve the gods. The symbolism is clear: Babylon's patron deity overcomes primordial nature by violence (Moholy-Nagy 1968:83).

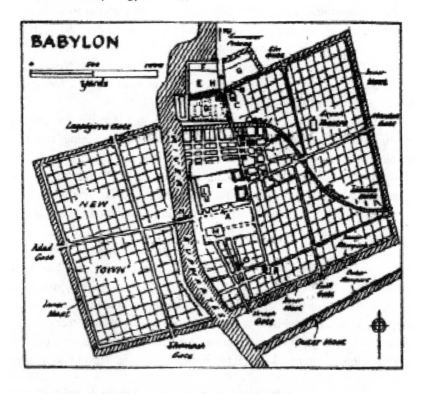

Babylon's Grid (Moholy-Nagy 1968:92)

As Cain sought to re-inaugurate the world, as Marduk conquered chaos, so the city renders nature (and people) servile and domesticated.

Babylon was the world remade by empire, its grid etched indelibly onto the complex, mosaic landscape of the alluvial plain.

III. Daniel: Hidden Transcripts, Trickster Tactics, and Wise Ones

The ancient book of Daniel can serve as a guide for those navigating the urban grid today, and the imperial ideology that undergirds it (Smith-Christopher 2002). The first half of the tale tells of court intrigue involving Daniel and his friends, while the second half records apocalyptic visions. Each genre animates resistance to empire in its own way; and by weaving these strands together, the book moves from individual stories of defiance to sweeping forecasts of imperial fall. This focus on both individual discipline and large-scale events assures readers that mundane yet faithful actions do make a difference in the movement toward liberation that will prevail in God's time.

The origin of the book underlines its character as a handbook of resistance. While undoubtedly inspired by escapades of Jewish exiles in Babylon, most scholars believe that these stories were compiled in the book of Daniel in the second century BCE (Collins 1994:31). As Jews experienced oppression at the hands of the Greek Seleucids (most infamously Antiochus Epiphanes), heroic tales of faithful resistance to Babylonian rule gained renewed traction. Those trying to imagine how to live out their faith under foreign occupation naturally found inspiration in the exploits of Daniel and friends. And Daniel the seer, who interprets dreams and envisions an alternative future featuring the demise of empires, offered a prophetic promise of the end of Seleucid rule.

Anthropologist James C. Scott, in his influential book *Domination and the Arts of Resistance* (1990), has proposed that in situations of oppression people find subtle ways to express their outrage, resistance, and noncooperation. Scott calls these "hidden transcripts": offstage narratives—away from the public spaces where the authorities monitor speech and actions—represent the true feelings of the marginalized. Anathea Portier-Young calls the book of Daniel such a text, a tool of people who experienced subjugation in order to subvert the dominant narrative. "In private," she says, "the dominated dream out loud; they sing and tell stories of reversal; they paint pictures of another kind of life" (2011:33). Hidden transcripts enable the oppressed to survive and even celebrate in spite of the repression they experience. Stories of faithful opposition to empire in the past are such texts, inspiring current practices of refusal.

The beginning of the book presents Daniel as a trickster figure, who with the help of God, outwits the machinations of the king and his imperial court. This is a common trickster trope: it features an underdog who "brings about change in a situation via trickery" (Niditch 1987:xi). Daniel, however, does not utilize deception; rather, he appears to elicit reversals of fortune with a combination of skilled wisdom and divine help. The text delights in putting Daniel and his friends in precarious situations, only to be rescued by divine aid and vindicated in the court. In the most famous example, when rival courtiers attempt to get rid of Daniel, he evades a den of lions while his competitors become feline fodder.

The text also highlights the acumen of Daniel and friends. From the outset in the first story, Daniel is associated with the "wise ones" (Dan 2:12f; Heb. maskilim, used thirteen times in Dan 2–5). Later in the text the maskilim play a role in Daniel's prophecy regarding the oppression of the Jews at the hands of foreign kings (Dan 11:3, 35; 12:3, 10). These maskilim teach the people how to be faithful and model nonviolent resistance, even to the point of martyrdom. Commenting on the Hebrew root skl Klaus Koenen writes: "The focus is not on any one, specific intellectual ability, but rather on the more general use of common sense" (2004:117). Embodied in both Daniel and the heroes of the riverbank prophecies later in the book, the maskilim see through the propaganda of empire, which legitimated the exploitation of nations and peoples. Moreover, they model how to navigate their perilous and tenuous position of privilege. Living in the royal court and sitting at the royal table were hazardous jobs; kings could be finicky, prone to fits, prideful, and above all, intent on getting their way.

James C. Scott's Seeing Like A State (1998) is also helpful for interpreting Daniel. These studies show that operating with a different sort of knowledge is another important "weapon of the weak." Scott highlights the Greek word metis, which connotes local, practical knowledge, as another resource for resisters of empire. If imperial logic is universalized to the detriment of the particular, metis is used in "situations which are transient, shifting, disconcerting and ambiguous, situations which do not lend themselves to precise measurement, exact calculation, or rigorous logic" (1998:320). I propose that this is what the book of Daniel means by maskilim. The tacit knowledge of metis is gained not by privileged study, but by action and experience—it is the embodied, applied knowledge of a carpenter or marine navigator. And in the treacherous waters of empire, political navigation and survival require such practical skills, as the following reading of Daniel suggests.

In Daniel 1 the author sets the tone by portraying Daniel and his friends as ones who, despite being captive to empire, seek to live faithfully within it. They are introduced as intelligent members of Jerusalem's elite taken into royal service: "Young men without physical defect and handsome, versed in every branch of wisdom, endowed with knowledge and insight, and competent to serve in the king's palace" (Dan 1:4). Forced assimilation of the captive elites of a conquered people was (and is) an important imperial strategy of social and political control. The renaming of these Jewish managers was a means to reshape their identity as retainers in the Babylonian court (1:7)—just as later nation-states developed surnames in order to track and tax populations (Scott 1998:70).

Daniel's refusal of the king's food constitutes the crux of the story: "But Daniel resolved not to defile himself with the royal rations of food and wine" (1:8). The term *patbag* refers to the allotted meal taken from the royal treasury to meet the needs of courtiers.[2] Most interpreters take this refusal to be a religious one—Jews in antiquity often maintained their ethnic and religious distinction by observing dietary rules. Indeed, food remains important as an expression of cultural sovereignty for modern diasporic communities as well (see for example Mares and Peña 2011). But we should not overlook the political economy of food as an issue here.

The royal table (and court system as a whole) depended upon the extraction of luxury and staple goods from the margins of empire. Indeed, wresting resources from conquered peripheries to urban elites was and is the defining feature of empire: "Adam Smith said it once and for all . . . the essence of imperialism lies in the metropolitan domination of the weaker economy (and its political and social superstructure) to ensure the extraction of economic rewards" (Williams 1980:7). And in fact "the procedure of funneling resources from the subject populations to the heartland through seizure and exaction was no less important to the Babylonians as it had been to the Assyrians . . . Nebuchadnezzar campaigned almost yearly in the west, in part to insure order, but also to fill the royal coffers" (Vanderhooft 1999:62). The king's table in Daniel would certainly have reflected

---

2. See Collins (1993:140). The only other occurrence of the term in Daniel is 11:26, in which the fall of the king of the South is blamed on his advisors—literally "those who eat his *patbag*" (1993:383).

this; meat and wine would be sourced from the tribute of conquered nations, since livestock were transportable and wine a commodity which could travel distances without spoiling. Meanwhile, the average diet of urban dwellers in Babylon depended upon grain taken from the surrounding countryside. Babylon's "foodprint," according to one catalogue of grain imports, extended from the Sippa in the north to Sealand in the south, a length of over 190 miles of irrigated land (Pedersen et al. 2010:135).

In contrast, vegetables do not travel well, so must be grown nearby. Thus Daniel's refusal of the king's food, and requested alternative of vegetables and water, can be read not just as a dietary preference but as an act of defiance of the extractive economy of empire in favor of local fare that was not stolen (though scholars have not recognized this aspect of his resistance). If, as Collins suggests, acceptance of the king's *patbag* symbolized political allegiance, this alternative fare was an implicit rejection of empire (1993:146). The four friends might have to reside in the king's court, but they sought ways to noncooperate with the politics of plunder.

The story of Nebuchadnezzar's dream of the coppiced tree is another expression of Jewish critique. The king relates it to Daniel:

> Upon my bed this is what I saw;
> there was a tree at the center of the earth,
> and its height was great.
> The tree grew great and strong,
> its top reached to heaven,
> and it was visible to the ends of the whole earth (Dan 4:10–11).

However, the tree is then ordered by God to be axed: "Cut down the tree and chop off its branches" (4:14). This echoes other prophetic allusions to the arrogance of civilization, such as Ezekiel's comparison of Pharaoh to a great cedar with its top "among the clouds" (Ezek 31:3), only to be felled due to pride. The Genesis tale of Babel is even clearer: people plot to build a city and tower "with its top in the heavens," which the divine council then "deconstructs" (Gen 11:4–9). So with Nebuchadnezzar's tree—human hubris will not be tolerated. Babylon in fact becomes the archetypal evil empire in post-exilic Scripture, including the New Testament.[3]

Daniel rejects the Babylonian theology of sacred urbanity. Nebuchadnezzar, who rebuilt Babylon, saw the city as a created world which made nature legible. The bricks in the city walls were imprinted with his name as

---

3. The classic case is, of course, the book of Revelation; but see also the parody of Daniel 4:12 in Mark 4:31–32 (Myers 1988:177–81).

testament to his taming of nature. Much of the city was laid out roughly in what planners call an orthogonal pattern, in which streets intersect at approximately right angles, a grid that sought to emphasize the imposition of order on a chaotic world. "The role of the city as an organizing principle in the universe was also the role of its god Marduk, the one who brings order to the universe" (Van de Mieroop 2003:273; 2005).

In the dream-vision, Nebuchadnezzar is returned to a place among creation and given "the mind of an animal" (Dan 4:15–16), an episode usually interpreted as connoting insanity. However, could we not rather see this as his healing from a madness resulting from his separation from nature by brick and grid? Such alienation eco-philosopher David Abrams also attributes to Western civilization.[4] Daniel's interpretation of the dream tells the king that he must live outside among wild animals and "eat grass like oxen" (Daniel's diet?! 4:25), reminding Nebuchadnezzar of the true order of the world and his place in it. Only when Nebuchadnezzar has learned that "heaven is sovereign" will his kingdom be restored (4:26).

Wendell Berry's essay "Two Economies" argues that the industrial economy both destroys and is dependent upon what it does not comprehend—the holistic reality of nature. The kingdom of God, on the other hand, which Berry also calls the "Great Economy," includes and connects everything (2003:186). The "sovereignty of heaven" referenced in Daniel is, I suggest, analogous to this Great Economy. Babylon represents human hubris, the project of civilization to harness nature. But without recognizing that we *depend* on nature, these civilizations will pulse and die—as eventually happened with the ecological collapse of Mesopotamian irrigated agriculture. Nebuchadnezzar's seven years' "exile with the wild animals" thus represents an extended re-initiation into nature, a baptism by the "dew of heaven" into the Great Economy, where no roads or walls separate or insulate humans from creation (Dan 4:23). This "rewilding" outside the city reiterates First Isaiah's prophecy about the demise of Babylon: "Wild

4. "Caught up in a mass of abstractions, our attention hypnotized by a host of human-made technologies that only reflect us back to ourselves, it is all too easy for us to forget our carnal inheritance in a more-than-human matrix of sensations and sensibilities. Our bodies have formed themselves in delicate reciprocity with the manifold textures, sounds, and shapes of an animate earth—our eyes have evolved in subtle interaction with other eyes, as our ears are attuned by their very structure to the howling of wolves and the honking of geese. To shut ourselves off from these other voices, to continue by our lifestyles to condemn these other sensibilities to the oblivion of extinction, is to rob our own senses of their integrity, and to rob our minds of their coherence. We are human only in contact, and conviviality, with what is not human" (Abram 1997:22).

animals will lie down there, and its palaces will be full of howling creatures" (Isa 13:21).

If the grid testifies to our attempt to control and even disappear nature, Nebuchadnezzar's dream is a counter-testimony that humans live not by roads, bricks, and mortar, but rather by those fleeting photons captured by the chlorophyll in grass and every green plant. In the poetics of Second Isaiah, "all flesh is grass" (Isa 40:6). The web of life will endure beyond the grid.

IV. Resisting the Grid Today

The orthogonal grid, I have argued, is a tool of the colonization, control and alienation of citizenry, in order to efficiently move goods and military assets across the landscape. Such grids are unprecedented in the breadth and depth of their imprint on our modern world, having moved beyond the metropolis to the global from transcontinental highways to transoceanic pipelines, underground cabling to overhead power lines, satellites to microchips, and wired and wireless networks. Watershed Discipleship in our historical moment, therefore, must pursue tactics that undo the power of the grid, using practical, place-based knowledge rooted in one's bioregional literacy to foment resistance and seed renewal (see Odum 2007).

One organization doing notable work in this regard is the City Repair Project in Portland (http://www.cityrepair.org/). Founder Mark Lakeman, with a background in architecture and city planning, understands the grid's power of alienation (his analysis provided the inspiration for this essay). One of the main tactics of City Repair is the artistic painting of cross streets, called "intersection repair." It recognizes how streets divide houses from one another, and how cars intensify this division by endangering pedestrian access across the paved partition. Intersection repair addresses these problems in multiple ways. First, the visual art slows traffic, creating safer streets so that children can play in yards with less danger. Second, it provides opportunity for neighbors to interact and work together. The grid isolates urban residents, who tend to live in one area, shop in other parts of the city, and work elsewhere; by bringing neighbors together around a common project, intersection painting helps foster "re-villaging." Third, as neighbors participate in painting their intersections they gain a sense of agency, symbolically defying the grid and related zoning regulations which seek to control where residents live and work and how they move across the landscape. Intersection repair is a trickster tactic that "takes back" streets as true public space which can unite rather than divide neighbors (see the related work of the "Reclaim the Streets" movement discussed in East and Beck's Chapter Eight of this volume). When the first neighborhood group painted their intersection in Portland, any marking of a street that was not mandated by City code was considered illegal. But since the intersection was painted by an entire neighborhood, the law was difficult to enforce. The city eventually changed its code, and now intersection painting is not only allowed but encouraged by authorities.

De-paving city lots represents another way to defy the grid. Long urban stretches of paved landscape destroy watersheds, preventing rain from sinking into the soil, where water can percolate into underground currents that feed into river systems. Paved areas create torrents of water that rush over hardened landscape and inundate streams, rivers, and aqueducts, causing flooding that harms native wildlife and disperses pollutants associated with city streets. De-paving parking lots and driveways not only helps the local ecology through promoting permeability; it also functions symbolically as resistance at two levels. First, it helps participants break from the unhealthy cycle of paving and piping water strategies (Dolman 2008:7; see also Fahey, Chapter Five). Second, it subverts the urban grid, which depends on built infrastructure to divide people and control nature, by literally breaking it down, tearing through the artificial membrane that separates humans and water from the soil. In Portland, churches like Pilgrim Lutheran have committed to "slowing, spreading and sinking" water runoff on their land by de-paving their parking lots. Watershed Disciples can challenge every church lot to become a demonstration site for such practices.[5]

A third tactic is to follow Daniel's refusal of the *patbag*. As is well documented in the contemporary food justice movement, the modern food system is based on an industrial apparatus that depends on fossil fuels, immigrant labor, and toxic chemicals. Cheap grains and meat are predicated on an extractive economy. Local food movements defy the imperial grid by insisting, like Daniel, on sustainable sources of food. By "eating locally," watershed disciples reduce their participation in an unsustainable system, keeping the energy cycle closer to home. Consumers today have greater

5. In 2014 Maryland instituted a "stormwater remediation fee" that applied to all properties, including houses of worship. Many churches howled in protest, objecting that this represented a "tax on God's rain." A local interfaith effort, however, mobilized to help congregations see this instead as an opportunity to practice responsible water stewardship through rainwater catchment and permeability (Hernandez 2014).

knowledge about how food is grown, and about agricultural labor relations (see Nolan, Smith, and Ortega, Chapter Eight). Mennonites have started "Simply in Season" groups to relearn to cook with seasonable vegetables as a local food practice. In Portland, EcoFaith Recovery promotes such groups, which gather to cook, eat and celebrate their connection to the local flow of nutrients (http://www.ecofaithrecovery.org/).

Food-mapping is a related way for Watershed Disciples to learn to be *maskilim*, rooted and skilled practitioners resisting the grid. By mapping fruit and nut trees scattered throughout neighborhoods—a nutrition source which often lies rotting in the streets—local residents can become more resilient, combat food insecurity, and better come to know their neighbors and the topography of the area. This is another way to encourage human interaction and place-based knowledge and skills. Committed organizers might even care for these trees, ensuring better yields. Portland Fruit Tree Project is an organization which rose from such collaboration, annually coordinating teams to prune, manage, and harvest these perennial crops that would otherwise rot (http://www.portlandfruit.org/).

A weakness of the local food movement, however, is its lack of analysis of the deep social history of local water- and food-sheds. A better model is La Via Campesina, which leads the global movement for food sovereignty. Their organizing focuses on food as a human right, economic inequalities in labor relations, land access, and how global markets commoditize food (Alkon 2013; see also McRay, Chapter Three). The Watershed Discipleship movement should deepen local analysis of the historic colonialism associated with the urban grid—when and how it was constructed in our particular place, and how it commoditized land and resources to create the unjust economic power relations that exist today. I broadly noted above how the gridiron, through the Land Ordinance of 1785 and Dawes Act of 1887, functioned to undermine local and indigenous food sovereignty. A specific example can be seen in the experience of the Karuk tribe in Northern California. Their subsistence practices of hunting and fishing have been jeopardized over the last 150 years by colonization. Industrial logging and damming of rivers has both reduced Karuk access to land and depleted the salmon on which they have depended (Norgaard et al. 2011:40). Food insecurity forces assimilation, because the gridiron plan fractionized the land on which the Karuk live, subdividing it for private ownership. The Klamath River has become polluted with toxins and sediment, diminishing the population of salmon and other wildlife, and undermining the health of the surrounding forest and tributaries.

Teresa Mares and Devon Peña call for all food movements to be aware of the cultural element of food and the history of colonization that precedes "local" food production, and to recognize communities displaced by colonialism, historic and contemporary. They call for food to be recognized as *autotopographical*—that is, promoting the "grounding of self and communal identities through place making" (Mares and Peña 2011:198). It is crucial that we see the struggle of diasporic and historically marginalized communities to secure access to land, food and justice as intrinsic to the work of Watershed Discipleship in our home places.

V. Conclusion

In this essay, I have proposed that the urban grid operates as a physical and mental reality *opposed* to watershed consciousness and ecology. Where the watershed unites creatures and landform by the flow of water, the urban grid isolates them by parceling and commoditizing land. Watershed design is a function of landform and contours, whereas the grid is imposed irrespective of terrain, inscribing itself in lines and angles that disregard the particularity of place. As water flows beside or underneath or through the grid, it is manipulated and administered according to the interests of those in power. The pulsing, living flow of water is forced into a static grid.

If humans are to live in right relationship to the earth cycles of energy upon which we in fact depend, we must reconceive how the designs of our settlements relate to the watershed as the fundamental design feature of ecosystems. And if Christian disciples are to live in right relationship to the watershed, we must resist the geometric hegemony of urban grids that incorporates both land and people into a matrix of oppression, and promote instead webs of life and visions, like Daniel's, that transcend the imperial grid. Our own prophetic actions can animate hope for new life-ways in our watersheds—and a good place to start might just be "down by the riverside."

References

Abrams, David. 1997. *The Spell of the Sensuous*. New York: Vintage.
Adams, Robert. 1958. "Salt and Silt in Ancient Mesopotamian Agriculture." *Science* 128 (3334) 1251–58.

Adams, Robert. 1981. *Heartland of Cities*. Chicago: University of Chicago Press.

Alkon, Andrea Hope. 2013. "Food Justice, Food Sovereignty, and the Challenge of Neoliberalism." Conference Paper # 38, presented at *Food Sovereignty: A Critical Dialogue*, an International Conference at Yale University, September 14–15. (http://www.iss.nl/fileadmin/ASSETS/iss/Research_and_projects/Research_networks/ICAS/38_Alkon_2013.pdf.)

Barstad, Hans. 1996. "No Prophets? Recent Developments in Biblical Prophetic Research and Ancient Near Eastern Prophecy." In *The Prophets: A Sheffield Reader*, edited by Philip Davies, 106–26. New York: Continuum.

Berry, Wendell. 2003. "Two Economies." In *The Art of the Commonplace: The Agrarian Essays of Wendell Berry*, edited by Norman Wirzba, 219–35. Washington, D.C.: Counterpoint.

Carstensen, Vernon. 1987. "Patterns on the American Land." *Journal of Federalism*, 18(4) 31–39.

Collins, J. J. 1993. *Daniel (Hermeneia: A Critical and Historical Commentary on the Bible)*. Minneapolis: Fortress.

deBuys, William. 1999. "Saint Contrary: John Wesley Powell." *High Country News*, April 12. (http://www.hcn.org/issues/152/4945.)

Diamond, Jared. 2005. *Collapse: How Societies Choose to Succeed or Fail*. New York: Viking.

Dolman, Brock. 2008. *Basins of Relations*. 2nd ed. Occidental, CA: Water Institute.

Ellul, Jacques. 1970. *The Meaning of the City*. Grand Rapids: Eerdmans.

Hernández, Arelis R. 2014. "Churches Receive Stormwater Fee Discounts by Starting 'Green' Ministries, Sermons." *The Washington Post online*, November 16. (https://www.washingtonpost.com/local/md-politics/churches-receive-stormwater-fee-discounts-by-starting-green-ministries-sermons/2014/11/16/7bbb94e4-6914-11e4-b053-65cea7903f2e_story.html.)

Hutchinson, Christopher. 2000. "John Wesley Powell and the New West." *Cosmos 2000*. (http://www.cosmosclub.org/web/journals/2000/hutchinson.html.)

Koenen, Klaus. 2004. "*skl.*" In *A Theological Dictionary of the Old Testament*, Vol. 14, edited by G. Johannes Botterweck, Helmer Ringgren, and Heinz-Josef Fabry, 112–27. Grand Rapids: Eerdmans.

Mares, Teresa M., and Devon G. Peña. 2011. "Environmental and Food Justice: Toward Local, Slow, and Deep Food Systems." In *Cultivating Food Justice: Race, Class, and Sustainability*, edited by Alison Hope Alkon and Julian Agyeman, 197–220. Cambridge: MIT Press.

Moholy-Nagy, Sybil. 1968. *Matrix of Man: An Illustrated History of Urban Environment*. New York: Praeger.

Mumford, Lewis. 1961. *The City in History: Its Origins, Its Transformations, and Its Prospects*. New York: Harcourt.

Myers, Ched. 1988. *Binding the Strong Man: A Political Reading of Mark's Story of Jesus*. Maryknoll, NY: Orbis.

Niditch, Susan. 1987. *Underdogs and Tricksters: A Prelude to Biblical Folklore*. San Francisco: Harper & Row.

Norgaard, Karie Marie, Ron Reed, and Carolina Van Horn. 2011. "A Continuing Legacy: Institutional Racism, Hunger, and Nutritional Justice on the Klamath." In *Cultivating Food Justice: Race, Class, and Sustainability*, edited by Alison Hope Alkon and Julian Agyeman, 23–46. Cambridge, MA: MIT Press.

Odum, Howard T. 2007. *Environment, Power, and Society for the Twenty-First Century: The Hierarchy of Energy.* New York: Columbia University Press.

Otis, Delos Sacket. 1973. *The Dawes Act and the Allotment of Indian Lands.* Norman, OK: University of Oklahoma Press.

Pedersen, Olof, Paul J. J. Sinclair, Imgard Hein, and Jakob Andersson. 2010. "Cities and Urban Landscapes in the Ancient Near East and Egypt with Special Focus on the City of Babylon." In *The Urban Mind: Cultural and Environmental Dynamics,* edited by Paul J.J. Sinclair, Gullog Nordquist, Frands Herschend, and Christian Isendahl, 113–48. Uppsala, Sweden: Uppsala University Press.

Portier-Young, Anathea. 2011. *Apocalypse Against Empire.* Grand Rapids: Eerdmans.

Scott, James C. 1990. *Domination and the Arts of Resistance: Hidden Transcripts.* New Haven, CT: Yale University Press.

———. 1998. *Seeing Like a State: How Certain Schemes to Improve the Human Condition Have Failed.* New Haven, CT: Yale University Press.

Smith, Michael. 2007. "Form and Meaning in the Earliest Cities: A New Approach to Ancient Urban Planning." *Journal of Planning History* 6 (1) 3–47.

Smith-Christopher, Daniel. 2002. *A Biblical Theology of Exile.* Overtures to Biblical Theology. Minneapolis: Fortress.

Van de Mieroop, Marc. 2003. "Reading Babylon." *American Journal of Archaeology* 107:257–75.

———. 2005. *King Hammurabi of Babylon: A Biography.* Oxford: Blackwell.

Vanderhooft, David. 1999. *The Neo-Babylonian Empire and Babylon in the Latter Prophets.* Atlanta, GA.: Scholars.

Williams, William A. 1980. *Empire as a Way of Life.* Oxford: Oxford University Press.

Chapter Three

The Transfigured Earth
Bioregionalism and the Kingdom of God

JONATHAN McRAY

Do unto those downstream as you would have those upstream do unto you. –Wendell Berry (2004:135)

Summary: Prevailing understandings of the kingdom of God are alienated from the land, which is viewed as national territory or real estate instead of a community of creatures. Displaced political theologies consecrate or overlook social and ecological destruction, obscuring the reality that our lives depend on the health and hospitality of the earth. In contrast, Jesus's articulation of the kingdom of God envisions the liberation and redemption of the land and its creatures, in order to imagine healthier and more just ways to inhabit actual places. He affirms the biblical image for salvation as a *transfigured earth*, which recognizes the thread woven between human communities and the land. Jesus's spin on the story of a foreign leper healed in the Jordan imagines that river not as a violent border, but as reconciliation, drawing life together in the watershed. This chapter connects biblical readings that integrate social transformation, land care, and welcome to strangers to the bioregional imagination of reinhabitation, especially as

embodied by the Alliance for Appalachia and the Landless Workers Movement.[1]

I. The World and the Earth

On a July evening some years ago I sat in a hotel outside the Damascus Gate
of Jerusalem's Old City. Mahmoud Abu Eid, a Palestinian Muslim and close
family friend, was telling his story to a group of American travelers. He was
talking about checkpoints, home demolitions, and color-coded ID cards
that classified him as a resident alien with ephemeral rights, though his
family had lived in that city for seven generations. An exasperated visitor
finally blurted out, "Why do you stay in Palestine with so much persecu-
tion?" Mahmoud smiled. "Because we have no other choice. This is my
place. I don't want to quit it. I love this land. Jesus loved this land."

Like that American traveler, we modern white Christians often
struggle to understand someone like Mahmoud who expresses an intimate
affection for where he is despite the oppression he experiences. We do not
recognize the biblical prominence of place, though our hymns depict a
"holy land." One theological stumbling block is the fact that the kingdom
of God, a notion lying at the heart of Jesus's gospel, is understood by both
academic and popular readers as *geographically unattached*. Though they
concede that the Old Testament is concerned with land, they seem to think
that the New Testament uproots a holy people into a universal, extrater-
restrial kingdom. While theologians diverge as to whether the kingdom
of God should be seen as a social revolution, ethical lifestyle, existential
consciousness or future divine rule, most agree it is a *landless* mission. For
example, N.T. Wright argues that Jesus's command to renounce possessions
is a command to abandon land, the "central possession in that culture . . .
Jesus is urging his contemporaries to set loose the things that had become
inalienable symbols of national identity" (1999:62). Wright's interpretation
assumes that land is real estate or national territory, so that a critique of
ownership or patriotism means abandoning the land.

---

1. Versions of this essay were previously published in *Missio Dei: A Journal
of Missional Theology and Praxis*, Vol. 5:2 (August 2014), online at http://missio-
deijournal.com/article.php?issue=md-5-2&author=md-5-2-mcray; and *The Other
Journal*, September 29, 2014, online at http://theotherjournal.com/2014/09/29/
the-transfigured-earth-jubilee-and-the-transformation-of-watersheds/.

Such perspectives tend to equate statelessness with landlessness, obscuring the reality that our lives always depend on the renewing health and hospitality of the earth. Land is not a commodity but a community of soil, water, air, plants, animals, and humans. Osage theologian George Tinker claims that indigenous cultures feel a "kinship tie to the land itself," a steadfast sense of the interrelatedness of a community larger than human tribes or villages (2008:71). This larger community is not the state, but "all the living, moving things" (2008:9); kinship is not rooted in ownership, but in affection for particular places and a responsibility to relate to the land with care.

If the kingdom of God is an embrace of life, then it must also be grounded in the land. Territorial borders may be erased, but the need to sustain our lives from the earth is not. Though the polyphonic biblical narrative may not advance a uniform perspective about the earth (Habel 1995), neither does it suggest a heavenly afterlife for disembodied souls. From the Garden of Eden to the New Jerusalem, the biblical images for salvation that recur most often concern not a spectral heaven but a *transfigured earth*. When severed from this tradition, the kingdom of God becomes an otherworldly space, in which Jesus's vision of a radical ordering of wealth and power is also lost (see Myers 2001:30ff). Without this grounding, we lose the ability to imagine healthier and more just ways to inhabit actual places.

Displaced and displacing Christian theologies of dominion have for too long sanctified or ignored social and ecological destruction. Central to their devaluing stance is to equate the New Testament notion of "the world" (*kosmos*), a term often associated with the powers and principalities and which indeed "passes away" in apocalyptic texts, with "the earth" (*gē*), a word suggesting the biodiversity of ecosystems and human communities. These words can be synonymous in English, but their theological conflation is problematic. It allows the kingdom of God—which Jesus indeed opposes to the *kosmos* (especially in John's Gospel)—to also be alienated from the earth. This theological error has created the space for the modern ideology that earth has no value outside of human engineering to prevail in our churches.

This conflation is represented in, and reinforced by, three political theologies in wide circulation in contemporary Christianity.

1. *Radical Orthodoxy* is an intellectually influential movement that seems to exhibit a certain nostalgia for Christendom. It ties an all-encompassing vision of Christianity to Western civilization, as if pining for

the bygone days when the church ruled the world and anticipating a reinstatement of its dominion. A reunion of church and state is seen as a goal, in competition with secularism and Islam (Ralston 2014). This theology fervently condemns liberal individualism, capitalism, and Islam, yet tends to stay silent about Christendom's many sins, such as the countless imperial campaigns that evicted Indigenous peoples from their homelands (e.g., Milbank 2010). Radical Orthodoxy instead imagines that the kingdom of God and European civilization were spread in the same forceful stroke: the world was saved by being conquered. By romanticizing this history, this theology whitewashes the way that the cross was turned upside down and sharpened into a sword.

2. Various liberal and conservative versions of *Christian realism* in the United States are suspicious of this rerouting of all roads toward Rome. But they agree that the secular nation-state is the only possible way to distribute power and organize common life, and are utterly disinterested in the ecologies and cultures of Turtle Island that exist beneath the political jurisdictions of the U.S. In classic Nieburhian fashion, this approach sees the American empire as a lesser evil, which usually means ignoring or endorsing its violence to make the world safe for global capitalism instead of struggling for viable alternatives. These political theologies suffer from the amnesia named by historian Ronald Wright, who notes that the U.S. may not have committed more crimes than other nations, but "it forgets them more quickly and more thoroughly" (2009:15). The kingdom of God, meanwhile, is relegated to a spiritual realm, while modern empire globalizes placelessness, ignoring natural boundaries and ecological scale by redrawing borders in the interests of profit and power. Any place will do for development, because all places are equally expendable.

3. A third trajectory eschews these first two; instead, Christians are to act as *"resident aliens,"* in the world but not of it, refusing the authority and splendor of nation states and remaining perpetual exiles among them (Hauerwas and Willimon 2014). Christians are absolved from the wider work of social transformation, since the church is viewed as a distinct polis, putatively self-sufficient and untethered to economic forces or ecological energies. Like Radical Orthodoxy, this theology insists that modern liberalism should not determine how Christians exists in the world: let the "church be the church" (Hauerwas 1983).

But this idealized ecclesiology, which represents their primary expression of the kingdom of God, ignores the fact that real churches are located *on* the earth, *somewhere,* surrounded by neighbors they did not choose. And it too easily appeases historic beneficiaries of colonialism (not to mention current neoliberal exploitation), while relegating Indigenous peoples and refugees to *actual* exile: one scholar told me that he mourned for a Native American Christian friend who could not overcome his "Zionist connection to tribe and land" in order to see the church as a truer alternative community. We might rightly call this view "resident alienation": Christians will not likely care for land in which they insist on remaining "foreigners."

All three political theologies preserve the devastating conflation between "world" and "earth," see coercive power as the mainstay of politics, and are in varying degrees anthropocentric. The world is seen only as a web of human-constructed systems that we either control or from which we escape—which effectively overlooks the dependence of these human systems on the life and health of the earth.

Wendell Berry notes that most American Christians have no place to lay their heads; they are eternal strangers to their landscapes because their only Holy Land is one they may never see (2009: xii). For many of us, earth is just dirt, static and inert, something to be wiped from our shoes. We forget that earth is *soil,* humming with organisms and complex horizons.[2] Perhaps this mistake is inevitable, considering that our consciousness is far removed from the organic processes that sustain us. But no matter how mobile we are, we are always some*where* and deeply intertwined in the ecological web of life. Our political theologies, therefore, need to center on a resilience and regeneration that acknowledges the bond between human powers and the life and health of the earth. Instead of imperial nostalgia, we need liberation for the displaced and repentance from the displacers. Instead of baptizing the state in resignation, we need an anarchist imagination that invites participation and cooperation in sustainable political culture. Instead of resident alienation, we need a homecoming to the land community.

Contrary to the old Pietist hymn, this world's our *only* home; we're *not* just passing through. The Apostle Paul, trying to settle internecine ecclesial

2. Soil horizons are parallel layers often distinguished by color and texture and formed by geology, time, climate, and vegetation. These horizons are broadly classified as topsoil, subsoil, and parent material.

disputes about diet, may have insisted that "the Kingdom of God is not food and drink but righteousness and peace and joy in the Holy Spirit" (Rom 14:17); but for our lives on earth it must to some degree *also* be about eating and drinking. This essay proposes, then, that "transfigured earth" may be a more fitting translation for Jesus's metaphor of "the kingdom of God." Such a theology requires people to care about where and with whom they dwell, heeding Jesus's call to pay attention to the ravens and the lilies of the field (Luke 12:24–27; Myers 2009). To pay attention means learning the ecological patterns and social histories of the places we inhabit, and how these two have interacted, both beautifully and tragically.

II. Reinhabiting the Transfigured Earth

I currently live in the Shenandoah Valley, part of the Ridge and Valley subsection of the Great Appalachian Valley. This two-hundred-mile basin, shaped like an outstretched arm and open hand, is hemmed in by the Allegheny Mountains to the west, the Blue Ridge Mountains to the east, and the Potomac and James Rivers to the north and south respectively. Shenandoah is carpeted with mixed hardwood forests and fertile limestone soil, evidence that the valley was once under an ocean. This explains its long history of cultivation; I know a farmer who has uncovered agricultural tools over seven thousand years old in the streambed below his fields. Running down the valley's spine and its watershed is the eponymous river.

Shenandoah fits landscape architect Robert Thayer's description of bioregions as physiographically unique, geographically legitimate, and operative spatial units (2003:15). Bioregions are the confluence of patterns like watersheds and landforms, soil and vegetation, climate and human interaction. Even though their ecological boundaries are fluid, they are more viable than capricious political lines, says Thayer (2003:19). Bioregions are places in which we know the scale of our actions, which are sensitive to feedback, and all inhabitants can be included in making decisions that affect them. They are therefore the best context for a praxis of liberation, participation, and homecoming.

Loving our neighbors as ourselves must include those we did not choose and our nonhuman neighbors. Scale is central to bioregional imagination, founded on the premise that we create ethical relationships as our actions have consequences for others (Evanoff 2011:20). We need to see the effect of our lifeways through critical feedback loops. For example, the industrial food system upon which most of us depend causes soil erosion, water pollution, energy depletion, and worker replacement, while requiring increased chemical and mechanical inputs, irrigated water, imported fertility, and cheap migrant labor to maintain productivity. Attention to scale helps tear the veil from a global economy that externalizes costs through cheap nonrenewable energy and outsourced labor and resources.

My home, Appalachia, is one of the most biodiverse regions in North America, with a rich history of skilled communities inhabiting its hills and forests. But Appalachia is also one of the most socially fragmented and economically poor regions in the country, often demonized as a backward and dispensable culture. In the late nineteenth century, after most of the Cherokee were killed or expelled, Central Appalachia became the primary source of coal and timber for the U.S. economy, and was severely logged and mined. But mechanization and resource depletion forced millions to immigrate north for factory work. Thirty-six of the poorest one hundred U.S. counties are now in this region, with the greatest poverty found in rural counties with intensive coal production. Access to education and healthcare has been limited, and the region has high rates of diabetes, cancer, mental health issues, and drug abuse. State and federal regulations are inadequately enforced, and counties are often controlled by a powerful few. The land has also suffered from this pervasive mining and logging, its abuse substantially correlated with absentee corporate ownership. People often feel compelled to choose between jobs and their own health and that of the land. The industrial economy has not been the savior of Central Appalachia.

Bioregional boundaries will not completely supplant political ones in the near future, but partnerships like the Alliance for Appalachia are forming across state lines to address social and ecological issues. The Alliance envisions a world in which everyone has access to clean water and air, and healthy land that is owned and stewarded locally. They organize to end mountaintop-removal coal mining and other destructive extraction technologies, and to create a sustainable and just Appalachia. This work is founded on the belief that mountain people are the experts of their lives, that they should participate in determining the future of their communities, that regional collaboration builds local power, and that systemic change is necessary to achieve justice in the region. The Alliance acknowledges the historical and continuing oppression of the disabled, the working class, people of color, women, and LGBTQ communities in Appalachia. It seeks to unite the region for the common good, with member organizations from Tennessee, Kentucky, Virginia, and West Virginia who believe they can move the nation away from an extraction economy toward a new ethic of whole and healthy communities (http://theallianceforappalachia.org/).

The Alliance demonstrates that places are not only connected, but also ever-changing. There is no "pristine baseline" to which we can return (Flores 1999:50). Bioregions are grounded mosaics moving through time that do not accept a dichotomy between culture and nature. Like every other creature, we alter and adapt to our ecosystems, which in turn adapt to and alter us. We are, as historian Dan Flores says, "endlessly recreating place" (1999:52). Purist rejections of change are inattentive to the lively unfolding of place.

This approach shifts us from a culture of *occupation* to cultures of *reinhabitation* (Carr 2004:238), committed to the life and health of our places. Occupation controls, reinhabitation converses. If we observe and interact within our bioregions, recognizing that various contexts are dynamic and connected, we will find appropriate and transformative responses to social conflicts and ecological degradation. Political theologies of empire, the state, and resident alienation prevent diverse people from cooperating with one another for liberation, participation, and homecoming. A political theology of reinhabitation calls for conversion to the transfigured earth so that we might learn to dwell well together in the world's diverse places.

III. The River is Reconciliation

Reinhabitation makes possible, and can be made possible by, imaginative interpretations of biblical stories. The stories about Jesus arose from particular places, and need to be understood in their social and ecological context. This helps us appreciate how they make important connections between social transformation, land care, and welcoming the stranger. The land, which Mahmoud reminds us Jesus loved, is an intrinsic part of those stories, which challenges the landlessness of modern kingdom of God theologies.

Israelite agricultural practices were closely related to the land and seasonal changes. A keen knowledge of their regions was important because harvest times differed based on local climates (Freyne 2006:24). Jesus's vision of the kingdom of God grew from the soil, seasons, and stories of the Lower Galilee under Roman rule, where creation and empire overlapped. This region between the Jordan river and the Mediterranean sea is, like

Appalachia, a fragile place, but also astoundingly fertile, with diverse ecological niches close together due to uneven wind flows and rainfall across rugged terrain (Lowery 2000:9). Biblical scholar Ellen Davis suspects that its "liminal location gave that small corridor of land a gene flow with few parallels worldwide" (2009:50). This region is thus like an ecotone, the overlapping biodiverse edge between two ecosystems (Holmgren 2002:224). Bioregional boundaries are mosaic habitats, without rigid borders. According to Toby Hemenway, edges like ecotones "are where things happen. Where a forest meets the prairie, where a river flows into the sea, or at nearly any other boundary between two ecosystems is a cauldron of biodiversity . . . The edge is richer than what lies on either side" (2009:45).

Jesus's homecoming in the Gospel of Luke helps us imagine bioregional engagement with the land and its people. As was his custom, Jesus attends synagogue on the Sabbath in his hometown. According to Luke 4:16–21, he unrolls the scroll from Isaiah and reads about an anointing to preach good news to the poor, liberate the oppressed and imprisoned, heal the sick, and proclaim Jubilee. In a dramatic and concise "sermon" he announces, "Those words are fulfilled right now." Everyone nods in amazed approval (and perhaps the poor in attendance exclaim "It's about damn time!"). Peasants in Herodian Galilee were subject to multiple layers of colonial taxation, and those who could not pay were evicted from their ancestral lands, which were then consolidated into great estates (Horsley 2003:32). The land was not being shared fairly among its inhabitants as Torah intended (Freyne 2006:42–3).

The Jubilee tradition envisioned a restoration of the livelihood of agrarian peasants through an ethic of abundance, self-restraint and redistribution (Habel 1995:97; Lowery 2000:57; Myers 2001:10ff). It suggests that the central political and moral question of land stewardship is not ownership but care (Davis 2009:102). With his declaration of Jubilee, Jesus indicates that his vision of the kingdom of God is grounded in the liberation and redemption of the land and its creatures—the transfiguration of earth.

If possession is conditional on care, then Jubilee challenges not only old states, but also new ones (Davis 2009:107). The Landless Workers Movements (or MST) of Brazil, a vehicle of peasant resistance to neoliberalism, is one of the largest social movements in the world. According to Brazilian law, ownership of unproductive land can be challenged by counter-claimants. While this law was systematically manipulated by rich landowners to seize valuable land from peasants, the MST flipped its use to serve the dispossessed (Perfecto et al. 2010:110). This was accomplished through dramatic direct actions that gained land for almost one million families (Vergara-Camus 2014:3). For MST, land is not primarily for producing monetary wealth; it is the source of subsistence and well-being (Vergara-Camus 2014:183). Land reform means redistribution and radical democracy in order to resist oligarchic power, which cannot happen if unorganized people are continually forced to new frontiers by government interests and land barons. MST believes that people need to remain in their places, where they are familiar with soils, climates, and cultures, and that land redistribution can create sustainable communities (Perfecto et al. 2010:112).

Jesus announces that the ecotone of Galilee belongs to the people who care for it, not to those that own and exploit it. But as everyone nods in agreement, Jesus adds that Jubilee is not just for the chosen people (or some ideal church set apart): "There were many in Israel with leprosy in the time of Elisha the prophet, yet not one of them was cleaned—only Naaman the Syrian" (Luke 4:27). Naaman was not just an outsider; he was a major cog in the Aramean military machine (2 Kgs 5; see Spina 2005:76). Jesus thus pairs a tale about the healing of an unclean outsider with his vision of the social renewal of Israel.[3] Because of his audacious social ecology, Jesus's audience turns on him, and tries to throw him off a cliff (Luke 4:29).

There is never only one way to interpret sacred texts, because they must always be understood within and translated for a given time and place. Jesus reminds his people that welcoming the stranger is compatible with at least some of their political traditions (Havrelock 2011:16). Jesus confronts purist paradigms that see only good insiders and bad outsiders, because he understands that ethnic groups are often formed by selective memory and selective amnesia (Willis 2009:8). He juxtaposes Jubilee renewal with the old Hebrew tale of a leprous foreigner to reinterpret the

---

3. Though Naaman's military might is hardly comparable to the power of the oppressed, a contemporary and recontextualized analogy to the shock value of Jesus's midrash might be to assert that, for white American males like me, enslaved Africans were more responsible for building America than the Founding Fathers, that Indigenous peoples are just as responsible for democracy as Western civilization, or that Hispanic immigrants are returning this land to its multicultural roots. My point is that reinterpreting founding stories which define insiders and outsiders can be subversive (thanks to Rachelle Martindale for this nuance).

meaning of the kingdom of God—and the Jordan River flows through his reading in an important way.

In the story of Naaman, an enslaved Israelite girl recommends that her leprous captor go see a prophet in Samaria. She knows where the prophet lives but not his name; according to her folk wisdom, healing for the military leader Naaman can only "result from a nonmilitary encounter with Israelite rivals" (Havrelock 2011:178). At the encounter, the general scoffs at Elisha's advice to wash seven times in the Jordan River, a watercourse he dismisses as a mere trickle compared to rushing rivers back in his homeland of Aram (2 Kgs 5:11f). Once again servants (not advisors) intervene, convincing Naaman to perform the ritual. The healing is effected without the presence of the prophet, or priests, or the king of Israel, or economic exchange; the Judean river itself is enough (Spina 2005:81). We can read this as ecological restorative justice: Naaman has to be healed in the watershed that he had invaded and damaged.

Naaman crosses the rolling Jordan twice: once to attack Israel, then to find healing. This suggests "a link between invasion and illness as well as between peaceful contact and healing" (Havrelock 2011:177). Elisha tells the afflicted general to immerse himself in the river that separates, but also unites, Israel and Aram. The Jordan thus represents an ecotone edge, "places of transition and translation, where matter and energy change speed or stop or, often, change into something else" (Hemenway 2009:46). By combining the story of Naaman with his vision for social renewal, Jesus recognizes that rivers are not sites of separation, but of encounter, boundaries that join rather than divide. As Naaman discovered, the river is reconciliation, drawing life back together in the watershed. The movements of rivers tell us that strangers are always among us, that the familiar always appears in the foreign. We too must learn to see the border rivers of our contemporary landscapes not as walls but as bridges, whether it is the Jordan between Israel and Jordan, the Rio Grande between Texas and Mexico, or the Kagera between Rwanda and Tanzania. The river is local and global, the neighbor and the stranger in our midst, and we must attend to the movements of its waters.

Marianne Sawicki writes that the Herodians controlled Galilee through centralization and marginalization. They employed Roman technology in an early "pave-and-pipe" paradigm to erect massive aqueducts that conducted water from faraway streams to urban centers: "Caesarea sucked on Carmel" (Sawicki 2000: 61,100). This type of irrigation provides plentiful water during droughts or dry seasons, but has profound effects on watersheds. Groundwater is used faster than rainfall can recharge it, causing land to subside and salinization near coasts. When water is borrowed from other places (or from the future), the likelihood of nutrient leaching and soil erosion increases (Gliessman 2007:4).

In contrast, according to Sawicki, indigenous Israelites embraced a cosmology of circulation and grounding (2000:61). For them, the heavens poured down water to the earth, where it was grounded by crops; surplus was caught in cisterns or circulated through channels, forms of water catchment that imitate the natural contour patterns of water. Storing rainfall (as opposed to diverting surface water) demonstrates the people's dependence on the gifts of heaven and the earth. Circulation and grounding, Sawicki believes, is a better way to understand Israel's view of holiness than the notion of *separation* that still prevails among theologians: "A place is holy when things move rightly within it and, moreover, when it can rectify the trajectory of what crosses it. Thus, what profanes is whatever moves the wrong way" (2000:100, 34). Thus Naaman's movement of conquest through the land was corrected by the circulation and grounding of the watershed that healed him.

The contrast between these two ancient views of water harvesting is powerfully relevant today. Ninety-eight percent of the Lower Jordan is now diverted for domestic and agricultural use by Israel, Jordan, and Syria, while the remaining 2 percent is sewage from fish pond waters, agricultural runoff, and saline water diverted from salt springs around Galilee. As a result, the river has lost 50 percent of its biodiversity (Havrelock 2011:237). Israel not only controls the Jordan River, but also 80 percent of Palestine's groundwater sources; both are pumped to taps in Tel Aviv and farms in the Negev. This modern strategy of centralization and marginalization has severely diminished the ancient waterway, depleted essential aquifers which are now extremely vulnerable to salinization, and intensified the Israeli occupation of Palestinian land (Faris 2011). Water, and how it is used and controlled, will increasingly determine the shape of this conflict (El Houry 2012). The current Israeli occupation conceals the fact that the land of Palestine has always been shared, and that the stranger has always been our neighbor. Lines can be drawn, people can be displaced, histories can be rewritten, but in the end all of us dwell together in particular places. The rain falls on friends and enemies alike. According to Daniel Kemmis, places can breed cooperation when "people who find themselves held together (perhaps against their will) in a shared place" discover that their best chance for survival is learning to work together (1990:122).

Our best chance for justice and peace is to enact Jesus's blend of Jubilee and watershed transformation. Like Naaman, we must learn to move from profane control to holy conversation through acts of reinhabitation. Theologically we need a hermeneutic of reinhabitation because the ancient myths of Scripture about this place influence modern geopolitics, sometimes catastrophically. Zionist leaders like David Ben-Gurion hosted study groups on the book of Joshua with scholars, politicians, and military officials (Havrelock 2011:14, 246). The United States has considered itself both a new Chosen People and a triumphant New Rome (Horsley 2003:137). We can and should interpret these stories with a bioregional imagination that tends to the earth and its creatures. As Peter Manseau asks, "What is theology if not a kind of revisionism? In the landscape of human discourse, theology occupies the place between fiction and history, myth and memory" (2006: 387–8). Theology itself, like a river, is like an ecotone.

IV. Conclusion: The Kingdom of God as Ecosynthesis

Bioregionalism is a conversation between people and place, and conversations always hold open the possibility for mutual conversion. *Ecosynthesis* is a term that describes the evolution of native and exotic species into new ecosystems in response to novel conditions. Ecosynthesis has remarkably beneficial and restorative effects on devastated landscapes (Holmgren 2002:262). It is thus like the good news of the kingdom of God: an invitation to reinhabit the transfigured earth.

Imperial occupation both ancient and modern has relentlessly disrupted Galilee. Jesus's imagination of the kingdom of God was an ecosynthesis, stitching together Jubilee and the leper in the river, a patchwork of observation and interaction within an endlessly recreating place. Jesus embraces the buzzing biodiversity of the land as a parable for hospitality. But the reconciling river is not just the Jordan, but also the Shenandoah and every watershed in the world. Colonial forces have invaded, conquered and damaged these rivers (see Friesen, Chapter One), yet they are also where we are healed. We must move from displaced political theologies to reinhabitation, for the kingdom of God is among us (Luke 17:21) as the transfigured earth. The grounding soil and circulating water are our holy land.[4]

4. "Harlan Hubbard, when a local church asked him for a painting of the Jordan,

References

Berry, Wendell. 2004. "Watershed and Commonwealth." In *Citizenship Papers*, 135–42. Washington, DC: Shoemaker & Hoard.

———. 2009. "Foreword." In *Scripture, Culture, and Agriculture: An Agrarian Reading of the Bible*, by Ellen F. Davis, ix–xiii. New York: Cambridge University Press.

Carr, Mike. 2004. *Bioregionalism and Civil Society: Democratic Challenges to Corporate Globalism*. Vancouver, B.C.: University of British Columbia Press.

Davis, Ellen F. 2009. *Scripture, Culture, and Agriculture: An Agrarian Reading of the Bible*. New York: Cambridge University Press.

El Houry, Ramzi. 2012. "Water for All: The Case for a One-State Solution." *Al Jazeera*, last modified January 26. (http://www.aljazeera.com/indepth/opinion/2012/01/201211712183641435 4.html.)

Evanoff, Richard. 2011. *Bioregionalism and Global Ethics: A Transactional Approach to Achieving Ecological Sustainability, Social Justice, and Human Well-Being*. New York: Routledge.

Faris, Stephen. 2011. "Holy Water." *Orion*, November/December. (http://www.orionmagazine.org/index.php/articles/article/6473).

Flores, Dan. 1999. "Place: Thinking about Bioregional History." In *Bioregionalism*, edited by Michael Vincent McGinnis, 43–60. New York: Routledge.

Freyne, Sean. 2006. *Jesus, a Jewish Galilean: A New Reading of the Jesus-Story*. New York: T & T Clark.

Gliessman, Stephen R. 2007. *Agroecology: The Ecology of Sustainable Food Systems*. 2nd ed. New York: CRC.

Habel, Norman. 1995. *The Land is Mine: Six Biblical Land Ideologies*. Minneapolis: Fortress.

Hauerwas, Stanley. 1983. "The Servant Community: Christian Social Ethics." In *The Hauerwas Reader* (2001), edited by John Berkman and Michael G. Cartwright, 371–91. Durham, NC: Duke University Press.

Hauerwas, Stanley and William H. Willimon. 2014. *Resident Aliens: Life in the Heavenly Colony*. 25th anniversary expanded ed. Nashville: Abingdon.

Havrelock, Rachel. 2011. *River Jordan: The Mythology of a Dividing Line*. Chicago: University of Chicago Press.

Hemenway, Toby. 2009. *Gaia's Garden: A Guide to Home-Scale Permaculture*. White River Junction, VT: Chelsea Green.

Holmgren, David. 2002. *Permaculture: Principles and Pathways beyond Sustainability*. Hepburn, VIC/Australia: Holmgren Design.

Horsley, Richard A. 2003. *Jesus and Empire: The Kingdom of God and the New World Disorder*. Minneapolis: Fortress.

Kemmis, Daniel. 1990. *Community and the Politics of Place*. Norman, OK: University of Oklahoma Press.

Lowery, Richard H. 2000. *Sabbath and Jubilee*. St. Louis, MO: Chalice.

Manseau, Peter. 2006. "Revising Night: Elie Wiesel and the Hazards of Holocaust Theology." *Crosscurrents* 56(3) 387–99.

Milbank, John. 2010. "Christianity, the Enlightenment and Islam." *ABC Religion and News*, August 24. (http://www.abc.net.au/religion/articles/2010/08/24/2991778.htm.)

made them a painting of their own river, the Ohio" (Berry 2009: xii-xiii).

Myers, Ched. 2001. *The Biblical Vision of Sabbath Economics*. Washington, DC: Tell the Word.

———. 2009. "Pay Attention to the Birds: A Bible Study on Luke 12, Ecology and Economics," *Sojourners*, December (38:11) 29–31, 53.

Perfecto, Ivette, John Vandermeer, and Angus Wright. 2010. *Nature's Matrix: Linking Agriculture, Conservation and Food Sovereignty*. Washington, DC: Earthscan.

Ralston, Joshua. 2014. "Islamophobia and the Comeback of Christendom: Riposte to Adrian Pabst." *ABC Religion and Ethics*, August 4. (http://www.abc.net.au/religion/articles/2014/08/04/4060254.htm.)

Sawicki, Marianne. 2000. *Crossing Galilee: Architectures of Contact in the Occupied Land of Jesus*. Harrisburg, PA: Trinity Press International.

Spina, Frank Anthony. 2005. *The Faith of the Outsider: Exclusion and Inclusion in the Biblical Story*. Grand Rapids: Eerdmans.

Thayer, Jr., Robert L. 2002. *LifePlace: Bioregional Thought and Practice*. Berkeley, CA: University of California Press.

Tinker, George E. 2008. *American Indian Liberation: A Theology of Sovereignty*. Maryknoll, NY: Orbis.

Vergara-Camus, Leandro. 2014. *Land and Freedom: The MST, the Zapatistas and Peasant Alternatives to Neoliberalism*. London: Zed.

Willis, Lawrence M. 2008. *Not God's People: Insiders and Outsiders in the Biblical World*. New York: Rowman & Littlefield.

Wright, N. T. 1999. *The Challenge of Jesus: Rediscovering Who Jesus Was and Is*. Downers Grove, IL: InterVarsity.

Wright, Ronald. 2009. *What is America?: A Short History of the New World Order*. Toronto: Vintage Canada.

Chapter Four

God's Gonna Trouble the Water
A Call to Discipleship in the Detroit Watershed

LYDIA WYLIE-KELLERMANN

Summary: This chapter explores my own call to Watershed Discipleship through the waters of my life. I reflect on baptism in the stories of my mother, the work of solidarity in Palestine and El Salvador, the struggle against water shut-offs in Detroit, and beginning my journey as a parent.

DARK AND HEAVY CLOUDS are rolling in fast. The sound of the wind in the leaves marks the coming of a storm. "Hurry," my mom calls to us; my sister and I jump in the car and we speed off. We park just as the first rain drops start to hit the pavement. Barefoot, with inner tubes under our arms, we make for the water, pushing past the crowds fleeing the other direction, searching for cover. We try to keep up as we watch my mom wade into Lake Huron; as we are up to our shoulders, the clouds finally give way and release the storm. The rain pours, and we lift our faces to it, letting the waves hold our bodies.

Jeanie Wylie-Kellermann.

The memories I hold of my mom feel like tributaries of water. She loved water in all its forms. We climbed through streams, danced in thunderstorms, and feasted on bowls full of snow covered with stringy chocolate sauce. Quietly and slowly, we walked through newly fallen snow, admiring the tracks of creatures out of sight. We honored the Four Directions with rock circles beside the Atlantic Ocean. In the heat of Detroit's summers, we found relief for our feet in buckets of ice. She taught us from a young age not to fear the water. We would paddle out in the middle of Lake Esau and tip the canoe to practice floating, then hold her gently while she swam us to shore. Her voice drifted me into dreams with hymns and freedom songs about water: "Wade in the water. Wade in the water children. God's gonna trouble the water."

A quarter of a century ago, Christian theology was far more distanced than today from the environmental movement, care for creation, and the liberative, earth-based texts in Scripture. Ahead of her time, my mom yearned for, learned from, and honored indigenous and Celtic traditions, holding them in balance with her love of incense and the Episcopal Eucharist. With a circle of women, she would go deep into the woods on vision quests. When we picked a flower or cut down a Christmas tree, we asked permission and gave thanks in the Native tradition. Her parenting was a beautiful tapestry, woven of an uncompromising and indistinguishable love of both Christian theology and earth spirituality. Her spirit found a resting place in my blood stream; I too am seeking this way, expecting our Christian tradition to hold the earth at its root.

Water flows through our ancient Judeo-Christian texts. Righteousness pours down like a mighty stream (Amos 5:24), and Jesus offers relief to those who thirst (John 4:13–15). Before whales or eagles or humans did, God dwelt among the waters (Gen 1). The creation of heaven and earth commenced through a parting of the seas. Rains fell, destroying all creatures except those aboard an ark, awaiting a rainbow covenant that promised an end to the waters of judgment (Gen 9:11–17). The Israelites flee from their oppressors to freedom through the miracle of a parting sea that offered safe passage from empire into the wilderness (Exod 14). In the Gospels, Jesus was baptized into the wildness of the river Jordan (Mark 1:9f), became living water at the well (John 4), and shed tears over Jerusalem (Luke 19:41). From the beginning, water has offered a call to discipleship.

I. Empire's Control, Discipleship's Call

Water, which is neither renewable nor infinite, is in danger. Our capitalist, consumer, entitlement economies and lifestyles have perpetrated great violence on the waters, leaving a bleeding earth and our future in danger. Polluted and commodified, water has become the next battleground for corporate grabs, military conflict, and occupation.

After graduation from college in 2008, I stayed with a family in El Salvador for a few days. They were lucky to get running water once every two weeks, when basins and buckets would be filled. During the long dry spells, they carried their laundry down the side of a mountain to wash in a river. The health risks of doing this had been recently intensified because of a newly built private community of wealthy families upstream; I could see sewage and agriculture chemicals pour down the side of the mountain and into the river. We drank nothing but Coca Cola, because it was more accessible to the families in this village than clean drinking water.

A few weeks later I was in the West Bank of Palestine, visiting another family experiencing drought and without running water. Again to my dismay and disgust, nearby was an Israeli settlement that was well shaded with trees, sprinklers spinning water on green grass. Driving alongside the "security wall" built by the Israeli occupation force, I saw how it twists and turns according to water access instead of along the lines declared by the United Nations in 1948. Occupation has seized the water. In that place 2,000 years ago Jesus walked alongside those waters under a different occupation. Rome was constructing aqueducts to direct, hoard, and control access to water. The Sea of Galilee was being industrialized and overfished, with fish salted and preserved into both medicine and food for export, making it increasingly difficult for local peasant fisherman to sustain their livelihoods. Empire always keeps an eye on the water.[1]

When we read the stories of Jesus, we encounter the landscape and geography of his roots. These familiar Scriptures are neither timeless nor placeless. We know the names of cities, mountains, and bodies of water. Crowds gather for baptism at the Jordan River (Mark 1:9f); turbulent waves shake the boat in a storm on the way to Gerasa (Mark 4:35ff); the community gathers to share a simple meal of fish caught in the Sea of Galilee (John 21:12ff). These place names were written and remembered because they matter. Jesus walked on water, was immersed in it, ate from it, traveled on it, and healed with it. He was intimately connected to water, and critical of the imperial economy that sought to control it.

Ironically, it is likely that we know the names of Jesus's waters better than we know those of our own. We know our water as it comes from a tap or bottle, but are ignorant about from which stream, lake or aquifer it comes. What are their names? What would it look like if communities were defined by the watersheds that nourish us rather than by gerrymandered political lines? Today our lives are so fast-paced and mobile that there is no time to touch and know the waters. We have forgotten how to be still, to pay attention, to feel the earth below our feet, and to honor it as our home. If we are to follow the Jesus who knew his waters and his place, we must take the time for our roots to go deep, to know our place so intimately that

---

1. For the question of water justice in the Occupied Territories, see http://www.thirstingforjustice.org/ and https://www.oikoumene.org/en/resources/documents/wcc-programmes/justice-diakonia-and-responsibility-for-creation/climate-change-water/ewn-jerusalem-statement?set_language=en. On the politics of water in biblical Judea see also Pritchett, Chapter Two and McRay, Chapter Three; on the political economy of the fishing industry around the ancient Sea of Galilee see Myers 2009:22–30.

we cannot ignore the needs of our neighbors or the unjust history that has shaped us. We must be able to feel the waters drying up. The earth cries out to us like a voice in the night, pleading with us to walk gently, for she is tired. She calls on us to remember her history, to tell the stories of those who have walked before us, and to live in a way that honors those who will walk after us. The trees invite us to come and sit and watch them grow. The soil asks us to hold it in our hands and learn why it is disappearing. The birds, bees, creatures, and plants call on us to preserve and trust and honor diversity. The rain summons us to dance and rejoice in all that grows and is sustained, for without water there is no life. God has always called us to this work through every moment of history.

Watershed Discipleship requires us to be followers and learners, nourished and nourishers. We must grow to trust water like manna in the wilderness, taking only what we need without hoarding, profiting, or exploiting (Exod 16). Water serves all of creation, and in return we should serve the waters. It is a matter of dignity and justice for all people and for the planet.

II. Submerged into *Wawiatonong*

My own roots and discipleship have called me home to the watershed into which I was baptized and in which I was nurtured. The Detroit River Watershed holds me like the moon's pull on the tides. I have known her rivers, streams, lakes, thunder, and snow. The 70 percent of my body that is water comes from this river. The Ojibwa called this place *Wawiatonong*, which means "where the river goes round." The Detroit River winds its way between two countries, and connects the Great Lakes, which hold 20 percent of the world's fresh water.

But in the building of Detroit, as in so many urban spaces, the streams and rivers have been forced underground to accommodate freeways and built environments (see Fahey, Chapter Five). The Great Lakes are being damaged economically and ecologically by untreated sewage, industrial pollutants, and invasive species; yet in our age, as we no longer have enough clean water to support our rate of use, these lakes will be next to be commodified and privatized, piped and drained, bottled and sold.

Detroit today is under occupation. Michigan's Governor has illegally appointed an Emergency Manager to "fix" the city by rendering Detroit's elected officials powerless and seizing the power to break contracts, sell off city assets, and collaborate with banks and corporations to profit off of an economic disaster they created. Our schools, lighting, trash, and public spaces have all been privatized, and it is no secret that the water department is next. Under orders from the Emergency Manager, the Water Department announced in the spring of 2015 that it was taking serious action against customers behind on their bills; water would be shut off to anyone who owed $150 and was sixty days late. By fall they planned to turn off 120,000 homes—meaning that 45 percent of Detroiters (the same percentage as those in poverty) would have to live without running water. Each day since, pickup trucks patrol neighborhoods, turning off water with no warning and no final notices. Homrich, a private company, was hired for this massive undertaking—the same company that contracts with the City to do home demolitions. If the water bills are not paid, they are tacked onto one's tax bill, putting thousands of homes in jeopardy of tax foreclosure.

This is all part of the City's plan to put profit over people. one activist wrote in April 2015, the "water shutoffs made international news showcasing Detroit as a third world country. [The] water management plan sparked local, national and international protests bringing the United Nations to declare Detroit the site of a Human Rights Emergency."

III. Charity Waging Love

Shortly after the water shut-off announcement, Charity Hicks, a longtime water activist in the city, woke early and looked out her window to see contractors turning off her water. She grabbed her robe and ran outside barefoot to alert her neighbors. She banged on a neighbor's door where a single, pregnant mother with eight children were still asleep. Water was cut before the kids had time to use the toilet or brush their teeth for school. Charity begged the contractors: "Can you give people at least five minutes warning, so, we can fill up buckets and bathtubs?!" After pleading with them, and angry at their inhuman response, she called the police.

Charity Hicks, Erinn Fahey, Lydia Wylie-Kellermann, and Isaac.

When two white officers arrived, the contractors told them she had assaulted them. Without listening to her story or why she had called, they handcuffed Charity, still in her robe, threw her phone and keys on her front lawn, and said, "You need to be taught a lesson." They took her to the only processing facility operating since Emergency Management—a state run prison—where she experienced awful treatment. The day after Charity was released on medical necessity, I sat in a pew and listened to her speak, still shaking from the experience. She called for a campaign of love in Detroit: "Children and the most vulnerable around the city are living with no running water, no flushing toilets, sewage backups, and no fresh water to drink.

Parents are afraid to come out and say their water has been shut off, because that is cause for Child Protective Services to take your children."

There are neighborhoods in Detroit now where only one house on the block remains with running water. The number of children being hospitalized for sanitary related illnesses brings back fears of waterborne illnesses we haven't had for a century, and the National Nurses Union has declared this a health crisis. How soon will children in Detroit, like those in El Salvador, be in a situation where Coca Cola is more accessible than clean water? Meanwhile, as water is being shut off to the poor, the Palmer Park Golf Club owes $422,000 in unpaid water bills, the Veterans Administration hospital $131,000, the NFL Lions's Stadium $55,000, and the Red Wings Hockey Arena $80,000. But there, as with Israeli settlements in Palestine, sprinklers water green grass, while nearby families thirst for justice.

Charity's heart and feet mobilized while charges were still hanging over her head. "If I am going to go down fighting, it's going to be for water!" she proclaimed loudly. But tragically, just weeks after her arrest, while waiting at a New York City bus stop on her way to give a talk on water, she was hit by a drunk driver; after weeks in a coma, she joined the ancestors on July 8, 2014 (see Ristau 2014).

This is not the first time that one woman said no and a movement was born; Charity stands in a tradition that stretches from Shiphrah and Puah in Egypt (Exod 1–2) to Rosa Parks in Montgomery. Even as many of us in Detroit mourn the loss of this sister, friend, justice thinker, and water warrior, her vibrant spirit continues. Others are carrying forward her "campaign of love," a movement determined to carry on until the shut-offs have stopped, a water affordability plan is adopted, and Detroit's waters are permanently protected from privatization. The citizens of this city are going to love an alternative future into being.

Two weeks after Charity died, at 6:30 am on a hot July morning, a group of us crossed the street and blocked the entrance to Homrich, the company hired to do the shut-offs. Fifteen trucks stood inside with tools, compressors and a list of addresses for the day. Across the driveway, we held a banner reading "Stop the Water Shut-offs," framed on each side with a painting of a baby in a bubble bath and a child brushing her teeth. In a circle, we joined hands and invoked Charity's name, dedicating this action to her as an expression of waging love—¡Presente! We poured a line of water across the driveway, and passed a cup around the circle, drinking and blessing one another. Then we sang: "Who are these children dressed in red?

God's gonna trouble the water. Must be the ones that Charity led! God's gonna trouble the water." The police did not make arrests until two pm. Since these trucks do 500 shut-offs a day, many homes had water one more night because for seven hours the fleet did not move. Ten Detroiters were arrested that week, nine the next—teachers, organizers, grandmothers, pastors, professors, journalists, urban farmers. We can count on more to come.

Stop the Water Shut-offs Protest.

While the resistance has been gathering outside Homrich, the Water Department, Water Board meetings, and banks, it also is building in the heart of our neighborhoods. Organizers are walking door to door to let folks know what is happening, what they can do, and how they can support one another. Stories are gathered, yet as the national media descends on Detroit in hunt of a personal angle, we are careful to protect families from public exposure because of the real danger of Child Protective Services removing children from their homes. Neighbors are helping one another. On blocks where only a few homes remain with running water, hoses are stretched out on the front lawn for people to fill buckets. Those with water are washing laundry for others, securing the dignity of clean clothes. Churches are opening their doors and becoming stations for water distribution.

Around the world, outrage is growing. The United Nations has declared Detroit water shut-offs a human rights abuse. In a caravan of vehicles, the Council of Canadians drove 1,000 of water across the bridge from Windsor to Detroit as an act of "international aid." As Maude Barlow, a well-known water activist with the Council, put it, "I have traveled around the world and I see water issues like this in Third World countries, but never before in the United States!" Another Canadian mama of the movement, who lives in the same watershed with us, called this "a real watershed moment!"[2]

The convoy's water was delivered to St. Peter's Episcopal Church, my faith community, where my father pastors. We placed the water around the baptismal font, with a banner hanging above reading: "St. Peter's Water Station. Water is love." We blessed the water, singing "There's only one river, there's only one sea, and it's flowing through you, and it's flowing through me. We are one." My father intoned: "It is only right that this water be gathered at the baptismal font. Baptism is the way into the church. But it is also the way out into the world."

St. Peter's Water Station.

IV. Baptism as the Way into the World

Baptism laid its claim on me through the words of my mother, who loved sacrament and liturgy, but was challenged when it came to baptizing her baby. She felt keenly the dangers represented in the act of baptism facing the newborn in her arms:

2. On the U.N. declaration, see Abbey-Lambertz 2014 and the report by Barlow at http://www.globalresearch.ca/water-crisis-in-detroit-putting-corporate-profit-ahead-of-human-rights/5388726.

Water, words, community. Offering our child back to God. We would stand with Abraham at the sacrifice. We would give her to a God who models the cross. We would invite her to listen for a voice calling in the night, to vigil, to put herself at risk, to leave family and friends, to speak clearly a truth for which one can be executed . . . So, we baptize her into the risks we've elected for our lives. We take her, in utero, to Nicaragua. We share with her this broken, violent world. We baptize her into the communion of saints who have been crucified in every possible way. We baptize her into the grueling decisions at Gethsemane and into Easter hope. We lay her on the altar before a God who rejects our carefully laid plans and takes her life into His/Her own.

And in so doing, we smash an idol. The child is no longer a reason to flee from the voice of God. Instead, we carry the child, with our hearts, toward the one who utters us and calls us into being. We claim our lives in that voice and entrust each other to it (Wylie-Kellermann, 1986).

"God's gonna trouble the waters" into which we are invited—rocky and dangerous. Into these waters my mom carried us, tipping our canoe so we would be held by them, teaching us to trust, to not to be afraid of the storm, to know the love of God. During some of the scariest moments of my life, from El Salvador to Palestine to Detroit, the reminder of my baptism kept me standing, though my knees were shaking.

My knees still shake, my stomach turns, and my heart aches each morning when I look out my window, fearing that the Homrich truck will find its way to our street. In my neighborhood, being one month late on a water bill may mean not only that kids are removed, but that parents are deported.

Today humidity hangs in the air. Shrieks of laughter make me smile, as I sit and watch a dozen children run through the sprinkler. They maneuver around my wobbling toddler as he sticks his face right into the arc of water.

"What does his shirt say?" asks Nayeli, an old soul at the age of eleven.

"Water is a human right," I answer.

Jason, who usually moves too reckless and fast for conversation, asks, "What does that mean?" In the vocabulary of a child, I try to explain what has been happening with the water shut-offs, and ask whether anyone in summer school has talked to them about this. Though the trucks have been within four blocks of our house, it is clear from their faces that this is the first they are hearing of it.

"But then you can't take a shower!" Jason protests, and keeps asking questions. "What if you don't have any bottled water to drink in your house? What if you run out of water to drink? How do you flush your toilet?" Others on the soggy lawn grow quiet as the reality starts to dawn on them.

"Exactly!" I reply. "It isn't fair. Just because you can't pay the bills, you still need water!" Murmurs of agreement last for a moment, but then the sprinkler calls out their names again. I watch the kids play in the water, hoping that our brief conversation might combat the shame that could come if their houses are targeted by a shut-off, and instead generate collective anger at the injustice, and help us to lean on one another when the trucks do come.

This is the place to which my baptism is calling me today. It calls me back into the water—and into the communities where people have been denied this basic gift and necessity. I watch my toddler play in the water. He has joined us at every march, lifting his fist high as we chant "Water is a Human Right!" I can't help but wonder what the state of these waters will be when he is an adult, and whether they will be safe for his grandchildren to drink.

My son has loved water since before his mind and muscles could give way to a smile. We carried him into the Great Lakes when he was just months old, his grandmother's spirit clearly alive within him. I pause, mindful of the waters that held him in my womb before I could hold him in my arms. I breathe a prayer:

> My dear child, lift your face to the storm, feel the power of the waves as they knock you over, dance with me in the rain, feel no fear. Trust this water as the life force that runs through your body, catch a snow flake on your tongue and feel God incarnate, give gratitude again and again, stand in awe at the abundance and sacredness of it. And feel it, as I do, as a call to discipleship.

References

Abbey-Lambertz, Kate. 2014. "Why UN Experts Are 'Deeply Disturbed' By Water Shutoffs For Low Income Black Detroiters." *The Huffington Post*, October 22. (http://www.huffingtonpost.com/2014/10/22/detroit-water-shutoffs-un-black-detroiters_n_6016516.html.)

Myers, Ched, and Elaine Enns. 2009. *Ambassadors of Reconciliation, Vol. I: New Testament Reflections on Restorative Justice and Peacemaking*. Maryknoll, NY: Orbis.

Ristau Julie. 2014. "Remembering Charity Hicks, Ardent Advocate of People's Right to Water." *Commons Magazine* online, July 11. (http://www.onthecommons.org/magazine/remembering-charity-hicks-ardent-advocate-peoples-right-water).

Wylie-Kellermann, Jeanie. 1986. "Within a Communion of Children." *On the Edge,* cited excerpt September 30, 2014. (http://radicaldiscipleship.net/2014/09/30/within-a-communion-of-children/).

Chapter Five

Caring for Our Waters
Shifting the Engineering Paradigm

Erinn Fahey

Summary: In an historical era threatened by climate change, economic and technological greed, disregard for the poor, individualism, and white supremacy, we look in part to engineers. Their work has perpetuated many of these crises, but they also have the tools and problem-solving ability to help move us toward racial, economic, and environmental justice. This paper explores the vocational call to be a visionary engineer in light of the gospel and the times.

I. A Tale of Two "DamNations"

BEAVERS ARE NATURE'S ENGINEERS. They labor tirelessly in shallow streams building canals, lodges, and dams, relying on local materials. Such dams create wetlands, which in turn establish biodiverse habitats for many animals, including several threatened North American species that rely on these freshwater habitats for survival. A beaver makes its home upstream of a dam in a mound of sticks plastered together with sediment from the stream bed. Canals are dug to transport construction materials to the dam or lodge, but also to keep water onsite when levels are low. Stream water is cleaned as it filters through the wetland and dam. A beaver's dam is not permanent, but exists in a dynamic equilibrium with the stream bed to which it is anchored.

Humans build dams too, but with quite different impacts. Our dams are built to serve anthropocentric political and economic interests, most often food and electricity production—resources that rarely are distributed equally. With virtually every major waterway in the United States now dammed, we have seen massive displacement of people and destruction of ecosystems. As sediment and silt build up behind dams, the water quality and habitat downstream suffer. Built with concrete and steel, these structures are meant to be permanent. Indeed, efforts to remove them encounter huge obstacles.

These examples represent a tale of two contrasting engineering crafts. Beavers can show human engineers how to create ecologically rich and diverse habitats that uplift creatures, humans, and the earth itself. As Canadian professor Glynnis Hood writes, "Beavers are the great comeback story, a species that outlasted the Ice Age, major droughts, the fur trade, urbanization and near extinction" (2011:9). In the face of the historical ultimatums presented by our contemporary ecological crisis, can we admit that we do not have all the answers, and perhaps allow beavers to be our teachers to whom we listen and from whom we learn? This might begin to free us from our obsession with technological development and dependency, profits over people, and environmental exploitation. What would it look like if we, too, used resources found locally, and that would return to the earth? What if we only engineered in the places where we lived, and in ways that would support our bioregional ecosystem? How could human engineers leave a place healthier than when we arrived?

I am a white, Masters educated, employed, able bodied woman. I have lived twenty-eight of my twenty-nine years in the Great Lakes Basin. Native to the Cuyahoga watershed, I humbly strive to be rooted in the Detroit watershed. I am a partner, mother, daughter, sister, aunt, neighbor, runner, gardener, bicyclist, learner, teacher, listener, chicken nurturer, coffee roaster, and math nerd. I am also a practicing water engineer.

I spend my workdays designing and resolving issues related to water for a civil engineering firm. Most of my work involves storm water: designing water detention basins, managing drainage along roadways, analyzing sewer systems in areas prone to flooding, designing green infrastructure, and providing alternative design solutions to improve water quality to surface waters. For example, when waste water treatment plants are at capacity, sanitary sewer overflow events can occur, in which raw sewage is discharged to surface waters; my job is to evaluate why and design a fix. Though I am early into my career, the list of the issues I face grows longer every week. My work as an engineer arises from a vocational calling to merge my analytical and problem-solving skill set with a desire to care for the earth and the living things that inhabit her. It also emerges from my commitment to justice and my discipleship of inhabiting this place. As such, it presents real challenges.

II. Detroit, City of Hope

Detroit impacts me in profound ways. It is a place where I have clearly been able to see the attack on the urban poor. Structures of racism exist in plain sight, expressions of white supremacy and unbounded economic growth. At the same time, Detroit has been my greatest teacher concerning community, and how revolutionary and necessary it is. Knowing one's neighbors and lifting each other up is arguably our most important work, especially in a culture that promotes individualism and dominion over others and the earth. Detroit put me on a continuing journey of coming to terms with my own privilege, and understanding ways that I routinely benefit from the dominant economic and political system, often at the expense of others. Detroit has taught me the value of listening deeply to, and learning the histories of, place and people.

I have been amazed by how the people of Detroit—exploited by corporate interests, deserted by white elites and city government, and now preyed upon by re-developers and state government takeovers—are struggling to create a new alternative reality from the ground up. They are addressing issues that affect them on a daily basis: food, education, lack of city services, and water shut-offs. I have learned that it is not enough to say "No!" to these systems; we need also to start living and growing into the Beloved Community through a process Detroit activist Grace Lee Boggs—a Chinese American activist, writer, and speaker based in Detroit who passed away in 2015 shortly after her 100th birthday—called "visionary organizing."

Once a thriving city of two million, Detroit was considered a place to realize the American Dream—which in capitalism is built on the backs of the poor, with clear winners and losers. Many citizens were employed by one of the "Big Three" automakers in the city: GM, Ford, and Chrysler. In the 1950s, whites started leaving the city for the suburbs, aided by the Federal Housing Administration. As whites were out-migrating, new highways to enable them to commute back into downtown for their managerial jobs began to be constructed, tearing through black neighborhoods and displacing thousands. The metro Detroit area was redlined, ensuring housing discrimination, and the city became increasingly racially and economically segregated. Inequality in the workplace, the housing market, and law enforcement fed the frustration and pain felt in the black community, which was expressed in the 1967 rebellion, one of the major urban riots of that decade.

As more people left the city in the 1970s, so did small businesses and grocery stores. Currently a city of 700,000, Detroit has become a food desert; for most residents now, the only place to buy produce is at corner liquor stores. The middle class exodus left a myriad of vacant lots, on which some started farming in response to the food crisis. Urban agriculture was born here not as a hipster fad, but as a way for Detroiters to feed themselves and each other. This movement has expanded to provide work; farmers's markets have popped up in neighborhoods all over the city, along with more than 1,000 farm, community, market, and home gardens (see http://detroitagriculture.net/).

In response to lack of city services, Detroiters are "putting the neighbor back into the hood." Ron Scott, who came out of the Black Power movement of the 1960s, has helped found Detroit Peace Zones for Life, which facilitates the practice of Restorative Justice in communities experiencing violence among each other and with police, as an alternative to the criminal justice system. This coalition encourages citizens to participate actively in making their communities safer (see http://detroitcoalition.org/). Certain neighborhoods have been emptied and torched by the foreclosure crisis, literally in some cases.[1] In response, residents have organized block clubs and other groups to clean their streets, alleys and vacant lots, board up abandoned houses, and create public art and grow gardens to beautify the urbanscape. On my own block, several neighbors have come together for

1. Beginning in the 1980s in Poletown, arson has been used systemically to remove people from neighborhoods (Wylie 1989). Since the recent foreclosure crisis, banks profit more when houses burn by collecting insurance money on the original value of the home; the banks thus have no financial incentive to restore homes and put them back on the market.

cleanup days, getting to know one another as we share tools, work, laughter, and pizza. At our annual block party, a good friend organized local children to decorate and paint plywood to use in boarding up an abandoned house. Most recently, neighbors organized a festival of lights called "Iluminado" as a way to reclaim community space after recurring violence in the neighborhood. Lights were strung up and down the block, candles lit the stoop of every porch, and handcrafted lanterns were paraded over a three-block area. It has created so much joy and deepened relationships that it may become an annual event.

In March of 2014, the City announced an aggressive water shut-off campaign, with a goal of turning off water to 3,000 homes every week. Residents who were sixty days past due or $150 behind on their water bill were at risk of shut-off, for which they were given little or no warning, nor a process for disputing bills or making a payment plan. Meanwhile, commercial customers who were in delinquency were given ample time to pay and avenues to dispute bills (see Wylie-Kellermann, Chapter Four). Through the leadership of We the People of Detroit, water stations and hotlines have been set up around the city in churches and community centers (http://wethepeopleofdetroit.com/). Water has been donated from both domestic and Canadian groups. Outreach teams hit the street to check in with residents in hard-hit neighborhoods, coming away with heartbreaking stories: parents and children, elders and infants living with no way to bathe, brush their teeth, or clean up after bathroom use; no water for cooking or drinking; children at risk of being taken away by the state; homeowners forced into foreclosure as outstanding water bills are tacked on to housing taxes. But also emerging are stories of strength and perseverance: water hoses strung between houses; neighbors doing laundry for and delivering water to each other. This is Beloved Community, Detroit-style. And it is Watershed Discipleship in our place.

III. Engineering Challenges and Evolution

Though my discipline is directly connected to land and water, I often find my profession to be at odds with my vocational calling to justice and reinhabitation. This is no surprise; after all, the engineering field is embedded in a capitalist system predicated on technological control and economic growth. It is and will be an ongoing challenge to navigate between my values and professional duties, which so often serve political and economic interests before human and environmental ones.

Piping and paving waterways, for example, has been a common civil engineering design practice in the modern era. Impermeable concrete is laid down throughout a city for economically and physically efficient transport of water. A map of the metro Detroit region reveals an abundance of rivers: the Rouge and its capillary tributaries, the Clinton, and the Huron, which empty into the Detroit River, Lake St. Clair, and Lake Erie, respectively. However, in Detroit all surface waters have been forced underground and absorbed into the city's sewer system. For example, Baubee Creek, which used to flow just a couple of blocks from my house, was impounded by a set of two parallel tunnels in the 1960s in anticipation of urban growth. Paving and piping waterways has detrimental effects on the environment, such as increasing storm water runoff, interfering with groundwater recharge and sediment transport, degrading water quality, and destroying ecosystems.

Like any profession, engineering has been evolving with time. As engineers have recognized the detriments of the pave and pipe ideology, and face the needs of our aging infrastructure, there have been many strides toward more innovative and sustainable alternatives. Green infrastructure, for example, employs structures and practices that allow storm water to spread, soak, and infiltrate into the ground, instead of into pipes headed to waste water treatment plants or a nearby rivers. Bioswales may take the place of conventional concrete curb and gutter. Bioswales are depressed ditches with gently sloped sides, at the base of which is a couple of feet of compost soil mix that supports water tolerant native plants. Instead of the rain being guided into a catch basin via curb and gutter and on to the sewer, water would collect in the swales. There, plants and soil remove and filter pollutants as the storm water infiltrates the compost layer and surrounding soils (during large rain events, an overflow pipe will discharge excess flow into the existing sewer system). Other examples of green infrastructure include rain gardens, pervious pavers, infiltration trenches, green roofs, and rainwater cisterns.

In graduate school I was introduced to these practices in two key classes: river engineering and storm water management. With a good professor who promoted sustainable infrastructure and the daylighting (bringing culverted and otherwise undergrounded watercourses back to the surface) and restoration of rivers, these two classes helped me affirm that there was something for me in the engineering field. However, as I entered

into the workplace, I found that these practices have not yet gained significant traction. Green infrastructure is starting to be considered in more
projects, but rarely do experienced engineers see the need for alternatives,
or believe in their viability. And there are other complications. Even designs that involve green infrastructure can have contradictory political and
economic undertones. For example, in January 2013, a 347-page document
called the *Detroit Future City Strategic Framework* was published to serve as
a long-term planning guideline for city stakeholders. A pragmatic, logical,
and visually appealing document, the plan articulates a way to rebuild and
re-vision the city over the next fifty years, and proposes specific steps to get
there. It puts a heavy emphasis on environmental transformation and low
density areas that have been marked for rezoning as "innovative ecological"
areas. These areas would be criss-crossed by green and blue infrastructure
that would: manage storm water through ponds and wetlands; clean air
with carbon forests; uncover sequestered streams; create habitat for diverse
wildlife; nourish the earth; recharge the groundwater; and clean the rivers.

Unfortunately, this plan is predicated on the depopulation of neighborhoods, and is not the product of a democratic process. The strategy is
to neglect people presently living in impoverished areas; exercising emi-
nent domain is avoided by simply divesting in these communities so their
residents will "choose" to leave. Already in some of these neighborhoods,
schools have closed and churches have left; Public Works has stopped ser-
vicing city lights, keeping streets dark. Eventually, police, fire, and EMS services will not respond in these areas. This is known as "design apartheid."
Another problem with the plan is that it does not address how and why
the city got to where it is today. A plan that forecasts what Detroit will look
like in the next fifty years ought to consider the history of the place and
people. Race is an integral part of Detroit's history and current moment, for
example, yet is not mentioned once in this document.

The *Detroit Future City* plan is an example of an ambitious project that
utilizes creative and innovative practices as an alternative to our aging and
expensive urban infrastructure. However, it exemplifies a shortcoming in
the engineering design framework: making technological advances in the
environmental arena while neglecting the social needs of people. Alternatives such as this will only perpetuate problems if they are not rooted in
the history of the place. Engineering cannot make a paradigm shift in environmental design without also changing the dominant racial, economic,

and political paradigms toward environmental justice and participatory democracy.

Amidst these tensions and problems, the work of a water engineer is broad, expansive, and vital to the everyday lives of people. Whether it is pouring a tall glass of water from the tap, flushing a toilet, swimming in a nearby lake, fishing in a river, or driving during or after a big rain, engineers have had something to do with it. There is important history here, too.

One of the largest impacts engineers have had on communities was the sanitation revolution of the nineteenth century. In the early 1800s, people used chamber pots and outhouses to take care of human waste. Waste was then either thrown out to sit stagnant in roadside ditches, or dumped into cesspools, pits with concrete or brick walls where wastewater infiltrates into the ground. Improperly maintained cesspools contaminated soils, ground-water and surface water, affecting drinking sources. As cities developed and diseases such as cholera and typhoid became more prevalent, poor sanitation practices were recognized as the culprit of these epidemics. Local governments started investing in a network of pipes that would use gravity to carry storm and sanitary waste (combined sewers) away from residential and commercial districts to a receiving lake or stream. The frame of mind at the time was "dilution is the best solution." As raw waste poured into surface waters, engineers thought that nature would take care of the rest; physical and biological processes would dilute and clean the water back to its pristine condition.

Although local sanitary conditions improved and disease outbreaks dwindled, the sewer outfalls affected downstream communities, plaguing their water supply. This brought about the treatment of wastewater, a process modeled after nature's cleaning processes with an extra dose of chemicals added in. The plant is where physical, chemical, and biological treatment takes place. Water is slowed down to allow sediments to settle from the water column for easy removal. Oxygen and UV light are used to disinfect, organic matter is broken down, and pollutants are removed through the cultivation of microorganisms called activated sludge. Some of the sludge is reused in the cycle, and the excess is used for agricultural purposes such as fertilizer. Before the water is discharged back into the natural environment, it is disinfected with chlorine.

Engineers are constantly learning the impacts of their work, which shapes the evolution of the practice—in the case of sanitation, from chamber pots to cesspools to a central treatment plant. For example, a lot of industry attention has been centered on addressing combined sewer over-flows (CSOs). Most older cities have combined sewers, which collect storm water, sanitary, and industrial waste in a common pipe that is carried to a waste water treatment plant. During large rain events or when the system is at capacity, this waste overflows into lakes or rivers. In Detroit, with just one inch of rain, CSOs occur in the Detroit and Rouge rivers. Cities all across the country are required to have a long term plan to address CSOs that will reduce their frequency and impact, guaranteeing compliance with the 1972 federal Clean Water Act, which regulates pollutant discharges in U.S. waterways. As infrastructure ages and with the high cost of replace-ment, engineers are looking toward alternatives, such as CSO treatment facilities where waste is disinfected with chlorine before discharging, or green infrastructure that keeps storm water out of the sewers entirely.

As the world faces catastrophic challenges as a result of our domineer-ing human presence on the earth, it is important and even hopeful to frame this time as one of evolution. We must continue to evolve as humans and engineers and with the consequences of our actions, so that we might live and work in ways that are creative, considerate, and nurturing. For prob-lems such as climate change caused by our technological aspirations and limitless appetites, we need *all* the problem-solvers. However, a paradigm shift is needed in the way we approach these problems, to avoid the nar-row "bandaid fixes" and proceed more holistically by considering social and ecological as well as technical factors. This would create "legitimacy for engineers in proposing alternative, radical, and paradigm-changing solu-tions" (Karwat et al. 2014).

IV. Participatory and Visionary Engineering

Engineers have an opportunity to be visionary: to reimagine our work as a craft that manages the human footprint while also restoring right relation-ship with the earth; and to create opportunities for people to engage in self transformation. In *The Next American Revolution*, Grace Boggs calls people to be visionary organizers:

> Every crisis, actual or impending, needs to be viewed as an oppor-tunity to bring about profound changes in our society. Going be-yond protest organizing, visionary organizing begins by creating images and stories of the future that helps us imagine and create alternatives to the existing system . . . We must come together as

inventors and discoverers committed to creating ideas and practice, vision and projects to help heal civilization (2012: xxi, xxiii).

Engineers too, are called to this. Visionary engineering involves doing work that is rooted in place, democratizes the profession, engages citizen participation, and broadens the problem-solving capacities of the engineer. This involves moving away from reductive, economically driven approaches that put profits before people and freely exploit the environment. As Dr. King put it, such changes will require a "revolution of values" (1986:240).

Boggs's husband Jimmy said it this way: "Revolutions are made out of love for people and love for place" (2012:96). Before a system can be turned on its head and before we can bring peace and justice to people and creation, we must first become more intimately connected to our place. In our watershed the land, creatures, and people are all nourished by the same water; the more we come to know this, the more stake we have in its well-being, and the more accountable we are to it. As noted, this includes learning the history of the watershed in order to engage present challenges. This approach can change the way an engineer comes to her work. The task at hand is no longer "just another problem to solve," but how to make our communities healthier. Instead of being removed from the people and land the engineer serves, she knows exactly who her work is affecting.

Participatory engineering involves a partnership between the professional doing the work and interested and engaged citizens. While engineers with vision and problem-solving skills are needed to help guide projects and train citizens, everyone can help in exercising care for their place. In fact, participatory engineering is necessary to understand the root of a given problem, to identify all stressors a watershed or community faces, and to arrive at meaningful and long lasting solutions.

One struggle for participatory water policy is Detroit's People's Water Board, formed as a coalition of different organizations to advocate for water as a human right. The Board believes water should be held as a commons, free of privatization (http://www.peopleswaterboard.org/). Charity Hicks was the Board's cofounder, a water warrior who passed in 2015 after inspiring the "Wage Love" movement against the City's water shutoff campaign. Charity believed that everyone should be involved in these issues: "We are saying: you are part of this conversation, you are an expert, we are all experts. We have full agency. This is what democracy looks like" (Barlow 2013:133).

In Georgia, the West Atlanta Watershed Alliance's guiding principle is authentic community engagement and collaboration, which recognizes the importance and necessity of community support for any project to be successful. In order to lift up the community's voice and get them a seat at the table of stakeholders, the Alliance designed a program called "Street Science," in which citizens are trained in air and water quality monitoring by other community members with scientific training. Founder Na'Taki Osbourne Jelks relates how citizens were being dismissed because they were seen as too "emotional" and "uneducated" on the topic at hand, so this training program has been an attempt to "democratize science" and to help citizens become agents of change in their communities. Jelks leads field trips to illegal dumping sites and out-of-compliance waste water treatment plants, organizes creek and stream cleanups, trains citizens in water quality sampling, and teaches about Atlanta's aging infrastructure and the water quality issues affecting local watersheds. "Helping people who live in environmentally degraded areas find their voices and challenge polluters who impair their quality of life," she says, "is the way toward lasting change." Indeed, the Alliance has won significant environmental battles in their watershed.[2]

One of the best ways to learn how to be a visionary engineer is to learn and connect with those doing radical work—like Jelks. She studied civil and environmental engineering at Georgia Tech, and has an M.A. in public health focusing on environmental health and occupation from Emory University (see http://whsc.emory.edu/home/publications/public-health/public-health/fall2010/public-health-24–7.html). Driven by her experience growing up in Louisiana's "cancer alley" and her mother's cancer, Jelks took an interest in environmentally degraded communities where industry adheres only loosely to environmental laws, playing by their own rules. As a part of her work with the West Atlanta Watershed Alliance and manager for the Community and Leadership Development Programs for the National Wildlife Federation, Jelks empowers citizens of all ages to take active roles in advocating for the environmental health of their neighborhoods.

Donna Riley is a founder of the first engineering program at a U.S. women's college (Smith). She has been researching and engaging liberative and feminist pedagogies in her classroom. Rooted in the work of bell hooks

2. See http://wawa-online.org/. For more on the impressive watershed-based community organizing work of Jelks and the Alliance, see Thompson, Chapter Six; clip at https://www.youtube.com/watch?v=A1FA10cC6Xk; and an expansive 2015 interview at: http://www.chedmyers.org/ArchivedWebinarWorldWaterDay.

and Paulo Freire, Riley challenges the "banking system" of education, in which professors make deposits into the brains of students, who are then expected to withdraw the deposit for testing or at jobs. Rather than training students to think reductively or mechanistically, liberative pedagogies see them as whole persons who can think critically and actively participate in their education. Teachers are also students, and students have more of a vested interest in the material (Nieusma et al. 2012). In a thermodynamics course at Smith College, Riley seeks to incorporate such pedagogy to "engage students in collectively creating a democratic classroom that encourages all voices" (2003). Her course consists of key elements: connecting the material to everyday life; students taking responsibility for learning and participating as teachers; ethics and policy issues; and de-centering Western civilization.

In my search for a community of engineers that incorporate social justice into their work, I stumbled online upon the Engineering, Social Justice and Peace network (ESJP). ESJP is a conglomeration of academics, practitioners, and students who "envision and practice engineering in ways that extend social justice and peace in the world":

> Our approach works toward engineering practices that enhance gender, racial, class, and cultural equity and are democratic, non-oppressive, and non-violent. We seek to better understand the relationships between engineering practices and the contexts that shape those practices, with the purpose of promoting local-level community empowerment through engineering problem solving, broadly conceived (http://esjp.org/).

The group organizes an annual international conference that hosts presentations and workshops on a variety of topics that intersect with social justice and peace, with foci on both local projects and international topics. The 2014 conference in Buenos Aires, Argentina included round tables on the engineering profession, education, cooperatives, and community development. ESJP also publishes a peer reviewed journal once or twice a year. I believe there is tremendous value in gathering a group of vocationally driven engineers to network with one another and collaborate in ways that make social justice engineering possible. It feels like a breath of fresh air to know there are people I can look to who walk with the same tensions I do and who share my vocation.

V. An Engineer's Oath

When I matriculated from graduate school I took part in the "Order of the Engineer" ceremony. Together with my classmates, I recited the "Obligation of the Engineer," an oath pledging to "uphold the standards and dignity of the engineering profession and to serve humanity by making the best use of Earth's precious wealth." Then I put my right hand through a large symbolic ring, and a much smaller stainless steel ring was placed on my little finger, an outward sign distinguishing an engineer. The ceremony is a rite of passage symbolizing the transition from student to practicing engineer. I was drawn to this ritual, and moved by the idea of standing with a group of peers pledging to ethical values. However, the oath we took doesn't encompass the vocation to which I am called.

I am just at the beginning of my journey, and have so much to learn as an engineer, as a student of justice, as a citizen of Detroit, and as a watershed disciple. As I continue to discern my vocation, reinhabit this place, and walk the tensions between often disparate strands of my life, I felt called to write the following alternative oath that challenges me to be a visionary engineer:

> I pledge be a visionary engineer who is humbly rooted in this place, which is more than a thing to be controlled. This place includes a diversity of living things of which I am a part; soil, trees, plants, flowing water, animals, and human beings are all interconnected, and we desire a healthy place to live.
>
> I pledge to work in this place like the beaver, who is a great teacher calling me to trust in another way. I will connect with other place-based, justice-driven problem-solvers, to learn and expand my own practice as an engineer, and to engage my imagination, which "is more important than knowledge" (Einstein).
>
> I pledge to recognize that water is a commons in the public trust, to be managed, distributed, and protected for the health and life of all. Delivering life's essential water to people is part of the work of an engineer, and I name and claim publicly that "Water is a human right."
>
> I pledge that in each project I work on I will bring social analysis and historical questions, working toward a more holistic vision that stands against environmental racism, poverty, and exploitive economic gain. I will listen to all who inhabit the watershed in which I work, and recognize that all voices are to be heard, valued, and welcomed as a multitude of experts in my ecosystem.

On my twenty-ninth birthday, my beloved gifted me a key chain with a beaver holding proudly to a piece of gnawed tree. This key chain, like the graduation ring, serves as a symbol of my pledges. This beaver reminds me who my teachers are, and to what my vocation calls me.

References

Barlow, Maude. 2013. *Blue Future: Protecting Water for People and the Planet Forever*. New York: The New Press.

Boggs, Grace Lee, with Scott Kurashige. 2012. *The Next American Revolution: Sustainable Activism for the Twenty-first Century*. Los Angeles: University of California Press.

Hood, Glynnis A. 2011. *The Beaver Manifesto*. Calgary: Rocky Mountain Books.

King, Martin Luther Jr. 1986. *A Testament of Hope: The Essential Writings and Speeches of Martin Luther King Jr*. Edited by James Washington. San Francisco: Harper Collins.

Karwat, Darshan, W. Ethan Eagle and Margaret Wooldridge. 2014. "Are There Ecological Problems that Technology Cannot Solve? Water Scarcity and Dams, Climate Change and Biofuels." *International Journal of Engineering, Social Justice, and Peace* 3(1–2) 7–25.

Nieusma, Dean, Donna Riley, Jens Kabo, and Usman Mushtaq. 2012. "Editor's Introduction." *International Journal of Engineering, Social Justice, and Peace* 1(1) 1–6.

Riley, Donna. 2003. "Employing Liberative Pedagogies in Engineering Education." *Journal of Women and Minorities in Science and Engineering* 9(2) 137–58.

Wylie, Jeanie. 1989. *Poletown: Community Betrayed*. Chicago: University of Illinois Press.

Chapter Six

An Ecological Beloved Community

An Interview with Na'Taki Osborne Jelks of the West Atlanta Watershed Alliance

SARAH THOMPSON

Summary: This chapter is an intergenerational conversation between two U.S. American women of African descent who are
leaders in organizations that address inequality and violence.
Na'Taki Osborne Jelks explains how a sidelined community in Atlanta, Georgia successfully mobilizes residents of the watershed to
challenge environmental racism and change city policy. The West
Atlanta Watershed Alliance is a grassroots effort empowering residents to reconnect with the environment around them and build
collective power to have a voice in City decisions that impact them.
Christian Peacemaker Teams executive director Sarah Thompson
reflects on historic splits in social movement and societal dynamics that permit inequitable decisions about sanitation and land
use infrastructure on local levels; she concludes with thoughts
about how these dynamics play out on a global scale. What might
it mean to be in solidarity with struggles in other watersheds to
build the ecological Beloved Community?

I. "SSDP": Connecting Dots, Bridging Gulfs

I CURRENTLY SPEND MOST of my time and energy in the administration and promotion of Christian Peacemaker Teams (CPT), an international organization that does strategic nonviolent intervention in areas of lethal conflict. In many places around the world, marginalized communities are mobilizing to stop violence being perpetrated against them and the land on which they live. In the context of military and/or economic occupation, this violence is often expressed at the end of a gun pointed at them by military, police, corporate security, or other armed actors. Going only where invited, small teams of CPTers work alongside community leaders and grassroots organizations to reduce violence and promote alternatives.

CPTers are trained physically, spiritually, and mentally for this demanding work. We also seek to develop within our teams an analysis that recognizes that violence is not only expressed externally (through death threats, bombs, or martial law), but exists in each of our hearts. It manifests through personal prejudice and systemic oppression—racism, sexism, heterosexism, "Samcentrism," and/or Christian hegemony—which arise from intersecting political, social, and communal structures.[1] If committed peacemakers are not attentive to the dynamics of privilege and oppression—i.e. the violence we carry intimately with and within us—our work can make a situation worse, strain team dynamics, and exhaust the local communities and leaders.

The same structural and lethal violence that manifests across international terrain also appears locally at a watershed scale. Historic inequality is layered like calcified sediment in every place, representing an unstable foundation upon which social and political structures are built. This chapter looks at the metropolitan region of Atlanta, Georgia. In the early 1800s white Settlers arrived in the area and authored a genocidal expulsion of the Creek and Cherokee people native to that place. Trade in and enslavement of African peoples followed with the establishment of plantation agri-business, resulting in both social and environmental destruction. This area has been ravaged by numerous wars over conflicting understandings of freedom and equality. But Atlanta has also been a hub for civil and social rights

---

1. "Samcentrism" is a term coined during a 2014 CPT workshop in Concepción, Chile. More specific than the anti-imperial term "Amerocentrism," it comes from Uncle Sam, the iconic image of what are in fact the most oppressive elements of U.S. imperialism: the use of human bodies and public funds to fuel a military industrial complex and global dominance through war-making and economic hegemony.

movements through history. Both violent and nonviolent efforts have left their mark on the human, theological, and ecological landscapes.

Even though the American civil rights movement achieved most of its basic aims, ongoing structural and internalized racism means continuing exclusion of Black and economically disadvantaged people in Atlanta's western watersheds.[2] The most damaged watersheds around Atlanta today are inhabited by populations that have been targeted by past and present racial and economic exploitation. Many factors have contributed to this, including a general disconnection of Atlanta residents from the land and laws governing land use, and lack of knowledge about green architecture and environmental planning. But most determinative was sanitation infrastructure and land use decisions made by the Atlanta municipal government in the 1990s—*without* the input of the most affected residents—especially regarding development of a combined sewer overflow system. Na'taki Osborne Jelks stresses "the importance of meaningfully engaging those most affected by planning decisions at the outset of the environmental planning." The city of Atlanta's proposals "would have adversely affected already overburdened neighborhoods, and exacerbated the already existing discrepancy in quality of life" (2008:173).

CPT is involved in many places around the world. To communicate with dispersed colleagues about common issues I often use the acronym SSDP: "Same Struggle Different Place." SSDP reminds us that because patterns of suffering repeat in predictable ways throughout our global system, we are never alone in what we face in a given watershed. As the famous Atlantan Martin Luther King, Jr. put it: "Injustice anywhere is a threat to justice everywhere. We are caught in an inescapable network of mutuality, tied in a single garment of destiny. Whatever affects one directly, affects all indirectly" (1986:290). This means that both locally and internationally we must connect the dots and examine how structures perpetuate exclusion and violence.

Conversations like the one Na'Taki and I shared help bridge gulfs between us, help us see the repeated patterns of violence on the bodies and lands of marginalized people everywhere, so we can prepare ourselves to be open and ready to act. We are called to organize for collective well-being

---

2. I define racism here as prejudice plus power, which characterize various public systems in the U.S. (such as courts and the legal corpus) that were constructed on the cultural assumptions of European-Americans. I define internalized racism as a taking on of attitudes, values, assumptions, and practices of a broader white-supremacist society by those who are part of population(s) historically targeted by racism.

both within our own communities and at the direction of the communities most affected. Marginalized people who bear the brunt of injustice must mobilize through community education, mobilization, and advocacy. And the privileged—who receive economic and social benefit from exploitation and exclusive processes—need to do their own work of deconstructing inequities. Still, our movements haven't always embraced the breadth of an intersectional analysis of oppression that complex social reality demands.

For example, there has long been a gulf between social justice movements and environmental movements. The former tend to focus exclusive attention on advocating for people. Indeed, slowing the assault on human life and dignity, meeting basic needs for shelter, food, and water, and trying to create healthy communities and organizations is fulltime work! The task of coping with the growing demands and increasing numbers of marginalized people, while trying also to practice self-care, can be overwhelming. On the other hand, mainstream environmental movements in the United States have paid attention primarily to the biosphere, often excluding the human. Some conservation organizations are anti-immigrant; others either romanticize or are overly critical of Indigenous peoples. Again, facing the multiple ecological crises that stalk our history is demanding work. Yet we need to integrate these movements, because it is increasingly clear that social and environmental issues are inextricably related.

CPT is often in the middle of these strained conversations, attempting to hold the strands of "people" and "nature" together in specific places. Invitations pour in to participate in struggles for social justice where the central issue is ecological. For example, in Las Pavas, Colombia, we stood alongside small farmers as they strategized how to regain access to their food sustenance crops after a multi-national corporation (protected by armed security) destroyed much of their land and tried to displace them in order to monocrop palm-oil trees for export. We worked together across international lines to win back access to their land. In northern Ontario CPT stood with Anishinabek elders to resist ongoing cultural devastation, participating in a long running blockade of logging companies who poison the Great Lakes environment and Indigenous communities through mercury dumping in the rivers.

Environmental and social justice movements need each other, and *can* develop a strong partnership. CPT has recently begun to talk about its work in terms of people(s), nature, and place. Though we work in specific conflict hot-spots around the world, most CPTers are also rooted in their own geographical home spaces, and participate there in faith-based bioregional social justice and peace work. Our mission is about "building partnerships to transform violence and oppression" at home and abroad, "inspired by the vision of a world of communities that embrace the diversity of the human family and live justly and peaceably with all Creation."[3] This is why I am pleased to participate with the other voices in this volume, who share our conviction that environmental theology is *not* separate from people's movements. Social struggles are integral to what happens for the health of the watershed; conversely, including the welfare of nonhuman nature in the work of social change will bring healing power to people's movements.

My conversation with Na'Taki Osborne Jelks regrounded me in Atlanta, a place that has formed both of us through our shared experience at Spelman College, a historically Black college for women. I love to learn about people of the African Diaspora who are doing work to heal our broken relationship with this "unchosen land." By re-introducing people to the wild and natural parts of Atlanta around them, Osborne Jelks's work creatively addresses the trauma stemming from the generations of transatlantic trade in African bodies, which destroyed so much of our souls, stories, families, and land-based practices. She is "part of the solution that helps address our issues and gets down to the root causes."[4] I believe her work is part of the next wave of the civil rights movement—building a Beloved Community that extends King's vision of humanity's deep mutuality to include interconnectedness with the watershed we inhabit.

II. The West Atlanta Watershed Alliance

Na'Taki Osborne was born in Walnut Grove, Mississippi, and later moved to Baton Rouge, Louisiana. The corridor between her home and New Orleans is nicknamed "Cancer Alley" because of the many people who have been affected by chemical leakages from nearby industrial plants. Her mother's cancer diagnosis was a catalytic moment for Na'Taki, spurring involvement in environmental justice struggles. As an undergraduate student

3. "Mission, Vision, and Values," www.cpt.org. CPTers sign up for two-to-three year terms as a full-timer, part-timer (four to six months in the field), reservist (two weeks to two months volunteer in the field), or administrative team member.

4. See the profile of her work at https://www.youtube.com/watch?v=Xv2kD8U_uWk (uploaded January 4, 2011). See also the interview I did with Ched Myers on the Bartimaeus Cooperative Ministries Webinar for World Water Day in March, 2015 available at http://bcm.adobeconnect.com/p354nyafzai/.

at Spelman College and Georgia Tech, she participated in local efforts to restore the Proctor Creek watershed in west Atlanta, in which Spelman sits. "The Proctor Creek watershed is one of Atlanta's most impaired," Na'Taki told me, describing how people from the suburbs illegally dumped refuse there. Transient Spelman students were invited to team up with long-time residents to do community cleanups, and to organize community watches to hold those dumping trash accountable. Na'Taki's student involvement with this local but off-campus work inspired her for a lifetime.

Na'taki married Ken Jelks in 2007. They have one son, and live in the Proctor Creek watershed. As Manager for Education and Advocacy Programs with the National Wildlife Foundation, Na'Taki nurtured youth and adults of color toward civic engagement. This included

> leading coalition building efforts to get kids connected to nature through policy and programmatic avenues, and engaging under-represented communities in conservation efforts to combat global warming, restore habitat in Atlanta's diminishing urban forest, create green jobs, and train the next generation of environmental leaders. For her work on environmental justice issues, engaging diverse communities in conservation, and improving environmental quality and quality of life for low-income and communities of color in Atlanta, Na'Taki has been recognized by and received numerous awards from a diverse number of organizations and agencies.[5]

She continues part time with the Foundation and teaches adjunct at Spelman College. Having earned her Masters of Public Health in Environmental and Occupational Health from Emory University, she is currently finishing her doctorate.

Osborne Jelks serves as the board chair and volunteer executive director of the West Atlanta Watershed Alliance (with the appropriate acronym WAWA), and has become one of the most respected watershed activists in the United States. She writes about the context that gave rise to WAWA:

> In the 1990s, the Atlanta metropolitan area, nicknamed the "sprawl capital of the world," grew more than any other American city, except Los Angeles, California . . . Efforts by the City of Atlanta to improve and expand its wastewater treatment system to accommodate growth caused major controversy and intense

5. National Wildlife Foundation webpage: "Faces of NWF," at: http://www.nwf.org/news-and-magazines/media-center/faces-of-nwf/nataki-osborne-jelks.aspx.

public debate. This controversy centered on the City's strategies for meeting state and federal environmental mandates in two areas: abatement of combined sewer overflows and reduction of phosphorus levels in wastewater discharges . . . A major controversy developed in response to the lack of equity and justice underpinning the processes by which the City initially chose to implement these strategies . . .

At the heart of the citizens's arguments against the City's proposals were the following questions that have relevance to all environmental and city planning processes: (1) Did the potentially impacted community have adequate access to information about the proposed policies?; (2) Was the potentially impacted community engaged from the outset of the planning process?; and (3) Was there an equitable distribution of benefits vs. risks and burdens for the proposed policy? (2008:174)

I interviewed Na'Taki on December 27, 2014 at the Outdoor Activities Center, one of three properties that WAWA stewards.

How did the West Atlanta Watershed Alliance start?

The City of Atlanta made some decisions about its combined sewer system that resulted in open sewage flowing into Utoy Creek, which flows through some people's backyards in northwest Atlanta. Those people were not consulted, so folks from Utoy Creek watershed got together with those from neighboring watersheds—the Proctor Creek and Sandy Creek watersheds—which cover most of northwest and southwest Atlanta. They decided to combine forces, since what was happening in each watershed was similar. We formed an alliance of watersheds, hence the name.

There are other watersheds throughout the city, but these three were contiguous and each predominantly African-American. We had various incomes, but still faced some similar challenges. We hoped that if we could harness our collective power and voice then we could make a difference on the west side of Atlanta. We aimed to improve northwest and southwest Atlanta where African-Americans live and are inundated with environmental stressors, though often under-represented at environmental decision-making tables.

Some say that the Black community cannot organize like it used to. Yet, the way you all did this—successfully pulling together citizens of different socioeconomic class backgrounds from these three watersheds—shows that it can still happen.

Yes, we got in, built power, established some coalitions, were able to change the course of public policy, and got some corrective action for environmental justice in these communities. Our grassroots work on behalf of ourselves and our backyards demonstrated that we can make an impact that cannot be ignored.

In community organizing it's great to have a success to build on to keep momentum. What organizing tactics did you use?

Organizing in our watershed is mostly grassroots: going door to door, town hall meetings, phone trees, some social media. It's going to community meetings, where people are already gathered; working with faith leaders to some extent; and going to the Atlanta University Center and helping students to understand that as residents of these watersheds—even if only for four years—they have an impact on this environment. Our conversations focused on helping people connect to public decisions, to their neighborhood, and to how they can make a difference. We also invited people to connect to the land through our visitor's days, offering safe experiences with land and water . . .

Before the twentieth century, cities like Atlanta discharged household excrement and industrial wastes openly into the streets. Now we have a system that chemically treats everything, but which is overtaxed and full of toxins. Was there thought given to alternatives to increased demand on the system, such as instituting an infrastructure for compost toilets or outhouses? I've learned from CPT experiences around the world that many people do not use potable water to dispose of their waste!

WAWA was not necessarily confronting the city about *which direction* it was going with its sewer system. We were challenging the *process* by which they were making the decision. History was repeating itself, because many of us had been left out of the decision-making process about things that affects us directly.

I need to remember that just a generation ago for many people, outhouses were their only option, so suggesting a return to them would cause trepidation, since indoor plumbing is linked with a higher social status. I feel we are in a moment on our collective journey where most African-Americans must again encounter the land they live on in an empowered way, because we had such a disempowered relationship during slavery, in which we broke and extracted from the land while the U.S. economic and cultural system broke and extracted labor from our bodies. No wonder so many people of African descent want nothing to do with "back-to-the-land" movements.

WAWA's work is to encourage our population to care for the land on which they live. We've been able to get some traction on "green infrastructure," helping people see how you get the land to work *with* you, rather than decide to build something that works against it. That's why we have visitor's days at the three land areas we steward. A lifelong connection starts with a visit.

What does Watershed Discipleship look like in Northwest and Southwest Atlanta?

We have some structured "rituals," you might call them, and some more free flowing activities. One aspect of our faithfulness in this place is facilitating relationships, making it possible for people to visit the ecologies in which we live. The work we do in all three watersheds makes it possible for people to touch and feel and see, making connections with water and land *here*—not far away in the rural woodlands of Georgia, but right in the city. We began by doing weekly creek clean-ups and water quality monitoring. We take water samples to be tested by partner organizations, who analyze the data for contaminants. These efforts are focused on Proctor Creek, our most impaired watershed, which is where the most attention is needed now.

We are stewards of the water with a watershed understanding that what happens on land impacts the water. So we also take care of the land, organizing clean-ups at the twenty-six acres at the Outdoor Activities Center, and the 102 acres at Hampton Beecher Nature Preserve located along North Utoy Creek in southwest Atlanta. We've also saved over 400 acres of green space in the city from being developed!

I saw my first image of Jesus as a Black man when I came to Spelman. I can hear him saying, "Each time you visit this land, and touch this water, do it in remembrance of me."

Water is life; like faith, it sustains us. At the same time we are concerned with water quality we need to be concerned about the people through whose neighborhoods this Creek flows. If the city of Atlanta would have been successful with their policy plan to change the infrastructure, that creek would have been full of sewage flowing through our neighborhoods during heavy rains.

And at the same time we care about the health of neighborhoods and people, we need to recognize that the land carries the oppression of previous policy decisions (landfills, superfund sites, polluting industries), as well as the violations of those who came from the suburbs and dumped trash and tires into the Proctor Creek Watershed. Caring for both "people and nature" must be included in Watershed Discipleship.

To me an understanding of basic civil rights is very central to this movement, which should include having the right to clean water, clean air, and soil that's free of contamination so we can grow healthy food in it.

What you're doing seems to be the next wave of the civil rights movement: reconnecting with land and working for human and ecological justice seems a natural continuation of the Black freedom struggle!

I do look at what we do in this vein as the next wave of the civil rights movement. When I think back to Dr. King's last mission, before he died in Memphis, he was there to support Black sanitation workers. They were striking not only because they felt that they needed to address racial disparity in wages, but also because of the abhorrent health and safety conditions that threatened their health as a part of their work environment.

So functional sanitation systems and access to environmental policy decisions, like voting rights and school integration, are part of the ongoing civil rights movement!

When we talk about environmental justice issues, it's about where we live *and* where we work, where we worship *and* where our kids and grandkids learn. When we think about the environment, we need to take into consideration both the natural *and* the built worlds.

This is exemplified in the connection between lead poisoning and the 2015 Baltimore uprising. The young man who was killed by the police officers had a high lead concentration in his blood, simply from living in the neighborhood where he grew up. When where you live is determining whether you live; that's both a civil rights and environmental struggle.

I think environmental justice is a convergence of environmental and public health, health equity advocacy and civil rights. To me an understanding of basic civil rights should be very central to this Watershed Discipleship movement. The reality is that there are [historic and structural] challenges for some communities to have access to clean air, water, and soil.

What are the ages and demographics WAWA engages?

Sitting at the feet of my elders and learning from how the youth organize are both important. Some of the elders here have civil rights and social justice backgrounds, and bring that context and work to these present-day struggles around environmental issues and city planning. Many elders say,

"Sustainability? That is just what we did!" The vision they have, coupled with the tools and expertise that we have, makes for the best possible solution. Regardless of formal education levels, local community knowledge is very important. They can teach us about history through their life stories, telling us about changes over time in the area. And they can inspire us about the vision they have for the future. But it's still a work in progress, because some elders say, "You're calling those spots 'green spaces,' but to me those are 'the woods.'" Because of the racist history here, these types of natural spaces do not have positive connotations. There are lots of folks whose awareness needs to increase, and many more people that we want to engage; so our work continues.

How does WAWA change that perception of the woods?

First and foremost it's having access to those spaces, and then having experiences that are positive there—such as at places like the Cascade Springs Nature Preserve.

As an undergrad in Atlanta I knew of Cascade road, where many prominent African-Americans lived, but I did not imagine that name corresponded to a real waterfall and nature preserve inside the city limits! What's the story of Cascade Springs Nature Preserve?

WAWA helped to open the preserve to the general public at reasonable hours. Until two years ago, people didn't have much awareness about this 135 acres owned by the City. Cascade Springs is gated, and was only open Monday to Friday from eight a.m. to three p.m.—just not accessible to working people. WAWA asked the City if we could open the place up on Saturdays, and they told us, "Absolutely not." They claimed they didn't have the personnel to work on weekends or to do a night closing. It clearly wasn't a priority for them, and they claimed that if the preserve was open late, the neighbors would complain about the crime. So WAWA bargained with the City, offering to take care of opening and closing it. And the City turned over the keys to us!

Then we did a lot of publicity: door knocking, flyers in mailboxes, going to gatherings. Some people told me that they had lived for thirty years in this community and had never been inside that park! This is not in an economically unstable neighborhood; just down from Cascade are homes that sell for half a million dollars. It was just always closed when people got home from work and on weekends. Some said, "I always wondered what was behind that gate."

There is a beautiful waterfall, with height and beauty that made me think I was in the mountains in north Georgia; I couldn't believe what I was seeing right here inside the I-285 beltway!

Cascade Springs was featured in a series on "sacred spaces" by the local interfaith television station. There are abundant natural resources there, and interesting historical and cultural aspects to the spring itself. When I walk the trails and check on the place (to see if there are hazards), I get to see who is visiting and inquire what draws them there. Whether they are first timers or regulars, I ask, "What are you getting from being in this place?" In conversation with visitors, WAWA members discern if they may want to have a deeper connection with that place, or engage in its maintenance or stewardship. We've been working to get more community attention to all the places that WAWA caretakes.

Sounds like another ritual of WAWA's Watershed Discipleship—organizing to open places in order to provide people adequate access and relationship to the land.

Another part of our ritual is visiting these spaces ourselves, and intentionally inviting both neighbors and those beyond the community to visit. During the week there can be school kids coming to play and to learn or for an after-school program, or community folks just exploring to get to know the area. We are not yet trying to restore habit; we have a lot of species in these watersheds, some native, some not. We just need to know what is around us.

III. Black to the Land

Connecting people to land connects us with one another, enabling us to re-knit kinship ties that were broken by enslavement. In the Diaspora, Black folks have had a primarily extractive relationship with the land, and later in industrial factories. We were seen as people whose worth was in our productive capacity, but beyond that, as disposable. It is easy to understand, therefore, why we have had an extractive relationship with one another, and use a lot of disposable things. But this cycle is spiritually devastating.

Many come out to our preserved lands to connect spiritually with the beauty God has created. WAWA's invitation to visit is not about getting African-Americans or others to *work* the land or do active stewardship of any kind. Rather, we want people to have access to these spaces to enjoy and rest, to get the restorative benefits from being active in the outdoors in whatever way they choose.

And we've had a disempowered relationship with bodies of water—from the Atlantic Ocean as a site of separation from Africa and death during the Middle Passage, to racially segregated swimming pool throughout the South. For many African-Americans the natural world is interwoven with a lot of social trauma; I see your work as healing that trauma and re-establishing an empowered relationship with our lands and waters.

We must remember that after slavery legally ended, public parks and natural spaces such as the ones WAWA stewards now were segregated. We didn't have access to most of them for a hundred years. But even after they were legally integrated, many African-Americans still do not feel welcomed in certain public spaces like parks, public campgrounds or green spaces. Yet these spaces belong to everybody and we ought to be welcome!

Despite all the trauma, there have always been healers, lovers, keepers of wisdom and stories—elders who take risks for the sake of youth, and children who hold the community together. They remind us that we are not separate from all that is—both in our specific watersheds and in the wider universe.

Yes, we're all about relationship and valuing one another's lives and recreation. We're a watershed group, but we're a community group too. You don't often see the two in one, but we've been successful in connecting those ways of being. I guess we defy the mold of what one might perceive a watershed group to be. For example, each of the last three years we have hosted a "Great American Backyard Campout," where now sixty to seventy tents and 250 people sleep under the stars—primarily, but not exclusively, African-Americans. Since many don't have camping materials, or prefer not to go the long distance to a campground where they might not feel welcomed or safe, we create these spaces in the middle of the city.

When we first did it, we had to pound the pavement to get our neighbors here. We knew if we advertised in the *Atlanta Journal Constitution* it wouldn't necessarily be our neighborhood folks who showed up. Our goal was to get first time campers and people of color to come. We work with everybody, but we have to make sure our community is here too, so we need to be intentional. A woman said to me, "I wouldn't have done this, but I did this for my grandchildren, and I feel safe with your organization." People might feel that because of their history and background—because they picked cotton in the field, for example—they'd have no interest in doing something like this. But because WAWA is a trusted organization in the community we were able to break down some of those barriers.

And when people get connected to a sense of place, that's just the beginning!

They want to keep coming out, they want to be stewards, to be engaged. They start to connect the dots between what's going on politically, how the environment plays a role in some of the things that are happening, how we need to safeguard what is precious to us, and why it's important for us to endeavor to be more sustainable. And in many cases, people then connect the dots with their upbringings.

Some people think that people who are oppressed don't have the capacity to take care of the environment around them because of the other pressures on their life. Your response?

Everything is connected. I do think people do get it. People who live in the Proctor Creek watershed, one of the most blighted communities, still care. Even though they struggle to meet their basic needs, there is something about these natural resources in our communities that compels them to care beyond their circumstances. Proctor Creek has been significant for people in northwest Atlanta: kids used to swim there; people fished; were baptized in this Creek; even bottled spring water there. There is a lot of history in that place, and recognizing that what used to be an amenity has become a polluted eyesore that detracts from the community gives people's motivation to change things. That transformation has to be driven by the people themselves, and that is what WAWA is fighting for.

Is the term "watershed" known and used among WAWA's constituents?

We meet people where they are. We do use the term "watershed," and many people don't know what that means. But many identify with the creeks themselves, so we teach about how those creeks are related to a broader ecosystem of which we are a part. But as organizers, we are also learning— that's what is most effective about our approach. We don't see ourselves as experts on anything, and don't prop ourselves, because we value local community knowledge. We might be able to teach people conceptually what a watershed is, but they teach us about what they've seen in this watershed over time. We're constantly giving *and* receiving, not only from the elders, but by all who have lived experience in the community.

Another example of what I call "SSDP"! In Atlanta and the places where CPT works, it's about taking direction from local folks and leveraging a groundswell of engagement.

The community sets the direction for the work that we do. We're advocating at policy levels and in decision-making spaces, but also just trying to get folk to visit the land. There we learn about what's going on in people's lives, which helps to facilitate relationships among people and with the land. We learn about their vision for making west Atlanta cleaner and greener, and they start to connect the dots between what is going on in City politics, why it's important for us to be more sustainable, and what we need to do to safeguard places.

Is it possible, then, to expand King's idea of Beloved Community beyond an anthropocentric definition?

My concept of the Beloved Community is not just the people, but all those natural resources that sustain us as well. Because for low income communities of color, social justice, public health, environmental justice, and energy equity intersect. When people can connect to a sense of place, things start clicking. They see how they can work to clean up drug houses and dealing on the corner *and* work to restore the watershed at the same time. They see how they can feed and clothe and house people *and* revitalize their community's natural resources.

IV. Christian Peacemaker Teams and Watershed Discipleship

King's vision of Beloved Community was one in which everyone's voices are heard in conflicts or questions of direction. As we pay attention to this critical movement in our history, it is critical to pay attention to who is at the table and how decision-makers relate to *all* impacted communities, human and nonhuman. In our time, this must include not only people, but all of the denizens of the habitat—an ecological Beloved Community. We must build partnerships with those who are most affected and targeted by violence in all its forms.

A primary strength of WAWA's organizing is that they've taken leadership direction from the community, building on decades of community struggle for justice in that place. Newer activists working in a particular place need to learn the history of social movements and social life in their home and/or adopted watershed, as well as to examine how their identity and social location play into existing dynamics of social privilege and oppression there. Visiting people *and* nature and understanding how human, ecological, and political rights interconnect is critical.

Back-to-the-land and environmental justice movements are growing in the United States, building an ecological Beloved Community. They are helping expose how globalized behaviors can damage local watersheds—rejecting, for example, clothing, food, or other commodities manufactured in far-away places in favor of upcycling, local markets, and biodegradable material usage. However, those working locally by intention can be—and often are—disconnected from those working with global realities. They sometimes harbor animosity toward those of us whose work carries us across the world.

To be sure, such challenges are warranted; after all, U.S.-based peace, mission, social justice and environmental movements have historically often only addressed problems or foreign policy issues as they pertained to "over there." For much of the last century, well-funded projects focused on changing or helping "those people," reproducing colonial-era objectification or paternalism rather than examining our own complicity in cycles of violence in our own contexts. Many contemporary activists thus understandably prefer a "deep local" ethics as a crucial alternative to this legacy, and a direct response to our ecological crisis. Experience has shown that land-based struggles prevail only where people live, know, and love their land, as suggested by Ched's paraphrase of Baba Dioum's classic litany (see the Introduction to this volume). This is what happened in Atlanta with WAWA—people saving land they are (re)learning to know and love.

Conversely, we must always be mindful of how people in one watershed affect the lives of those in other watersheds. If *only* focused locally, watershed work will find itself limited. We have a lot to learn from those around the world who have been place-rooted activists for centuries—whether their protection and resistance projects efforts succeeded, failed, or continue today. We of African descent in the Diaspora of the Americas can learn, for example, from Indigenous peoples in the Pacific, who still have an empowered relationship with their land and waters. By connecting with and standing in solidarity alongside them in their ongoing quest for self-determination, we can find our way back to our stories, souls, indigeneity and land.

CPT is a North America-based, global organization, with workers from fifteen different countries and projects on all peopled continents. Talking with Na'Taki helped me see that the CPT experiment will only survive and thrive into the next era if we commit to learning from Watershed Discipleship experiments and other collective efforts that cultivate an ecological Beloved Community in specific places. WAWA is a great model for connecting grassroots relationship building with public policy advocacy, and ecological restoration with civil rights. As we build relational and analytical capacity among communities struggling in specific places, making connections between watersheds will enable us to cultivate multi-layered expressions of justice and righteousness. For just as every watershed is connected through the hydrological cycle, so too, though we work in different places, are we part of the same struggle and story.

References

Jelks, Na'Taki Osborne. 2008. "Sewage in Our Backyards: The Politics of Race, Class and Water in Atlanta, Georgia." *Projections Volume 8: MIT Journal of Planning* 8:172–188.

King, Martin Luther Jr. 1986. "Letter from Birmingham City Jail." In *The Essential Writings and Speeches of Martin Luther King, Jr.*, edited by James Washington, 289–302. San Francisco: Harper.

Chapter Seven

A Pipeline Runs through Naboth's Vineyard
From Abstraction to Action in Cascadia

M ATTHEW H UMPHREY

Summary: This essay calls for North American Christians to move
from a posture of *abstraction from* to one of *action for* the land
they inhabit. It offers an "unsettling" reading of the story of King
Ahab and Naboth's vineyard that confronts our inherited histories
of dispossession and settlement in North America. On the heels
of the release of the Canadian Truth and Reconciliation Com-
missions Report on Indian Residential Schools, I argue that it is
incumbent upon our churches in Cascadia and beyond to become
"Settler allies" distinguished by meekness, repentance, and action
for the sake of the land and all who inhabit it.[1]

---

1. Material in the first half of this essay appeared in another form in "Reinhabiting Place: The Work of Bioregional Discipleship," *The Other Journal* (online), October 14, 2014, available at: http://theotherjournal.com/2014/10/13/
reinhabiting-place-the-work-of-bioregional-discipleship/.

I. "Abstraction is the enemy wherever it is found."

"FOR MOST OF MY life I've tried not to worry too much about the environment," a student at the Bible college where I occasionally teach told me. "I just figure, I do my thing and let the environment do its, and we're all good, right?" An admission this honest is rare, yet he detected none of its irony. He was surprised he was required to take a course on environmental issues, and had many questions about how this fit within his expectations of a Bible college education.

His sentiment is shared broadly, and not only among young evangelical students. Even in a city as eco-friendly as Vancouver, British Columbia, on whose outskirts my family and I reside, there is a vast gap between what people *think* about the environment and their daily patterns of life. Indeed, most of our day-to-day lives betray a fundamental alienation from creation—yoga pants and green tea lattes notwithstanding. Wendell Berry writes, "Abstraction is the enemy wherever it is found" (1992:23). Yet far too many of us share the approach of my student—even those of us who study the planetary crisis closely. It is easy for the interlocking ecological crises we face to induce apathy, despair, or a detached attitude.

To inhabit our place in creation as people committed to the way of Jesus is to recognize that this journey is not about adopting new green fashions or technologies, but a call to deeper *metanoia* (repentance). Facing the reality of the threats to creation and our own complicit lifeways challenges us to rethink many of our comfortable assumptions and rechart our most familiar paths. In my classroom, a moment typically comes about halfway through the semester, when a quiet but attentive student will state: "It seems like these problems require the complete reordering of human society." Yes, I reply, that will be necessary. The response is a familiar litany of how difficult, or impossible, such change is. This unveils some key assumptions which lurk deep in the cultural milieu, and which present a serious roadblock to action.

Included are the following three:

1. *We don't have the right to advocate for large-scale social change unless we are willing to undergo a complete and radical personal transformation first.* This is most often expressed as a concern about hypocrisy. How can Al Gore advocate sustainability and still fly around the world? My students routinely chastise me for calling for an end to Tar Sands development in Alberta while still driving my car to class. This

personalist approach to social change is common among conservative Christians. The desire for congruity is commendable, but leaving change at the individual level alone fails to address the systemic dimensions of the problems we face.

2. *It is someone else's job to effect real social change—politicians, business owners, or some other "change makers."* The assumption here is that whatever change we might make in our personal lives is dwarfed by the impact of potential changes which those in power might make. Why should I go without meat or take public transit when meat consumption in Brazil and China is skyrocketing and India is adding thousands of cars to its roads daily? While contradicting the previous assumption, it similarly divorces individual from systemic change and exonerates us from real action in the sphere within which each of us can most readily make change. We need *both* personal and political transformation.

3. *We are locked into the way the world is because we cannot imagine another way of life and/or because we don't believe building an alternative is realistic.* Such lack of vision is unconsciously rooted in a presumption of the fundamental stability, sustainability, or inevitability of the prevailing political economy. This is represented by statements such as, "The oil in Alberta *will* be developed, one way or another." This sort of resignation strengthens apathy about the possibility of change and betrays a lack of faith—and is often found among conservative Christians who nurture an other-worldly vision of salvation.

Collectively these assumptions blind us to our complacency and complicity, confirm our anxieties, and absolve us of responsibility, while alienating us from the power of collective action. As Berry puts it: "The great obstacle is simply this: the conviction that we cannot change because we are dependent on what is wrong. But that is the addict's excuse, and we know that it will not do" (1990:201).

Berry's warning hits particularly close to home for me. As a newcomer to British Columbia, I am still struck by how dependent our regional economy is on resource extraction (see the analysis of a former Canadian Imperial Bank of Commerce chief economist of world markets regarding Canada's petro-dependence in the face of a "carbon bubble," Rubin 2015). A quick poll of a class on Resource Management revealed that well over half of my students had family members working in forestry, oil, or gas.

The majority of North Americans maintain a very high carbon lifestyle, but in this corner of the continent a larger percentage derive their daily bread from its extraction. According to Naomi Klein,

> the real reason we are failing to rise to the climate moment is because the actions required directly challenge our reigning economic paradigm . . . the stories on which Western cultures are founded . . . as well as many of the activities that form our identities and define our communities . . . Only when we identify these chains do we have a chance of breaking free (2015:263).

Challenging broken identities and false narratives is familiar work for those who have answered the call to discipleship. This requires that we confront the idolatries which have alienated us from God, one another, and creation; that we repent; and that we follow the way of Jesus, which reorients our action and identity in the world. But to do this we must get to know our local place in creation, which is an increasingly foreign concept in our mobile, globalized culture.

II. "In America we have careers, not places"

Alan Durning tells the story of a trip he took to the Philippines to document the impacts of environmental destruction on Indigenous peoples there. After interviewing several elders, he was introduced to a frail old priestess who, through a translator, asked him, "What is your homeland like?" Durning pondered his neighborhood in Washington, D.C., where he had moved to be able to lobby politicians (though he admits he spent most of his time "jet-setting on behalf of future generations"). He realized how little connection he had to his home as a place, confessing: "'In America . . . we have careers, not places.' Looking up, I recognized pity in her eyes" (1996:4).

This Filipina elder helped Durning realize that in choosing career mobility first—a path into which he was socialized to consider normative—he had "gained the whole world but forfeited his soul." *This Place on Earth* narrates Durning's remarkable conversion from deep alienation to deep belonging to place. He describes how though he worked for an environmental NGO, the ecological crisis remained an abstract issue which he cared about, but that scarcely impacted his daily life and practice. His story is uncomfortable because it is so familiar to those of us who have been socialized into mobility; we remain alienated from the world that sustains us even as we desire to "care for creation," as Myers points out in his Introduction.

Berry warns against this crucial contradiction:

> The abstractions of sustainability can ruin the world just as surely as the abstractions of industrial economics. Local life may be as much endangered by those who would "save the planet" as by those who would "conquer the world." . . . In order to make ecological good sense for the planet, you must make ecological good sense locally. You *can't* act locally by thinking globally (1992:23).

The modern tradition of bioregionalism takes up this insight and focuses the scale of human engagement within our local ecosystems. It challenges each of us to get to know our place and the manifold ways our health is tied to the health of our local habitat.

"At the right scale human potential is unleashed, human comprehension magnified, human accomplishment multiplied," contends Kirkpatrick Sale. "I would argue that the optimum scale is the bioregional, not so small as to be powerless and impoverished, not so large as to be ponderous and impervious, a scale at which at last human potential can match ecological reality" (1985:55). A bioregional identity recognizes we are heirs to a deeper identity as neighbors and members of a shared place—a whole family we never knew we had. This is neither a new parochialism nor a bland locavorism that abandons concern for others across the planet. Rather, it is predicated on the honest admission that, as Myers puts it, "if we are going to stand *for* something we first are going to have to stand *somewhere*" (Introduction). My own journey bears this out.

For the last five years, my family and I have lived in the Little Campbell River Watershed, where we work with A Rocha Canada (www.arocha.ca). The river that runs through my backyard is just thirty kilometers long, yet crosses two countries and five municipal jurisdictions, all on the unceded traditional lands of Semiahmoo First Nation. Into the Little Campbell flow two additional streams that originate south of the U.S. border in Whatcom County, Washington. This river is thus implicated in over ten different political jurisdictions. Yet the salmon that return to spawn every fall do not carry passports, nor are the rare and at-risk species who live here (such as the red-legged frog, the Pacific water shrew, and the Oregon forest snail) given a vote in important land use decisions affecting their habitat or health.

Five species of salmon still spawn each fall in our little river—Chinook, Chum, Coho, Cuttthroat, and Steelhead trout (also of the salmonid family)—despite enduring pressures from urban encroachment, mismanaged agriculture, and suburban pollution. This keystone species of our bioregion connects me to a broader community. The Little Campbell (which drains just seventy-four square kilometers) discharges into the massive body of water the Salish Sea, which covers over 18,000 square kilometers of water.[2] And the salmon that spawn in the Little Campbell River travel along the entire western coast of our continent, from Alaska to Northern California.

The watershed in which I reside joins many other watersheds in the bioregion known as Cascadia, which stretches as far as the salmon run. Living in this place links me to this broader ecological community whether I acknowledge it or not. Following Saint Paul (and Wendell Berry), I recognize that just as I am a member of Christ's body, I am also a member of the Little Campbell River Watershed and the Cascadia bioregion. Getting to know this geography and affirming my membership in it has proven indispensable in deepening my efforts to care for my place. Nor does it limit my care for other places. Quite the opposite: it implicates me in a web of relationships across space that span from California to Alaska (and indeed to all coastal inhabitants of the Pacific region), and across time to the people who have inhabited these places throughout human history.

Gary Snyder writes that a community working to rehabilitate a salmon stream "might find itself combatting clear-cut timber sales upstream, water-selling grabs downstream, Taiwanese drift-net practices out in the North Pacific, and a host of other national and international threats to the health of salmon" (1995:230). By engaging with our watershed in actions such as riverside cleanups, nature walks, or invasive weeding parties, we indeed find ourselves thrust into broader action, often in unexpected ways. Bioregionalism recognizes that our modern political frameworks have failed to provide meaningful governance over or cultivation, protection and distribution of creation's resources, and our human and nonhuman neighbors are suffering as a result. In addition to demanding that our policy makers remedy that situation, we must foster solutions to these problems together in community. As Berry puts it, "Everyone can make ecological

2. The Salish Sea includes the Puget Sound and the Straights of Georgia and Juan de Fuca; its recent renaming is a rare and compelling story of conservationists working across political boundaries to achieve common ends (see http://staff.wwu.edu/stefan/salish_sea.shtml).

good sense locally, *if* the affection, the scale, the knowledge, the tools, and the skills are right" (1992:23).

III. "Becoming Native to This Place"

Cultivating affection for place is a major theme of the Hebrew Scriptures. When Christians nurture biblical literacy alongside bioregional practice, we find that these disciplines shed light on one another. Unfortunately, when modern readers of the Bible consider issues of land and place, two interpretive strategies typically cloud the waters.

One, a product of modern fundamentalist dispensationalism, conflates God's ancient promises to Israel of safety and security in the land with support for the modern state of Israel. Christian Zionism rightly acknowledges the centrality of land in God's covenant with Israel, but fails to understand what right covenant relationship means in our present context. Israel's flourishing in the land is meant to be a light to the nations, but as the Law and prophets make clear, is conditional upon her practice of justice, including specific commitments on behalf of the poor and the land itself. Such texts problematize the modern Israeli occupation of Palestine and Zionist claims to absolute ownership.[3]

A second and equally problematic reading strategy derives from supersessionism, which spiritualizes the Hebrew Bible's claims about land just as it pits Law against grace or the new covenant against the old.[4] Torah's intense concern for right relationship to the land is deemed irrelevant for faith communities today. We must grapple more deeply with how place functions for God's people past and present; Jonathan R. Wilson (2013) has helpfully elaborated upon this point in his work on the doctrine of creation.

Both theological reading strategies misconstrue the meaning of land in the biblical history and further estrange us from a sense of place today. In turn, our contexts of alienation have made it difficult to hear biblical texts; as modern readers we come to the text earth-illiterate, and thus derive earth-illiterate conclusions. But for the ancient writers, concerns over the

3. For a Christian critique of Zionist ideology, see Ateek (1989); Raheb (1995 and 2014); Ateek, Duaybis and Tobin (2005); Burge (2010); Munayer and Loden (2012); and most recently Wagner and Davis (2014). See also McRay, Chapter Three.

4. This tends to characterize the theology of Martin Luther and the later Reformed tradition. For critiques of supersessionism see N.T. Wright (2013) and the "New Perspective on Paul" school (see for example http://www.patheos.com/blogs/jesuscreed/2013/10/15/nt-wright-and-the-supersessionism-question-what-did-paul-do/).

health of land and all its inhabitants were a daily, lived reality with immediate implications. In attending to the ancient context we can discover deep wisdom for our ecological crisis.

Scripture does not present us with a uniform understanding of land (Habel identifies six distinct land ideologies in the Hebrew Bible, 1995). Nevertheless, there are several consistent features of Israel's land ethic. Throughout the Hebrew Bible we find a triangular covenant narrated between YHWH, Israel, and the land (see C. Wright 1990), which animated a unique ecological and social ethos in Israel grounded in care for people and place alike. Deep memories of slavery in Egypt and decades of wandering in the desert forever reminded the people of the pain of placelessness; the covenant at Sinai, conversely, described a way of relationship with specific land through which the whole community of creatures might flourish. Ignoring these statues would result in the renewed placelessness of exile (see Marlow 2009).

Torah is thus not concerned only with the spiritual relationship between Israel and YHWH, but equally with "creaturely" life. Ellen Davis writes:

> Taken as a whole, biblical law seeks to inculcate a precise awareness of physical being: of human life in a particular place, the land of Canaan, shared with other creatures—trees and birds and animals—whose own lives are precious and vulnerable. The legal codes . . . offer guidance for how the people Israel may order its life—including its work, its eating practices, and its worship—in conformity with the larger design of that place (2009:82).

Read in this way, the Hebrew Bible offers Israel an invitation to "become native to this place," to borrow Wes Jackson's phrase (1996). It is through knowing and treating the place as home that Israel secures both its own future and the health of the land. "Land tenure is conditional upon proper use and care of land in community" (Davis 2009:2).

This ethos is articulated variously throughout Torah, such as in Leviticus 26:3–5:

> If you follow my statutes and keep my commandments and observe them faithfully, I will give you your rains in their season, and the land shall yield its produce, and the trees of the field shall yield their fruit. Your threshing shall overtake the vintage, and the vintage shall overtake the sowing; you shall eat your bread to the full, and live securely in your land.

Safety in the land, an abundant harvest, and dependable rains are all premised upon God's gracious gift *and* Israel's obedience to Torah. Failure to live rightly before the Creator thus has the real possibility of upsetting the natural order of things, with weather patterns and food security the most obviously felt impacts. Living in the arid hill country of Canaan, Israel had to pay particular attention to the rhythms and seasons of Creation *in that place* (see Hillel 2006 and Hiebert 1996).

One of the ways Israel's life in the land is tied to their covenant obedience is through a particular system of economic exchange, anchored in the Sabbath (see Myers 2001). Once a week the community is commanded to rest from labor (Exod 16), and the soil is given further respite every seventh Sabbatical year, while the fruit of the field returns to the commonwealth (Exod 23). And after seven cycles of seven years, on the year of Jubilee, the land is to be redistributed equitably, and all those who have fallen into debt slavery are to be released (Lev 25). Such laws were intended to keep Israel oriented toward just and sustainable stewarding of the good gifts of creation, rather than the power and wealth stratification exhibited by Israel's imperial neighbors—which lessons Israel had only mixed success in embracing.

Tim Gorringe notes that these texts warn that if the people "think that they can manage land and resources on arbitrary principles which they themselves devise they will end up in the house of slavery" (2010:377). Israel had to acknowledge that it was not the *owner* of their place; as Leviticus states, "the land is mine; with me you are but aliens and tenants" (25:23). This stipulation, however, was particularly difficult for Israel's kings, whose claims over land and labor inevitably conflicted with the sovereignty of YHWH (see, e.g., 1 Sam 8; Howard-Brook 2010). This conflict is poignantly illustrated in the tale of Naboth's Vineyard.

IV. "Have you killed and taken possession?"

The story is found within the extended drama of King Ahab and the prophet Elijah. Ahab has done "evil in the eyes of the Lord" more than all Israelite rulers before him (1 Kgs 16:25). He marries Jezebel, daughter of King Ethbaal of the Sidonians and sets up an Asherah pole and worships Baal in blatant defiance of Torah prohibitions. Ahab's actions kindle the jealousy of YHWH, but also betray a broader socio-political conflict between Israelite identity and surrounding nations. The contest between the prophets of Baal and Elijah to end a drought, Gorringe notes, epitomizes "a standoff between two cultures, two economies, and their two legitimating deities, YHWH and BAAL" (2010:369). This drama also articulates a struggle between two systems of land tenure, as the story of Naboth's Vineyard makes clear.

King Ahab has a palace in Samaria and desires Naboth's vineyard in nearby Jezreel. The Jezreel valley, Davis notes, was "the richest agricultural region in the country, close to the major trade route running through Megiddo" (2009:111). Ahab makes what appears to be a fair offer (at least by modern standards): he'll either trade comparable land or pay fair market price (1 Kgs 21:2). The response from Naboth is perplexing to modern readers used to market transactions: "The LORD forbid that I should give you my ancestral inheritance" (21:3). Davis points out that Naboth's objection is based upon religious purity (the Hebrew word is *halila*, whence *halal*), so the phrase is better rendered: "I would be defiled before YHWH." Moreover, Davis says, the Hebrew word *nahalah* is often translated "portion," "possession," or "inheritance," all of which denote some form of property ownership. But this is precisely the connotation this word undermines: *nahalah* represents land given as a gift or trust, hearkening back in the original distribution of land to the twelve tribes. "Tribal ancestral lands" is a better translation, and thus carries an implicit judgment upon King Ahab, whose offer represents a betrayal of the traditional system of land tenure established by YHWH which a king is supposed to uphold.

When Jezebel finds Ahab sulking in his bed in the aftermath of this encounter, she sweeps into action, falsifying a letter from the king to the village elders and paying scoundrels to bring false charges against Naboth, who is ultimately stoned to death (21:7–14). She then goes to Ahab and challenges him to "take possession" (21:15; the Hebrew verb here connotes expropriation or displacement by conquest). The king does, not to turn Naboth's vineyard into a vegetable garden as he had proposed, but to take its wine for his own table as well as for export. Ahab has forcibly "integrated" Naboth's land into his project of transforming Israel's economy "from one focused on local subsistence to a state-controlled economy designed to generate surplus of the key crops" (Davis 2009:113). Naboth's commitment to his land in terms of the triangular covenant is eclipsed by Ahab's commodification of land as an abstract asset whose value should be maximized. But before the story ends, Elijah unmasks the truth of Ahab's murderous scheme: "Have you killed and taken possession?" (21:19).

The legacy of dispossession for the sake of economic profit remains one of the defining features of both our history right up until the present time in North America. It is unsettling to realize that we affluent Settlers stand in the tradition of Ahab, having expropriated the *nahala* of Indigenous peoples through official duplicity and murder.[5]

I have just read the summary report released by the Truth and Reconciliation Commission of Canada (available at http://www.trc.ca/websites/trcinstitution/index.php?p=890). This commission was charged with hearing and recording the stories of survivors of Indian Residential Schools, which operated between 1886 and 1996 across Canada. After a five-year process, Commission chairperson Justice Murray Sinclair said the following at the report's release:

> Removed from their families and home communities, seven generations of Aboriginal children were denied their identity. We heard how, separated from their language, culture, spiritual traditions, and their collective history, children became unable to answer questions as simple as: "Where do I come from? Where am I going? Why am I here? And, who am I?" . . . Survivors were stripped . . . of the love of their families. They were stripped of their self-respect . . . and of their identity (2015).

These violent acts were carried out in schools run by churches and funded by the Department of Indian Affairs. Children were forbidden to speak their native language, practice native customs, or disobey school authorities. Thousands of children died from disease, and far more were subjected to physical, psychological, and sexual abuse.

The TRC report concludes that what occurred in Residential Schools was nothing short of "cultural genocide." What prompted that tactic, however, was the longer-term process of dispossession of native land and resources. As Mi'kmaq lawyer and Chair of Indigenous Governance at Ryerson University Paula Palmater states: "They weren't killing us because of our culture. They were killing us because we were Indians, and we stood in the way of accessing all of the lands and resources and settlement in this country" (2015).

Residential schools were seen by government officials as the "final solution" to the "Indian problem" as articulated in the Indian Act of 1876. This Act was written with the express intent of driving native peoples to

---

5. Laurel Dykstra has argued similarly that privileged North Americans should read the Exodus story from the perspective of Pharaoh's household (2002:196).

renounce their Aboriginal identity, to adopt a European way of life, and to become Canadian citizens through a process known as "enfranchisement": "Voluntary enfranchisement was introduced in the *Gradual Civilization Act of 1857* and was based on the assumption that Aboriginal people would be willing to surrender their legal and ancestral identities for the 'privilege' of gaining full Canadian citizenship and assimilating into Canadian society" (Crey). The 1876 Act further limited what rights Canada recognized on Reserve lands (which differed from property rights recognized elsewhere in the country), and restricted possibilities for broader enfranchisement. An amendment in 1884 established the legal requirement that all Indigenous children attend school, backed with threats of fines or jail time for parents who did not comply. This series of laws and practices underwrote a century of cultural genocide.

And the long story of dispossession and resource extraction continues, from the beaver pelts first traded on Hudson Bay in the seventeenth century to the forestry and gold rush booms of the nineteenth century to the current race to extract oil from the tar sands of Alberta. Standing in the way of that extraction are Indigenous peoples who have inhabited this land for more than 12,000 years. Of course, many contemporary Canadians will protest that *they* have not killed anyone to take over their land. They have little or no sympathy regarding the dispossession of indigenous culture, land, and lifeways, and assume we have somehow "moved on." This is where the deep wisdom of the TRC is vital for disciples of the Jesus Way—committed as we are supposed to be to truth-telling and the work of reconciliation. It simply will not do to treat the historic dispossession of our Indigenous brothers and sisters as lost history; we must instead repent of our complacency regarding this ongoing legacy, and work to become Settler allies in caring for the land together (see Heinrichs 2013).

In *We are all Treaty People*, Roger Epp warns against the danger that "reconciliation to a liberal society may turn out to mean only the ability of strangers to live together in pursuit of individual projects" (2008:126). Modern liberalism's forward-looking, progress-minded, ahistorical consciousness is often either unable or unwilling to grapple with our collective and conflicted history. But to recognize, with Epp, that "we are all treaty people" commits us to facing our own complex and violent history, which alone makes real reconciliation possible. That journey requires us to move from abstraction to action, especially in the bioregions we inhabit. This should be a fundamental commitment of Watershed Discipleship.

V. "The meek shall inherit the earth"

With the other contributors to this volume, I believe that the bioregion is the most appropriate setting and scale for meaningful action to take place. In Cascadia we are encountering profound environmental challenges. Close to my home we have just experienced a small oil spill—2,700 liters of bunker fuel from a container ship anchored in English Bay. The city of Vancouver was not notified until twelve hours after the incident, and local beaches were shut down for several weeks. The spill has sounded an alarm for local residents who have been confused by the propaganda over the past year concerning the proposed expansion of the Kinder Morgan pipeline, which would bring oil from Alberta to a port in Burnaby, B.C., in the heart of the Salish Sea.

When consultants hired by Kinder Morgan began test drilling within a conservation area on Burnaby Mountain last year in defiance of a municipal bylaw that prohibits such action, several dozen people were arrested for blockading the work. One was Lynne Quarmby, a professor of biochemistry at Simon Fraser University, whose campus sits atop Burnaby Mountain. Kinder Morgan slapped her and four others with a court injunction against speaking out in opposition to the project, claiming that protestors at Burnaby Mountain are costing them $80 million every month in project delays. This charge was not blasphemy against God and king, as in the trumped up case against biblical Naboth, but blasphemy against future profits of the pipeline company. Standing in the way of "progress" is indeed blasphemy of the highest order for the ruling ideology of our time!

Though Quarmby realized that the company could come after her personal assets, she was motivated by other possible effects: "What is the value of owning my home and having retirement savings, if our world is spiraling into this negative space? . . . If there's no freedom of speech in Canada . . . If there's no intergenerational justice . . . If there's no global justice—then what's the value of my home?" (Prystupa 2014). This represents a modern invocation of *nahalah*—refusing to put market value ahead of intergenerational justice, not only for herself but for the original inhabitants of this land. Quarmby is on a journey from abstraction to action, and it has made her an effective leader and organizer in rallying to protect the place she calls home (she is now campaigning on the Green Party ticket in Burnaby).

In Cascadia our current political rulers are pulling on all possible legal and jurisdictional levers to extract and market local natural resources, even in the face of a growing popular resistance movement led by First Nations of this region. These forces mean to commodify the *nahalah* of B.C. First Nations, and no environmental or social barrier is too great. How is the community of faith to respond? Beyond repentance and confession of past wrongs, what sort of work might we commit ourselves to? For a start, we must disavow ourselves of what Teju Cole calls the "white savior industrial complex" (Cole 2012). As Paulette Regan has noted, such an approach "merely encourages passive empathy or a neutral distancing from the Other that is insufficient to effect social and political change"; radical change is not going to come about by white posturing or hashtag activism, but by embodied relationships with honest dialogue that will "unsettle the Settler within" (2010:51).

Epp asserts: "The most meaningful work of reconciliation . . . will lie in small, face-to-face initiatives for which the imperative is greatest where communities exist in close proximity" (2008:138). In Cascadia, this entails engaging the difficult and complex issues of resource extraction that are advancing all around us in genuine dialogue with the First Nations of this place. What sort of character will this require of us, and what sort of skills?

"Blessed are the meek, for they shall inherit the earth," said Jesus (Matt 5:5). Of all that has been written concerning the ecological crisis, meekness is rarely a virtue named. Yet, as Wilson argues, it is essential to the sort of life to which Jesus invites his disciples. Typically perceived as weakness or passiveness, Wilson claims that meekness "is power under control. It is not an absence of power, nor is it an inability to act on the basis of one's power. Rather, meekness is the disposition of one who has power and who could act on the basis of that power but restrains or directs that power in such a way that the act of power is properly proportioned to the circumstance and the proper *telos*" (2013:226). This is the character we must achieve as Settlers living in a land that is not our own. Putting our privilege and power under the constraint of meekness helps us become allies.

What is perhaps most stunning about the Ahab story is that once challenged by Elijah's prophetic word, he actually repents, and publicly (1 Kgs 21:27). Confronted with the legacy of his actions, he turns from his own violent history. This suggests that there is hope that even the worst perpetrators can be redeemed and transformed. And perhaps even the most abstract among us can be moved to action.

Back in my classroom at the Bible college, I've just finished up a day of dialogue between Indigenous and biblical worldviews concerning care for creation. My students have participated alongside some seventy local church and community members. I share the podium with Eddie Gardner, a Sto:lo elder from the Skwah First Nation. He thanks me for sharing a vision of the biblical worldview that leads toward healing and wholeness for creation rather than the typical "pie in the sky" dualism he has encountered his whole life in church. I recognize him as my elder, and tell him I am honored to learn from what he has shared. "You know," he tells me with a gleam in his eye, "if you really believe this stuff, you need to come up and join me on Burnaby Mountain." My own abstraction exposed, I gaze down at the floor for a moment to consider what this means. It is only a week after Lynne Quarmby's arrest, and my mind buzzes with concern about my image, safety, and comfort—all signs of my privilege and abstraction from the land. What should I do?

Dusk, some days later. I am sitting in the car with the windshield wipers going, as a light mist of rain falls. I turn the motor off, lock the doors, and follow the crowd up a long road to the top of Burnaby Mountain. I hear drums. Ten minutes later, I join Eddie and a circle of elders, all in traditional regalia, singing songs in a language, and with a passion, I cannot fully understand. A crowd of some 600 witnesses who've come to listen and participate surround us. That night I learn, in word and action, that we are all members of this place and its challenging history. The threat to Naboth's Vineyard continues, but the drums still beat and the prayers still rise. Perhaps, if we Christians listen to Creator's call and walk in the Way of Jesus, we too will find ourselves standing with those who stand up for this land.

References

Ateek, Naim Stifan. 1989. *Justice and Only Justice: A Palestinian Theology of Liberation.* New York: Orbis.

———. Cedar Duaybis and Maurine Tobin. 2005. *Challenging Christian Zionism: Theology, Politics and the Israel-Palestine Conflict.* Jerusalem: Sabeel Liberation Theology Center.

Berry, Wendell. 1990. "Word and Flesh." In *What Are People For?*, 197–203. San Francisco: North Point.

———. 1992. "Out of your Car, Off your Horse." In *Sex, Economy, Freedom, Community: Eight Essays*, 19–26. New York: Pantheon.

Burge, Gary M. 2010. *Jesus and the Land: The New Testament Challenge to "Holy Land" Theology.* Grand Rapids: Baker Academic.

Cole, Teju. 2012. "The White-Savior Industrial Complex." *The Atlantic*, March 21. (http://www.theatlantic.com/international/archive/2012/03/the-white-savior-industrial-complex/254843/).

Crey, Karrmen. No date. "Enfranchisement." Indigenous Foundations, University of British Columbia. (http://indigenousfoundations.arts.ubc.ca/home/government-policy/the-indian-act/enfranchisement.html).

Davis, Ellen. 2009. *Scripture, Culture, and Agriculture: An Agrarian Reading of the Bible.* Cambridge: Cambridge University Press.

Durning, Alan. 1996. *This Place on Earth: Home and the Practice of Permanence.* Seattle: Sasquatch.

Dykstra, Laurel A. 2002. *Set Them Free: The Other Side of Exodus.* Maryknoll, NY: Orbis.

Epp, Roger. 2008. *We are all Treaty People: Prairie Essays.* Edmonton: University of Alberta Press.

Gorringe, Timothy. 2010. "Idolatry and Redemption: Economics in Biblical Perspective." *Political Theology* 11(3) 367–82.

Habel, Norman C. 1995. *The Land is Mine: Six Biblical Land Ideologies.* Minneapolis: Fortress.

Heinrichs, Steve, ed. 2013. *Buffalo Shout, Salmon Cry: Conversations on Creation, Land Justice, and Life Together.* Waterloo, ON: Herald.

Hiebert, Theodore. 1996. *The Yahwist's Landscape: Nature and Religion in Early Israel.* New York: Oxford University Press.

Hillel, Daniel. 2006. *The Natural History of the Bible: An Environmental Exploration of the Hebrew Scriptures.* New York: Columbia University Press.

Howard-Brook, Wes. 2010. *Come out, my people! God's Call out of Empire in the Bible and Beyond.* Maryknoll, NY: Orbis.

Jackson, Wes. 1996. *Becoming Native to This Place.* Washington, DC: Counterpoint.

Klein, Naomi. 2015. *This Changes Everything: Capitalism Vs. Climate.* New York: Simon and Schuster.

Marlow, Hilary. 2009. *Biblical Prophets and Contemporary Environmental Ethics.* Oxford: Oxford University Press.

Munayer, Salim J. and Lisa Loden. 2012. *The Land Cries Out: Theology of the Land in the Israeli-Palestinian Context.* Eugene, OR: Cascade.

Myers, Ched. 2001. *The Biblical Vision of Sabbath Economics.* Washington, D.C.: Church of the Savior.

Palmater, Paula. 2015. "Cultural Genocide: Landmark Report Decries Canada's Forced Schooling of Indigenous Children" (Transcript). (http://www.democracynow.org/2015/6/3/cultural_genocide_landmark_report_decries_canadas.)

Prystupa, Mychaylo. 2014. "SFU scientist worries she'll lose home over Kinder Morgan lawsuit." *Vancouver Courier*, November 14, 2014. (http://www.vancouverobserver.com/news/sfu-scientist-worries-shell-lose-home-over-kinder-morgan-lawsuit-video.)

Raheb, Mitri. 1995. *I am Palestinian Christian.* Minneapolis: Fortress.

———. 2014. *Faith in the Face of Empire: The Bible through Palestinian Eyes.* Maryknoll, NY: Orbis.

Regan, Paulette. 2010. *Unsettling the Settler Within: Indian Residential Schools, Truth Telling, and Reconciliation in Canada.* Vancouver: University of British Columbia Press.

Rubin, Jeff. 2015. *The Carbon Bubble: What Happens to Us when It Bursts?* Toronto: Random House Canada.

Sale, Kirkpatrick. 1985. *Dwellers in the Land: The Bioregional Vision.* Athens, GA: University of Georgia Press.

Sinclair, Murray. 2015. "For the Record: Justice Murray Sinclair on Residential Schools." *Macleans,* June 2. (http://www.macleans.ca/politics/for-the-record-justice-murray-sinclair-on-residential-schools/.)

Snyder, Gary. 1995. *A Place in Space: Ethics, Aesthetics, and Watersheds.* Washington, DC: Counterpoint.

Wagner, Donald and Walter Davis. 2014. *Zionism and the Quest for Justice in the Holy Land.* Eugene, OR: Wipf & Stock.

Wilson, Jonathan R. 2013. *God's Good World: Reclaiming the Doctrine of Creation.* Grand Rapids: Baker Academic.

Chapter Eight

Growing from the Edges
Conversations on Land and Labor, Faith and Food

Sarah Nolan, Erynn Smith, and Reyna Ortega

Summary: This chapter explores one small grassroots group that is
attempting to live out the practices of Watershed Discipleship in
its local context. During the 2015 Bartimaeus Cooperative Ministries's Festival of Radical Discipleship, Sarah Nolan, the Director
and Chaplain of The Abundant Table, a faith-based community
non-profit and small organic farm in Ventura County, California,
interviewed two core members of organization, Erynn Smith
and Reyna Ortega. These two women, from very different backgrounds, here share the journeys that led them to The Abundant
Table. They then talk about their experiences of challenge and
hope as they try to practice ways of life and agriculture that offer
alternatives to the destructive and unhealthy farming that surround their community.[1]

---

1. The inspiration for our chapter title comes from Katerina Friesen, an alumnus of
The Abundant Table intern program and fellow contributor to this anthology. For more
information go to: http://theabundanttable.org/.

I. Introduction

IN 2006, A SMALL Episcopal and Lutheran campus ministry was established at California State University Channel Islands in Camarillo, California. Sarah was hired in 2007 as a lay chaplain to help build community and discern outreach on campus and beyond. Over the course of the next few years, through thoughtful conversation, visioning and prayer, our worshipping community decided to launch The Abundant Table, whose mission was to change lives and food systems by creating sustainable relationships to the land and local community. This ongoing experiment attempts to connect theory and practice through worship, theological reflection, organic market gardening and community building. In 2009, we inaugurated a year-long Episcopal Service Corps internship program for young adults to work on a local, sustainable farm and to engage in social justice service and advocacy in the local community.[2] We quickly expanded our commitment to youth through the development of a farm and nutrition education program. Today, The Abundant Table houses a four-acre vegetable farm, the young adult internship, several farm education programs and our Farm to Faith initiative, which nurtures a distinctly ecumenical Christian, but also interfaith, narrative of restoration and renewal for the earth and its inhabitants.

THE
ABUNDANT
TABLE
FARM
PROJECT

Situated in Ventura County, a coastal agricultural community north of metropolitan Los Angeles and south of Santa Barbara, The Abundant

---

2. The mission of the Corps is to develop and support a national network of intentional communities in the Episcopal Church. Young adults serve others in solidarity: promoting justice in community; deepening spiritual awareness and vocational discernment; and living simply in intentional Christian community. For more information see http://episcopalservicecorps.org/.

Table farm is one of a handful of small scale sustainable farms within a sea of industrial agricultural operations. As an almost all-female and cross-class operation with college graduates under the tutelage of immigrant farm workers, we probably look strange to other growers in our county, even some of the sustainable ones. Moreover, Ash Wednesday, Good Friday, Easter, Pentecost, Dia de los Muertos, Las Posadas, Sukkot, and other religious ceremonies are celebrated publicly on the farm. Salsa dancing is as important as a good composting system, and conversations about race, identity, sexuality, and God are as common as we weed a row as are questions about which seeds to plant or how much nitrogen is in the soil.

Members of the Abundant Table Farm Team.

It is in this context that we engage the kinds of questions raised in this volume about Watershed Discipleship, wrestling with their implications and embracing the power of transformation they offer. What does it mean to be a "people of a place" and a community of bioregional resilience in the midst of a dominant agricultural system and economic culture that is primarily characterized by extraction, consumption, and death? How do we sustain ourselves when we have to keep moving from watershed to watershed in search of affordable land on which to grow food? How can the labor of our hands undergird our worship, and our worship strengthen and sustain our daily work, and both animate our journey toward justice and liberation?

Mindful of the importance of sharing our own stories of struggle and resilience, as a plenary presentation at the February 2015 Festival of Radical Discipleship in Oak View, California, Sarah interviewed two core members of The Abundant Table: Erynn Smith and Reyna Ortega. Each is an amazing woman in her early to mid-thirties with a unique journey. As a fifth generation resident of Ventura County, who grew up in the Santa Clara and Calleguas watersheds, Erynn shares about the path she took away from her childhood home, which in the end brought her back to that same community with new eyes and renewed engagement. Reyna explores leaving her birth place of Mexico City to find a new home, and the bittersweet nature of living away from her birth family and country on one hand, while building a new family and community in a new place on the other. They reflect on their respective vocational *caminos* (paths) and what it looks like to embrace a calling to both a place and people.

I. Erynn Smith

Share the journey that brought you to the Abundant Table.

I was born and raised in an upper-middle class community in Ventura County, California, minutes away from neighboring agricultural fields and communities. I regularly drove by strawberry fields, played in "strawberry soccer tournaments," and attended the Strawberry Festival with my family, gorging on strawberry funnel cakes and strawberry chili. The strawberry was a ubiquitous image in my childhood—yet the fruit was completely disconnected from the realities in the fields that lined the main freeway artery through our area, and of the farmworkers who tended and harvested the vast acres of our county's top crop. The fields, the farmworkers and their communities, and the agricultural practices that leave them with higher rates of cancer were invisible to me, though in plain sight. My food source was a high-end grocery store, where every type of produce was available year round. No one in my family, educational, or cultural networks worked in the fields or sought connections between farms, farmworkers, agricultural practices, the environment, food access, or health.

My years in university were an unsettling time of coming to consciousness about many oppressive systems to which I was blind during my childhood. I learned stories of peoples who suffered from historical oppression, which continues today. Living near South Central Los Angeles, I could see evidence of racism, poverty cycles, food deserts, and chronic disease. It became a time of deconstructing the self-serving narratives of privilege and hyper-individualism in which I was raised. I felt ashamed of and alienated from my own roots, and longed for a community with whom I could honestly confront broken systems while nurturing loving, whole ways of being.

A few years after graduating, I went to live in Cuenca, Ecuador, where I was immersed in a very different kind of food system. Daily farmer's markets were permanent establishments, accessible and affordable in every poor and working class neighborhood. Buying fresh and seasonal produce from local farmers was the norm, as it had been for centuries. Only in upper-class neighborhoods could one find expensive sugary, salty, processed foods, and only wealthy families could afford fast food. Schools served meals "from scratch" that contained fresh local produce found in neighboring fields. Having experienced the food and agricultural disconnects of my childhood, seen the food deserts in Los Angeles, and learned about the disproportionately high rates of diet-related chronic disease affecting low-income communities of color, I began to realize how off track we were in the suburban U.S. compared to this Third World country. If food could be produced and consumed differently in Ecuador, why not in Ventura County? Slowly it sank in that there would be no going back to my insular blindness.

When I moved back to Ventura County to pursue a bilingual teaching credential at California State University Channel Islands, I was ready to dig into food justice activism—and there I found The Abundant Table. I'll never forget meeting Sarah Nolan, the Abundant Table chaplain and now director. She had long, beautiful dreadlocks and piercings, and shared about her experience with the South Central Farmers' Cooperative during their land struggle in Los Angeles.[3] She was unlike any Christian person I'd ever met, and soon my skepticism about a campus minister gave way to a sense that I'd found a place to grow and deepen my work in food justice.

---

3. In 2006, after a three-year campaign to save their fourteen-acre urban farm, the South Central farmers (and solidarity activists from around the world) were evicted from the land after a multi-week occupation. Following the eviction, many in this mostly Mesoamerican farming community developed the South Central Farmers' Cooperative. This grassroots economic development project is committed to engaging and empowering community members to attain food sovereignty and access to high quality organic produce. Farmers from SCFC provide The Abundant Table with technical support and partnership in developing a stronger local food system for all. For more information see www.thesouthcentralfarmers.com, and the Academy Award-nominated documentary *The Garden* (http://www.thegardenmovie.com/).

I began attending The Abundant Table's weekly campus liturgy, and grew into a discipleship that is rooted in seeing and naming oppression and responding with love and compassion. At The Abundant Table we felt righteous anger and a desire to change oppressive systems; at the same time I began to know a Christ, a Christian faith, and a discipleship community I'd never experienced in the Catholic Church of my childhood. I'd found a community that shared a radical understanding of Christ and his teachings, and a desire to grow an alternative local food system out of a decaying and crumbling industrialized agricultural system. This was exactly what my heart had longed for!

The Abundant Table Farm Project set up an initial five-acre organic farm on the fertile Oxnard plain, and we grew produce for our weekly Community Supported Agriculture (CSA) subscriptions. As part of the inaugural class of year-long interns, I and four other women worked in the fields; sold our produce at local farmer's markets and through the CSA program; cultivated intentional community life in a rambling one-story farm house; and connected with the local food justice network. Since then, I have worked as the Abundant Table CSA coordinator, farm manager, and now as director of farm education. Currently our farm grows produce for over 100 families through our CSA, and thousands of pounds for local school districts to serve to students in school lunches. In addition we have a very active Farm Education program, which I had the opportunity to build and now lead, cultivating the next generation of healthy conscious eaters!

Say more about your role with The Abundant Table.

When I started as an intern in 2009, I had just completed my teacher credentialing program. I was eager to use the farm as an outdoor classroom to create learning opportunities for youth. A farm is an ideal place to learn about the interdependent relationships between farming practices, soil, watersheds, botany, human health, and economics. We observe, experience, and understand the impacts of sustainable and industrial practices on farmworkers, soil, the environment, ourselves, and our community. I wanted to help facilitate learning opportunities I did not have growing up, the kind that facilitate both awe and anger. Students come to our farm and experience the wonder of life: from micro-organisms in the soil to worms in the compost, from ladybugs eating aphids to hawks circling for rodents, and from pulling weeds to putting a freshly harvested carrot right in their

mouths. They also intuitively compare the life-giving and sustainable growing practices we use with the soil-depleting, water-contaminating, and hu-
man-oppressing practices of surrounding industrial agriculture. Students
feel a relationship with their place and community, and are upset that environmental resources and human lives are treated poorly in our dominant
food system.

Erynn Smith and students looking for "good bugs."

As director of farm education for The Abundant Table, I coordinate a
variety of programs: farm field trips year-round for students of all ages; a
YMCA farm day camp for two weeks in the summer; and "Farmer in the
Classroom," which brings our programs into local classrooms. Our grant-
funded education programs also bring nutrition, agriculture, cooking, and
food security education to under-resourced schools and farmworker communities. This past year I co-created with colleagues from the Wilderness
Way community a day camp we call "Alive: Eco-Faith Farm Camp," which is
designed to inspire and educate the next generation of watershed disciples![4]

4. Wilderness Way is a worshipping community in Portland, Oregon, that seeks "to
"re-wild Christianity" through collective public action, teaching, mentoring, training,
retreats, relationships, and sharing of resources, and to "open up creative space in which
to un-tame the language, ritual, prayer, song, sacraments and movements of the church."
See http://www.wildernesswaypdx.org, and community member Pritchett's Chapter
Two.

Another of our education programs, "Rooted Futures," is currently helping change school food practices in the local community of Santa Paula, California. This largely agricultural community has the highest rates of obesity in the county due to poor access to the very fruits and vegetables that farmworker residents harvest for a living! In 2013, I began meeting regularly with a Santa Paula High School student activist club to explore food access, agriculture, and how their own families and communities are impacted by our food system. Students decided to focus their advocacy on their own school food system, developing a "Harvest of the Month" program to serve one kind of local, seasonal produce each month in the cafeteria. They create a monthly calendar that highlights local, seasonal produce; develop a local produce purchasing guide for food service staff; and create a simple recipe featuring the highlighted produce that can be served in the cafeteria. Students and food administrators met throughout the school year to plan a launch for May 2015. They selected *nopales* (pads of prickly pear cactus), a Mexican food staple, and developed a *nopales* quesadilla recipe with a local chef. The administration has shown full support in adopting Harvest of the Month program throughout the entire school district.

How would you describe the community that has grown out of The Abundant Table?

Community is one of the reasons I have stayed with The Abundant Table. I love our authentic, diverse, and complex family, that is developing a longevity and sustainability that is critical during our struggles. When we started we were white and privileged persons wanting to deconstruct the systems that unfairly benefitted us. Then our farmers Reyna, Guadalupe, and their family joined our farm team. Reyna's experience migrating to the United States from Mexico and working over a decade as a farmworker added a depth to our community. It helped us reframe questions about what justice meant in a larger agricultural system into what it looks like in our work together. For us justice is not just a value or ideal, but the fabric of our relationships with each other. This work is hard and personal, complicated and human, but it's the right place to start!

I love the layers of community within The Abundant Table. CSA members have joined our Farm Church, church members have become my closest friends and mentors, former interns have met their life partners here, and Sarah and Reyna have become my sisters. And many of us have intentionally moved into the same neighborhood in Oak View.

What have been the ongoing challenges for The Abundant Table and how do you see them connected to systemic issues facing our communities?

Some are practical; we struggle to find consistent access to land, adequate equipment and capital, sustainable agriculture resources in Spanish, and to cover our monthly costs. Some are cultural; CSA customers turn over because eating in season and preparing fresh whole fruits and vegetables "gets old," and some realize they are "farmer's market people" instead. But each of these challenges is connected to larger systemic issues facing our communities. The dominant agro-industrial growing model extracts (and contaminates) resources pursuing the objective of "feeding the world" at a maximum profit for corporate landholders and managers. Food policy, regulations, and the market economy fuel this system. The collateral damage, however, is costly: degraded water and soil; food contamination; diet-related chronic disease; and food insecurity among the agriculture labor force. But these costs are externalized from production: we all pay for them through federal programs to support families that can't afford food due to low agricultural wages; healthcare costs; and environmental programs to clean up disasters related to agricultural chemical use. Consumer demands for "cheap everything!" and "tomatoes year-round!" pose tremendous challenges to small scale, diversified agriculture. The real costs of sustainable agriculture that embraces fair labor practices make it impossible to be competitive in much of our local food system.

Land access is a huge challenge in our community. High land values make ownership virtually impossible for younger farmers who have inherited neither land nor capital. Leasing from land owners has been our only option; but tenant farming is difficult, since landlords have so much control over how land is used. We've had to move our farm twice in six years due to rent increases and changing usage needs for the property. Every growing season we face the depressing financial reality that it could be our last. Every one of us working and growing *from* the edges of dominant systems and *into* alternative systems knows that life at the edge is precarious. Farmworkers have been my best teachers when it comes to dancing with grace and joy on those edges—which at The Abundant Table means salsa dancing!

What inspires you to continue your work?

I have been inspired by the growth of my relationships with self, place, and community during my time with The Abundant Table, and I've seen others move into their callings as well. That's one of the greatest gifts of this community: we mirror the goodness or the "God-ness" of each other. We let the miracles of each other, the soil and our watershed be revealed through our life and work. Our acts of resistance bring us to places of such life and wholeness that our eyes are opened to see the disorder and disconnection that characterizes our larger food systems. We can participate fully in life through the farm and the relationships that grow from and around it, which is a powerful way to break down our crumbling food system.

And at the core of this work is love. If we didn't love ourselves, each other, and our place we wouldn't have made it past our first growing season. To see what our love can grow has been one of the greatest gifts of my life.

III. Reyna Ortega[5]

Share about the journey that brought you to The Abundant Table.

I was born in Mexico City, and grew up in a touristy area. I was fortunate enough to learn about my culture, food, arts, folklore, and music. Unfortunately, it was also a place where there was a lot of violence, corruption, and poverty. I believe that poverty is the thief of innocence. By age eleven I was seeing my friends, brothers and neighbors losing their innocence little by little by stealing, smoking, using drugs, and having sex. It was like a plague. I tried to make good decisions, but I knew that sooner or later I would also succumb to this plague, possibly making bad decisions, like becoming a prostitute.

I had the opportunity to immigrate to the U.S. when I was fourteen years old, which offered hope and dreams for a different life. When I arrived in Oxnard, California I started to work in the fields. Even though I had worked a few jobs in Mexico, I never imagined how difficult fieldwork would be. My first day lasted twelve hours, and most of my coworkers didn't think I would last. Though still a child, I dug deep to find the strength to finish that day. Every time I felt pain, I would tighten my jaw as forcefully as

---

5. This interview was conducted in Spanish, and later translated to English by Leticia Sandoval and Erynn Smith.

possible in order to mask it. The next day, when I woke up, I couldn't move my legs to get out of bed, or sit down to use the toilet, or open my mouth to eat. I became so scared. I think my body experienced all the pain I had suffered in my life on that day. But despite these challenges, I didn't really have an option to quit if I was to survive, not having friends or family here. So, my body had to get used to it, and eventually did.

On my fifteenth birthday I awoke to heavy rain. I should have been wearing a princess dress to celebrate my *quinceañera*; instead, I donned a plastic bag and giant rubber boots. As I worked that day I cried uncontrollably, and the indifference of my coworkers confirmed the loneliness that I felt. I was miserable; my dreams and hopes for a better life had turned into a nightmare. My tears mixed with the rain, as if the sky was crying with me. I had lost everything. My parents, siblings and friends were all far away, as was the celebrative culture that made me feel proud to be Mexican (such as the mariachi songs I heard from my crib). On the contrary, my nights were filled with a loud silence. My homeland was distant and I did not belong to anything. It was a painful loneliness.

As a child in catechism class the teacher would tell us that we shouldn't sin or else God was going to punish us. I felt I was paying for some sin I had committed, and asked God why this was happening, and interrogated myself about what I might have done to be punished in this way. I wondered, "Which is the worst reality, the one I had escaped or this one?" There were so many times I was angry with God, believing God had forgotten about me, because I saw others who were so much more fortunate. I couldn't understand what God's plan was for me, and began asking God to give me the opportunity to have a different life.

Fifteen years later, I am seeing the fruits of my labor that were watered with so many tears. I have formed my own family and have four wonderful daughters. I have a partner that supports me on my journey, and have found a community of people that are passionate about a different type of agriculture. I was blessed to discover The Abundant Table and its commitment to justice for the earth, for the community, and for farmworkers. They have taught me so much and been a "family" that values, loves, and respects me for who I am. I have also reconciled my relationship with God. I am still working in the fields, and though it is still just as hard as before, it is work that I enjoy and that gives me dignity. Not only do I have friends now, but lots of sisters and brothers, like when I was a little girl. But I'm still very Mexican and love my culture; I continue to miss my country, its celebrations, and my parents and siblings. My wounds have healed, but my tears are still close, and the scars will always be with me.

Why was it so important for you to celebrate a "Treintañera"?

In Mexican culture, celebrating a young woman's fifteenth birthday (*Quinceañera*) represents a formal transition from girl to woman. This is when your hopes and dreams begin, a day you will remember for the rest of your life. For me, celebrating my thirtieth birthday (*Treintañera*) was incredibly important, not just for superficial reasons (having a party and wearing a princess dress), but because it helped me fulfill the dream I had yearned for on my fifteenth birthday. At fourteen, with the soul of a little girl, I was forced to become an adult, and had to fight for survival. Now I was able finally to present myself formally before the community as a true woman.

Reyna, Erynn and Sarah at the "Treintañera."

Each immigrant has a different story and different reasons for being in this country. I still have many dreams, and a desire to go out into the world and live life to its fullest. I now know that I am part of God's plan and that God has a mission for me. Poverty is a thief of innocence, and stole a lot from me. However, it couldn't steal my belief that one day I would have a better life, my dreams or my love for and faith in God.

What is your role with the Abundant Table?

I'm the farm manager, supervisor, and a farmworker who does almost everything in the field. I grow the vegetables, take care of the weeds, irrigate, harvest, and pack produce. Recently I've had the opportunity to lead spiritual practices on the farm, write liturgies and sermons for community gatherings, and even coordinate a stations of the cross on the farm. So though initially I was hired to be a field worker, I ended up in charge of the farming and as a spiritual leader. This has been a challenge, because in U.S. society there's not much confidence that a woman can run a farm. I had to learn many jobs that require the strength of a man. And even though I had worked on farms since I was fourteen, I had no knowledge of how to supervise an operation. My jobs before were very different; since work in conventional agriculture is very large scale, you have specific positions where you only pack, or harvest, or irrigate.

What is the most difficult part of running a small sustainable farm?

When I began as a farmworker at The Abundant Table and realized we were growing vegetables for a CSA, schools, and farmer's markets, it motivated me. When the farm manager position was offered to me, I was excited. I didn't think much about my lack of experience; I'd fallen in love with the farm and had come to feel that it was "mine." So I have worked with even more enthusiasm for our values at the farm. There are highs and lows, but because I feel ownership of this project, I fight every day. But let me answer your question as if I were an owner. The lack of information, money, and workers are the most difficult things facing a small farm. Most things happen that are out of your control. You plan, work, and do the best you can, yet from one day to the next a pest infestation can come and finish off everything. It shouldn't feel personal but it does.

When I began working at The Abundant Table they told me the mission was "Justice for farm workers, for the earth, and for the community." Though I didn't believe in it at first, perhaps because I didn't understand it deeply, this mission is what has hooked me! In conventional agriculture there's not much valuing of the earth, and even less of the workers, who are treated as statistics. Because of this we farmworkers tend not to value ourselves as human beings. When I talk to other farmworkers about my work now, they don't believe in this different way to run a farm. But I feel so valued and respected for who I am and what I do, and I want my friends and family to be a part of this different system. I've invited them to work on the farm, and they come, but they don't stay. I believe this is due to their lack of hope that there are truly ways of working and producing food that value workers and the earth. It is also difficult that there is so much lack of understanding and support in the wider community about why it's important to take care of the environment, those who consume the produce, and farmworkers.

Why is it important to show youth the dignity of working with the land?

It's important that all work be dignified. As a farmer in a Latino community, it's been very sad to hear that many of our youth don't want to be like their parents who work in the fields, bent over all day in the mud and sun. Of course it's good that our kids want to better themselves and have good jobs, but we as farmworkers don't give ourselves the credit that our work deserves. Before I was ashamed to go into a bank or store in farmworker clothes, even in a farmworker neighborhood! Now I respect my job just as much as that of a nurse or teacher. My dirty clothes are my professional uniform. I believe it's very important that youth have opportunities to work in the field and grow their own understanding of farm work, so they can begin to respect and value this work and the tremendous physical strength and earth-literacy it requires.

I have four daughters, and I want my daughters to be proud of their parents's work in the fields and with the soil. They come to the farm and work with me, and experience how difficult it is; and so now they give me massages when I get home from work. I'm so happy they can have these experiences at The Abundant Table. In our county, where agriculture is one of the principle sources of income for many families, it's crucial that youth learn to value farm work and its importance for everyone. Farmworkers deserve to *feel* dignity in, and respect for, their work.

What was your experience working with young adult interns on the farm?

Supervising interns was really strange at first! I am accustomed to having white people as my superiors. When I learned about our internship program, I didn't understand it, and couldn't see interns working in the field. I thought they would come and enjoy the open air of the fields, write a bit of poetry, and get a good tan. Truthfully, I felt bad for them, thinking, "Poor things! They don't have to work in the field to make their living." I didn't feel comfortable asking them to work or demand that they work harder, and so would often end up doing a lot of the work myself. In our group reflections and discussions I would hear them speak about justice and equality for all, so once I had to sit down and talk with them about the fact that while I was working as hard and as fast as I could, they were taking excessive breaks to chat with each other. I told them, "We can talk and talk about values of justice and equality, but if we ourselves don't begin to practice these here and now there's no way we can think about changing the world." I learned to respect them by deeply respecting myself, and came to feel that because white and brown people are equal, I'm not going to do *their* harvest!

What is the relationship between God and your work, and how do you see your dreams connected to that relationship?

It's difficult to get out of bed so early every morning. But when I arrive on the farm, I have a feeling of deep satisfaction. I have more opportunity to see the wonders of the earth. In breathing the fresh air of the morning and seeing the sunrise I've created a deeper relationship with God. I am fortunate to witness the miracle of life everyday on the farm: in seeing a seed germinate or the compost dying to give nutrients to the soil's life. The miracle also exists in creating family among friends, in having dreams and fighting for them, and in believing that life is God's creation. I know that my job does so much good for the community, farmworkers, and the earth; but I also want to work with more farmworkers, with children, with prisoners. Working here has taught me that when you see the miracle of life every day, you are inspired to live in deeper relationship with God.

What inspires you?

Working on our farm gives me the opportunity to experience challenges and overcome them. I realize that I have more abilities than I ever could have imagined! It's given me the chance to understand that women are inspirational, that we can dream the impossible and make it happen. I would never have believed that there could be a place where women are such powerful activists and run a farm! But that is exactly what our team at The

Abundant Table is doing. They inspire me not only to dream big, but to fight for those dreams to come true!

IV. Conclusion

As this chapter was being completed, The Abundant Table was in the process of its third move in six years. Our new piece of land will hopefully allow us to continue growing in a way that embodies our mission and values, but is also financially viable. Our staff, worshipping community and land base now inhabit three different watersheds within the same county: the Ventura River Watershed; Santa Clara River Watershed; and Calleguas Creek Watershed. As we get to know new types of soil, water systems, micro-climates, and the neighbors we will be working with, we are again challenged to understand better what it means for our community to develop a relationship to a bioregion—from the microorganisms to human organisms.

Erynn and Reyna's stories point to the importance of restored relationship to one another, to the land and to God. We still have a lot to learn, and some days it seems like this work is a constant uphill struggle. However, the transformation that happens through the power of relationships and community offers a reminder that a different way is possible. But this way is not a straight path like the political borders of Ventura County, but rather like the undulating lines of the watershed map, proceeding more like water winding through multiple landscapes, with pools of calm and wild rapids along its course—ultimately seeking level.

Our lives are deeply interconnected with the created cosmos as incarnated in our place. It is in the call to a Watershed Discipleship that we begin to wrestle with those intertwined relationships in ways that lead toward restoration and life. For The Abundant Table, this occurs by practicing thoughtful stewardship of the earth; advocating for farmworker rights; growing good food for local people; inviting others to share in the joys and miracles of plants, bugs and soil; and challenging one another to nurture visions and dreams for a world fully restored.

Chapter Nine

Plastics as a Spiritual Crisis

SASHA ADKINS

Summary: Disposable plastics are paradigmatic of a culture that has lost its ability to form healthy relationships. We vilify the plastics that infiltrate our oceans, our water, and our bodies without reflecting on why we produce over 300 million metric tons of it a year. While plastics are only one of many unhealthy components of a society premised on planned obsolescence, I single them out because not only are they inherently toxic at each stage of their "life" cycle, they may become even more dangerous once they are thrown away. This is fundamentally a spiritual problem, which technological fixes will not resolve, but only a cultural transformation concerning disposability.

WRITING ABOUT PLASTIC BY industry employees or environmental activists, whether scientific or literary, invariably begins with a paean. The authors remind us how lucrative the plastics industry is, how dependent we've become on the "convenience" plastics provide, and how unrecognizable life would be without them. Some hearken back to a famous scene from the 1967 film *The Graduate*: Mr. McGuire offers career advice to recent college graduate Ben at a cocktail party, conspiratorially whispering, "I have one word of advice to you, just one word: *Plastics*." Mr. McGuire's faith in the great promise of plastics has, in the view of most commentators, been fulfilled. Even those who enumerate the ways that plastics are harming us feel obliged to assert a basic loyalty to them—an expression, I suppose, of the Stockholm Syndrome.

I feel no such obligation, and see the abundance of plastics as a profound problem, not a point of pride. Plastics are a convenience only to the short-sighted. In 1950, the world produced 1.7 million tons of cellulose, urea formaldehyde, Bakelight, PVC and nylon. By 2012, we were making 288 million metric tons of synthetic polymers a year (UNEP 2014; see http://www.statista.com/statistics/282732/global-production-of-plastics-since-1950/). When will we reach a saturation point? Plastic medical equipment, from disposable gloves to pacemakers, has prolonged many lives; yet plastics themselves are suspected of contributing to many of the diseases we try to cure. In my opinion, we would have been better off without plastics, but I believe it is still possible to break free from and relearn to live without them. I think our survival depends on it.

I. Plastics in Our Food

Let's begin this overview with how we are ingesting plastics at a far higher rate than we realize. For example, many time-release medications and vitamins are microencapsulated in plastics (see presentation at http://www.authorstream.com/Presentation/vamshi767-2066171-microencapsulation/). Fresh fruit may be coated in vinyl chloride-vinylidene chloride copolymer (similar on a molecular level to an invisible layer of Saran Wrap) or oxidized polyethylene to prolong its shelf life (see FDA's "Everything Added to Food in the U.S." site: http://www.accessdata.fda.gov/scripts/fcn/ fcnNavigation.cfm?rpt =eafusListing). Chewing gum bases made of natural chicle or beeswax have been replaced with sugar-coated polyvinyl acetate and synthetic elastomers like styrene-butadiene. Some exfoliants and toothpastes also contain plastic microbeads (http://www.ctvnews.ca/business/crest-removing-controversial-microbeads-from-toothpaste-after-outcry-1.2013155). Cows chew cud instead of gum, but a U.S. patent for "artificial roughage" eliminates the need for them to graze: yet "synthetic hay" is simply strips of shredded polyethylene (http://www.wikipatents.com/US-Patent-3876793/method-of-aiding-digestion-with-artificial-roughage-materials). Fortunately, this practice is not yet widespread.

We also add plastics to our food indirectly. Many studies demonstrate that the plastic containers in which we store, heat, and freeze food and beverages leave traces of themselves behind in the food (Adkins 2014). Many of us try to avoid microwaving plastics, place our leftovers in glass or stainless steel, and avoid brewing coffee in plastic. However, most of the contact between food and plastics is invisible, occurring long before we bring it home. Martin Wagner and Jörg Oehlmann compared snails living in mineral water from plastic bottles to snails living in mineral water taken from glass bottles (2009). The former had many more offspring, which is one indirect way to measure their estrogen levels. The confusing part was that sometimes the water from glass bottles seemed to have high levels of estrogenic chemicals, too. The mystery was solved by a visit to the bottling facility: it turned out that the glass bottles were inert, but that the water had been stored in plastic *before* being transferred to glass bottles!

Even before food is processed, it may be grown in plastic. Produce grown in greenhouses constructed with plastic panels may contain significant levels of bisphenol-A (BPA), a hormone-disrupting component of polycarbonate plastic (Sajiki et al. 2007). Researchers suspect that this chemical might be transferred through the air. Another potential source of indirect contamination is the post-consumer polystyrene pellets that are sometimes mixed with the soil in which some crops grow in order to "hold water, minerals, and nutrients" (http://tamgreen.com/gaia_soil). We know that heat increases the rate of transfer of chemicals from plastic into whatever it is touching. When soil is steamed (as is often done as a non-chemical means of sterilizing it), or on hot summer days, are plants taking chemicals from these pellets up into their root systems? We do not know enough about how much of a risk this could pose to people or to the plants themselves. Rhizobial bacteria fix nitrogen, communicating with their host plant using phytoestrogen signals (the plant version of our bodies's estrogen signals); BPA disrupts this process (Fox et al. 2001, Vivacqua et al. 2003).

It is in the oceans, however, that plastic's impact on the food chain is most worrisome to me. Some of the physical hazards of plastic are readily visible: plastic marine debris strangles, suffocates, and drowns birds and marine life. Some seabirds seek synthetic rope as a building material for their nests, which can result in entanglement (Votier et al. 2011). Over 260 species of marine wildlife, including whales, turtles, birds, and fish have been observed feeding on pieces of plastic large enough to choke them or to obstruct their digestive tract (see https://www.mcsuk.org/press/view/181

and http://www.seashepherd.org/reef-defense/marine-debris.html). Large pieces of plastic debris slam into coral, breaking off pieces of fragile reefs and ruining habitat for the prey; the smaller pieces the coral eats (http://www.thehindu.com/todays-paper/tp-national/corals-feeding-on-plastic-debris/article6930514.ece).

Plankton comprises the base of the marine food chain, and along with krill, is the largest animal biomass on our planet. One type of plankton often used as a biodiversity indicator is the copepod (https://en.wikipedia.org/wiki/Copepod). Without it, many small fish would go hungry. Plankton feed at the surface, where lighter plastic debris is abundant. Could plankton be eating it, and what impact would that have? A lab experiment attempted to answer these questions (Cole et al. 2015). Finely powdered polystyrene was added to the water in the tank of a copepod, which did indeed feed on the polystyrene; subsequently its ability to ingest nutritive food decreased, and its survival rates plummeted. It is not clear whether this is because the plastic was a physical obstruction in its digestive tract or whether it was acting as a poison.

Whole plastics are called *polymers;* their chemical building blocks are referred to as *monomers.* To further complicate matters, each polymer also contains a blend of other chemicals that do not contribute to its structure, but instead confer properties such as color, texture, or durability. These are called *additives,* and their particular combinations, which vary from batch to batch during production, are closely guarded trade secrets. Many legal additives in plastics are acknowledged as being toxic, such as lead, cadmium, phthalates, organotins, and tricresyl phosphate. In the case of plastic marine debris, we need to know the fate not only of the polymer, but also of its monomers and additives.

Chanbasha Basheer and colleagues bought seafood from a market in Singapore (2004). They tested five samples each of prawn, crab, blood cockle, white clam, squid, and a pelagic species of fish, *Decapterus russelli,* for BPA, the building block of polycarbonate plastic. BPA was present in *every* sample, at levels that ranged from 13 to 213 parts per billion (ppb) wet weight, with the highest levels found in the crabs. We can begin to comprehend this ratio of concentration through analogies: one part per billion as one pancake in a stack 4,000 miles high, or three seconds in a century. Though these are infinitesimally tiny amounts, a concentration of BPA in the six to ten ppb range or even less has been shown to have adverse effects (Peretz et al. 2014). As endocrinologists know, the effective dose of many pharmaceuticals falls into this low-dose range (for example, the NuvaRing contraceptive acts at 0.035 ppb, while an inhaler can relieve an asthma attack with a puff of 2.1 ppb of albuterol). Moreover, we are likely also exposed to BPA through other activities, such as touching cash register receipts made with a BPA or BPS (its chemical cousin), or eating canned food (in the U.S. many food containers are lined with BPA). Basheer et al. (2004) wondered whether the BPA was finding its way into seafood through the seawater. They tested six seawater samples at twenty-eight locations both near shore and offshore that represented diverse uses (industrial zones, beaches, marinas, etc.). The highest concentration they found, however, was only 2.47 ppb, much lower than that in the seafood. Does this mean that BPA is persistent enough to bioaccumulate? Or could it be that marine creatures had ingested plastics that were releasing BPA?

To make matters worse, petroleum-based substances like plastics behave in a curious way when placed in water. They actively seek out other petroleum-based compounds, with which they form nearly inseparable bonds. This property is called lipophilicity (*lipo-* meaning oily or fatty, and *-philicity* meaning love or attraction). Thus petroleum-based plastics become magnets for the trace residues of pesticides such as DDT and its breakdown products that linger in the environment. Another class of oily industrial chemicals that adsorb to marine plastics is polychlorinated biphenols, or PCBs. Though their production was banned in the US in 1979, they turn up mysteriously now and again in things dyed orange and yellow (http://www.scientificamerican.com/article/yellow-pigments-in-clothing-and-paper-contain-long-banned-chemical/). Another are phenanthrenes, part of a class of combustion byproducts collectively called polycyclic aromatic hydrocarbons, or PAHs.

Japanese scientist Yukie Mato and her team collected nurdles (pre-consumer plastic beads that are melted and shaped into roughly the size and shape of lentils) by hand from three beaches, and scooped floating nurdles from a canal using a stainless steel net (2001). They sorted the nurdles by resin type to find the polypropylene pellets (polypropylene is used for example in yogurt tubs). They measured how much DDE (a metabolite of DDT, an insecticide), PCBs, and nonylphenol (an endocrine-disrupting surfactant, which we will call NP for short) the pellets contained. They learned that nurdles in the ocean had soaked up so much of these chemicals that they contained up to one million times more of each contaminant than the seawater itself. This is likely because persistent organic pollutants (or

POPS, including DDE, PCBs, and NPs as studied by Mato) are lipophilic. Mato's team wondered if the nurdles might have had these contaminants in them before they fell into the ocean, so examined "virgin" nurdles from a plastics factory and found they did not contain any DDE, PCBs, or NP. Just to be sure, they put new nurdles into a fine mesh stainless steel basket and dangled them in Tokyo Bay for six days, then tested them again. Now all the nurdles had high levels of DDE, PCBs, and NP, demonstrating that plastics are binding to chemicals already in seawater and concentrating them.

Emma Teuten and her colleagues took this line of investigation a step further, documenting not only how plastics soak up poisonous chemicals but also how they release them into the food chain (2007). They first studied how much phenanthrene (a hazardous polycyclic aromatic hydrocarbon that serves a model for other POPs) each of three types of plastic (polyethylene, polypropylene, and polyvinyl chloride) could absorb from seawater. All three absorbed much more than did natural sand or pebbles. Then they placed lugworms (*Arenicola marina*) in sand that was contaminated with phenanthrene; some of the lugworms also had plastic added to their sand. Adding just one microgram of polyethylene per gram of sediment dramatically increased the amount of phenanthrene the lugworms accumulated. A complementary study by the University of Exeter has shown that elevated levels of plastics cause lugworms to eat less and to suffer from reduced energy levels (Browne et al. 2013).

Because "polycyclic aromatic hydrocarbons" and "DDE" are not household words, this phenomenon does not have the impact outside the scientific community that it deserves. I wondered if a similar process might be happening with a more familiar contaminant: mercury. The saving grace for our seafood seemed to be that mercury in its most toxic form is not particularly lipophilic. However, mercury *is* attracted to *mercaptans* (the Latin name indicates how sulfur molecules draw mercury and hold it captive). I decided to investigate whether these sulfur molecules could attract and bind mercury even when they themselves are already bound to another material. My proof of concept pilot study found that this was indeed the case. Styrene-butadiene block copolymers, used in automobile tires, contain these sulfur molecules as a residue of a particular type of vulcanization process. When pieces of this plastic were dropped into a seawater solution spiked with methyl mercury, it only took three days for the plastic bits to soak up over 70 percent of the mercury. If we were somehow able to submerge these particles in the ocean and then remove and dispose of them safely, we would be essentially purifying sea water. However, since the only ways plastic marine debris leaves the ocean are by washing up on shore (unlikely for materials this dense) or by being ingested and passing into the marine food web, the net effect is not removal of mercury, but its *concentration* in our seafood.

But how do fish come into contact with automobile tires? Off the Atlantic coast of Florida, two million used tires were spread on the seafloor in what Goodyear proclaimed was an ecologically friendly solution to the problem of old tire disposal, since on land tires tend to fill with rainwater and breed mosquitoes, when buried they have a tendency to resurface, and when burned they release toxic chemicals. So "artificial reefs," Goodyear reasoned, would provide a habitat for marine species, just as had been proposed for other artificial reef material such as scuttled ships, subway cars, and more recently, "Reef Balls"(including some made of PVC or concrete mixed with cremated human remains!). This is a classic case of one "solution" generating more problems.

II. From Washing Machine to Gyre

Plastics are paradoxical. Though in many cases they are designed to be discarded after a single use, they may outlast life on earth. No one actually knows how long it will take plastics to break down—or if they ever will (giving rise to the slogan, "Like diamonds, plastics are forever"). Unless it has been incinerated or digested by microbes, every piece of plastic ever made is still with us—or in some cases, *in* us. The conventional wisdom holds that if we "manage" our plastic properly, we will be able to maximize its benefits and minimize its risks. The truth is, we do not yet know how to contain our plastic trash, much less to detoxify it.

Much of what is "responsibly" tossed into recycling bins still finds its way out again. Light plastics such as Styrofoam and SaranWrap tend to blow out of open curbside receptacles, from the trucks that transport them, or from the facilities that receive them. Moreover, since these remnants have so little monetary value, there is little incentive to design and implement infrastructure that would prevent such loss. Since plastics do not break down in landfills, sooner or later their resting places will be disturbed, whether by storms or curious creatures. Incineration, meanwhile, transforms plastics into new molecules, some of which are unfortunately even more hazardous.

Many well-intentioned people have with great intelligence and creativity devoted themselves to figuring out how to scoop up and repurpose plastic debris. Various innovative technological fixes are being proposed, such as sweeping up larger pieces in the ocean with a giant trawl and melting them down for conversion into fuel or into new plastics. However, even if all the plastic in the oceans *were* cleaned up tomorrow, at the rate we are redepositing them, it wouldn't take us more than a few years to replace what had been cleaned up. I am drawn instead to trying to understand how we can stem the tide of garbage in the first place. First we must understand where it comes from.

In one sense, since all plastic is made by factories, it is all land-based. But those of us in the marine conversation field point out that 20 percent of debris is sea-based. It is now illegal to toss plastic overboard from ships, but we can confirm only the accidental spills. Cargo containers are not infrequently lost from freighters during storms. In one famous incident in 1992, a ship spilled nearly thirty-thousand Friendly Floatee toys. A citizen science project directed by Curtis Ebbesmeyer used these rubber duckies to study oceanic currents in the Pacific (see http://beachcombersalert. org/Rubber Duckies.html). The intentional disposal of plastic at sea, on the other hand, like other illegal activities, is hard to quantify. Dutch researchers have caught some ships shredding their plastic trash and mixing it with food waste before sending it illicitly overboard. According to some informants, the Italian mafia makes a lucrative business of disposing of society's toxic waste, including plastics, the disposal of which is more strictly regulated in the European Union. They charge their customers a fee for taking away their waste, which they then load onto ships and sink offshore, entitling them to insurance reimbursement (see e.g. http://www.spiegel.de/ international/europe/anger-rises-in-italy-over-toxic-waste-dumps-from-the-mafia-a-943630.html).

The issue of "upstream" microsplastics debris is much closer to home. Sixty percent of all fibers used in clothing and accessories are synthetic (Browne et al. 2011). Each time we wash a garment made of polyester, Lycra, nylon, or acrylic it sheds thousands of microscopic fibers. Experiments sampling wastewater from domestic washing machines demonstrated that a single garment can shed more than 1,900 fibers per wash. These are flushed through (usually PVC) outflow pipes with the greywater, and eventually pass through a wastewater treatment plant, because their filters are not designed to capture debris this small. In spite of my fastidious efforts to shop only for clothing made of hemp, wool, organic cotton, and bamboo, some plastic sneaked into my closet. My winter boots and coat are lined with fleece, which is typically made of polyethylene terephthalate, some from reclaimed plastic water bottles. The boots were made water resistant with perfluorinated compounds, another synthetic polymer found in wastewater. My bathing suit includes Lycra/Spandex, which is a polyurethane-polyurea copolymer. Tightly woven polyester gives my sun-protective jackets and hats their high SPF factor. My vegan shoes are PVC. I have nylon stockings and even an acrylic sweater (it was a gift). And this doesn't count all the plastic buttons!

Personal care products are another household source of plastic micro-debris. The Environmental Protection Agency confirmed that as of 2011, there were more than 2,000 products using polyethylene or polypropylene microbeads on the market in the U.S. These include exfoliating scrubs, lotions, and even some toothpastes (for example, there are approximately 330,000 microbeads present in a large bottle of facial scrub; http://ottawacitizen.com/news/local-news/environmentalists-drawing-a-bead-on-microplastics). Activists with the "Ban the Bead" campaign worked with manufacturers and state-level lawmakers to end this practice, which will be phased out by federal law beginning in 2017 (see http://www.5gyres.org/banthebead/).

In 1997, Charles Moore sailed through a remote spot in the North Pacific called a gyre, and was astonished to find that he was gliding through a plastic soup (2003, 2012). There were pellets and shards, threads and films. Many of the fragments bobbing at the surface or barely submerged were too small to identify; others were recognizable as having once been pen caps, shopping bags, and bottles. He noted ghost fishing nets and barnacle-encrusted buoys, but they were too heavy to retrieve. Deeply distressed, he struggled to convey the magnitude of his discovery. We now know these areas as "gyres," a convergence of currents into which much of the ocean's flotsam finds its way. In the gyre's swirls and eddies, the sunlight and the waves slowly break the flotsam into smaller and smaller pieces. We have learned that some of the pieces do leave the gyre—in the stomachs of migratory fish.

Scientists prefer to confront the world in managed, neatly measured increments, so Moore devised a methodology to quantify his discovery. He sailed back to the plastic soup, trailing a Manta trawl behind him. In this long, fine mesh net, held open by metal wings that resemble those of the eponymous Manta ray, he collected the skimmings of the sea. Back at the lab, he and his collaborators dried and weighed the samples. The abundance and mass of neustonic plastic was the largest recorded anywhere in the Pacific Ocean. While plankton abundance was approximately five times higher than that of plastic, the *mass* of plastic was approximately six times that of plankton. This means there are five microscopic plankton individuals for each fragment of plastic garbage, but by dry weight there is six times more plastic than marine life at the surface of the ocean. Moore's findings represented the highest recorded level of marine plastic to that date (much higher levels have been recorded since).

Other researchers raced to confirm or disprove these numbers. The more measurements taken, the more dismal were the findings. Miriam Goldstein's team found that microplastic (less than five mm) debris in the North Pacific had increased twofold between 1972–1987 and 1999–2010 (see http://www.miriamgoldstein.info/research.html). Another research team cautions, however, that surface measurements significantly underestimate plastic marine debris by a factor of up to twenty-seven due to wind-driven mixing in the upper water column (Kukulka et al. 2012). Ten years after his initial findings Moore estimated there was fifty to one hundred times *more* plastic debris than marine life in the Pacific gyre (2012).

Meanwhile, researchers have begun documenting abundant plastic debris outside the five oceanic gyres, from the Great Lakes to Antarctica. One team found a concentration on average of more than 43,000 microplastic particles, including microbeads per square kilometer in the Great Lakes, which increased ten-fold near major cities (Eriksen et al. 2013).

III. Learning to Love Trash

The ever-increasing abundance of plastic trash in land, sea and bodies is, fundamentally, a spiritual problem. Plastics habituate us to accept unhealthy relationships—and not only because our use of them is so typically fleeting. The foundation of a healthy relationship lies in a celebration of the Other's unique and intrinsic value; disposable plastics, however, are by design both fungible and instrumental.

We tend to project what we loathe onto "trash," and then hold to the fantasy that by throwing away what is "used" and/or "dirty" we will ourselves be purified. I contend that this relationship to disposables habituates us to project a similar shadow onto other people, thus dehumanizing them.

I have been wrestling for years with the memory of watching an infant die at the hands of the Kenyan police for the "crime" of being homeless. Their justification was: "We're cleaning up the streets. These people are garbage." The idea that people are disposable is reinforced by slurs like "trailer trash" or "poor white trash." The salient question, then, is how to unlearn this form of oppression.

At a class on environmental racism I taught at the Servant Leadership School in Washington, D.C. a few years ago we talked a lot about trying to love trash. I related a story of a client at an AIDS service organization who, after being estranged for decades from his family, was finally invited home to share Thanksgiving dinner. When he arrived, full of hope for a renewed connection, he was directed to sit outside on the back steps and to eat from disposable dishes while the rest of the family shared a meal on china around the dining table. We discussed how Jesus would have interacted with this modern-day leper, and reflected on times when we felt treated like garbage, or treated another person as if they were disposable. Then we each committed to choosing a piece of litter from the street to bring home to put on an altar. For one week, we would spend time contemplating what is beautiful and holy in it. After the week was up, I invited each person to share how this practice affected their prayer life. We found this exercise stirred up powerful, inexplicable, raw emotions, and many of us were nudged to get back in touch with people from whom we've been estranged. We then created a ritual together to bless our garbage. We each shared how special our piece of litter had become—a piece of ourselves we gathered to bless.

There is a connection between how we treat objects, how we view ourselves, and how we treat each other. My ecotheology of zero waste affirms that all that is has intrinsic value and is good. Everything that is belongs and contributes. By disposing of any part of the whole, we are all diminished. Everything and everyone, no matter how broken, is needed to re-member the body of Christ. As Jesus said to the authorities of his time:

> Have you never read in the Scriptures: "The stone the builders rejected has become the cornerstone; the Lord has done this, and it is marvelous in our eyes"? (Matt 21:42 citing Psalm 118:22; see Acts 4:11)

I see a parallel between this reference to the reclamation of material refuse and Jesus's other teachings concerning the reversal of social position ("the last will be first"), the centrality in God's plan of those on the margins, and the leadership of those who have been rejected. Conversely, throwing something away reinforces the mentality of a linear progression from birth to death, foreclosing the possibility of resurrection.

If we choose zero-waste as a spiritual discipline, we affirm that which is life-giving instead of toxic. We practice finding beauty, utility, and worth in the world around us and in each other. We call into being a world that is not a wasteland. And it is at the bioregional scale that we can most practically manage (and take responsibility for) our "garbage-shed."

An apple producer in British Columbia has recently marketed pre-cut, genetically modified apple pieces (no doubt wrapped in plastic) because "in a convenience-driven world, a whole apple is too big of a commitment" (http://greenecountynewsonline.com/2015/05/06/do-you-have-difficulty-committing-to-an-apple/). The temptation of such a "better apple" seems to me to be a parable of Eden's Fall. With our earth groaning under the toxic pressure of trash—especially plastics—we can no longer claim ignorance of the consequences of, nor displace blame for, eating *this* apple. As seductive as it may seem, we must wean ourselves off of disposable culture, and muster a commitment not only toward whole apples, but to a zero-waste world.[1]

References

Adkins, T. 2014. "Plastics." In *Achieving Sustainability: Visions, Principles, and Practices*, Vol 3, edited by D. Rowe, 588–92. Detroit: Macmillan Reference USA.

Basheer, C., H. K. Lee, and K. S. Tan. 2004. "Endocrine disrupting alkylphenols and bisphenol-A in coastal waters and supermarket seafood from Singapore." *Marine Pollution Bulletin* 48:1161–67.

Browne, M. A, A. Dissanayake, T. S. Galloway, D. M. Lowe, and R. C. Thompson. 2008. "Ingested Microscopic Plastic Translocates to the Circulatory System of the Mussel, Mytilus Edulis (L)" *Environmental Science Technology* 42:5026–31.

Browne, M. A., P. Crump, S. J. Niven, E. Teuten, E., A. Tonkin, T. Galloway, and R. Thompson. 2011. "Accumulation of Microplastic on Shorelines Worldwide: Sources and Sinks." *Environmental Science Technology*. 45:9175–9.

Browne, M. A., S. J. Niven, T. S. Galloway, S. J. Rowland, and R.C. Thompson. 2013. "Microplastic Moves Pollutants and Additives to Worms, Reducing Functions linked to Health and Biodiversity." *Current Biology*. 23:2388–92.

Cole, Matthew, Pennie Lindeque, Elaine Fileman, Claudia Halsband, and Tamara Galloway. 2015. "The Impact of Polystyrene Microplastics on Feeding, Function and

1. Two useful websites are http://zerowasteinstitute.org/ and http://www.zerowasteeurope.eu/2015/03/zero-waste-a-key-solution-for-a-low-carbon-economy/. Two popular practical household guides on zero waste are Johnson (2013) and Korst (2012); on plastics specifically SanClements (2014) and Freinkel (2011); on the waste crisis in general Humes (2013) and Palmer (2005).

Fecundity in the Marine Copepod *Calanus helgolandicus.*" *Environmental Science and Technology.* 49(2):1130–37.

Eriksen, M., S. Mason, S. Wilson, C. Box, A. Zellers, W. Edwards, H. Farley, and S. Amato. 2013. "Microplastic pollution in the surface waters of the Laurentian Great Lakes." *Marine Pollution Bulletin* 77:177–82.

Fox, J. E., M. Starcevic, K. Y. Kow, M. E. Burow and J. A. McLachlan. 2001. "Nitrogen fixation: Endocrine Disrupters and Flavonoid Signalling." *Nature* 413:128–29.

Freinkel, Susan. 2011. *Plastic: A Toxic Love Story.* New York: Houghton Mifflin Harcourt.

Johnson, Bea. 2013. *Zero Waste Home: The Ultimate Guide to Simplifying Your Life by Reducing Your Waste.* New York: Scribner.

Humes, Edward. 2013. *Garbology: Our Dirty Love Affair with Trash.* New York: Avery.

Korst, Amy. 2012. *The Zero-Waste Lifestyle: Live Well by Throwing Away Less.* Berkeley, CA: Ten Speed Press.

Kulkulka, Tobias, G. Proskurowski, S. Moret-Ferguson, D. W. Meyer, and K. Law. 2012. "The Effect of Wind Mixing on the Vertical Distribution of Buoyant Plastic Debris." *Geophysical Research Letters* 39 (7), DOI: 10.1029/2012GL051116.

Mato, Yukie, Tomohiko Isobe, Hideshige Takada, Haruyuki Kanehiro, Chiyoko Ohtake andTsuguchika Kaminuma. 2001. "Plastic Resin Pellets as a Transport Medium for Toxic Chemicals in the Marine Environment." *Environmental Science and Technology.* 35 (2):318–24.

Moore, Charles. 2003. "Trashed: Across the Pacific Ocean, Plastics, Plastics, Everywhere." *Natural History* 112 (9), November, 1–11.

———. 2012. *Plastic Ocean: How a Sea Captain's Chance Discovery Launched a Determined Quest to Save the Oceans.* New York: Avery.

Palmer, Paul. 2005. *Getting to Zero Waste.* Parkville, MO: Purple Sky Press.

Peretz, Jackye, Lisa Vrooman, William Ricke, Patricia Hunt, Shelley Ehrlich, Russ Hauser, Vasantha Padmanabhan, Hugh Taylor, Shanna Swan, Catherine VandeVoort, and Jodi Flaws. 2014. "Bisphenol A and Reproductive Health: Update of Experimental and Human Evidence, 2007–2013." *Environmental Health Perspectives.* August 122 (8):775–86. http://www.ncbi.nlm.nih.gov/pmc/articles/PMC4123031/.

Sajiki J., F. Miyamoto, H. Fukata, C. Mori, J. Yonekubo and K. Hayakawa. 2007. "Bisphenol A (BPA) and its Source in Foods in Japanese Markets." *Food Additives & Contaminants* 24 (1) 103–12.

SanClements, Michael. 2014. *Plastic Purge: How to Use Less Plastic, Eat Better, Keep Toxins Out of Your Body, and Help Save the Sea Turtles!* New York: St. Martin's Griffin.

Terry, Beth. 2012 Plastic-Free: How I Kicked the Plastic Habit and How You Can Too. New York: Skyhorse.

Teuten, Emma L., Steven Rowland, Tamara Galloway, and Richard C. Thompson. 2007. "Potential for Plastics to Transport Hydrophobic Contaminants." *Environmental Science and Technology* 41 (22) 7759–64.

UNEP (United Nations Environmental Program). 2014. *Valuing Plastics: The Business Case for Measuring, Managing and Disclosing Plastic Use in the Consumer Goods Industry.* http://www.unep.org/pdf/ValuingPlastic/#_blank.

Vivacqua A., A. Recchia, A. G. Fasanella, G. Gabriele, S. Carpino, A. Rago, V. Gioia, M. L. Di, A. Leggio, D. Bonofiglio, A. Liguori and M. Maggiolini. 2003. "The Food Contaminants Bisphenol A and 4-nonylphenol act as Agonists for Estrogen Receptor Alpha in MCF7 Breast Cancer Cells." *Endocrine* 22:275–84.

Votier, S. C., K. Archibald, G. Morgan, and L. Morgan. 2011. "The Use of Plastic Debris as Nesting Material by a Colonial Seabird and Associated Entanglement Mortality." *Marine Pollution Bulletin* 62:168–72.

Wagner, M. and J. Oehlmann. 2009. "Endocrine Disruptors in Bottled Mineral Water: Total Estrogenic Burden and Migration from Plastic Bottles." *Environmental Science Pollution Research International* 16 (3) 278–86.

Chapter Ten

Bioregionalism and the Catholic Worker Movement

Victoria Machado

Summary: The Catholic Worker started in 1933 as a way to carry out gospel works of mercy: offering food to the hungry, shelter to the homeless, and care to the sick through its various houses of hospitality. My experience with this movement, together with my studies in religion and nature, led me to explore how each Catholic Worker house adapts to its own *bioregional* context, rather than adopting a uniform model in every location. This is expressed through each house's use of resources, cultivation of community, and engagement of local social needs. With the rise of environmental consciousness among many houses today, bioregionalism's place-based approach to understanding the world may become more influential in the Catholic Worker movement.

CATHOLIC WORKERS ARE PROPONENTS of social justice. They feed the hungry; house the homeless; care for the unemployed and under-employed, the over-worked and under-paid; and take in the sick, downtrodden, marginalized, and others who don't quite fit in society (see Zwick and Zwick 2005). I spent five years working alongside members of the Gainesville

Catholic Worker in Florida, as well as interacting with many who serve or are served in similar houses of hospitality around the Southeast. For two of those years I was a live-in community member, experiencing the daily activities of serving food to the under-nourished, protesting against injustice, gardening in reclaimed parking lots, gleaning food from the local farmer's markets, tending chickens, making recycled art, and most of all, talking over coffee with homeless friends.

I discovered that Catholic Workers have been described in many ways: communists, socialists, anarchists, artists, idealists, pacifists, convicts, sinners, and saints. They have shown up in the *Los Angeles Times* and on the FBI's wanted list. Though it is rooted in Catholic social teaching, many Catholics have never heard of this movement, which boasts dozens of hospitality houses nationwide. The foundations of a Personalist philosophy and works of mercy are important to the mission of Catholic Worker houses, but their sustainability also comes from an adaptability and fluidity in how these concepts are implemented. They live the gospel with careful regard to location, each house and farm filling its own niche for the context in which it operates. I thus contend that the Catholic Worker Movement may find meaningful resonance with *bioregionalism*, a place-based framework of viewing the world.

I begin with a working definition of bioregionalism, drawing on the work of Michael Vincent McGinnis, then offer a brief history of the Catholic Worker movement: its founders, initial goals, and how the original framework was put into action, and an overview of houses and farms today. I then look at how the movement sustains itself through leading by *local* example as a way of engaging the larger social system. In addition to my own experience with and research on the Catholic Worker, I draw from recent literature, especially Dan McKanan's *The Catholic Worker after Dorothy: Practicing the Works of Mercy in a New Generation* (2008).

The parallels between bioregionalism and Catholic Workers are pertinent today because climate crisis is indivisibly about *both* environmental and social justice (Taylor 2005). Moreover, both movements exhibit similar anarchistic tendencies, though they have developed independently. As more Catholic Worker communities return to the land and/or focus more on environmental concerns, it is a good time to engage this conversation, as well as to study how intentionally *placed* groups impact larger environmental issues.

I. Basics of Bioregionalism and the Catholic Worker Movement

Bioregionalism is defined by political scientist Michael Vincent McGinnis as "both a philosophy and social activism that favors a small-scale, decentralized, and place-based approach to life" and observes the "organic interconnectedness of Earth systems" (2005:188). The foci of bioregionalism include how people relate to their surroundings (literacy in ecosystems), build relationships with living systems (inhabitation), and practice local responsibility and stewardship (including local economies; 2005:189). Bioregionalism is more than a contextualized notion of the local; it focuses on how a place defines itself topographically through watersheds and land formations rather than political boundaries, as Ched Myers points out in his Introduction (see also Aberley 1999).

In his book-length treatment of bioregionalism, McGinnis focuses on the importance of the interconnection and interdependency between humans and other creatures such as animals, plants, and insects. Bioregional thinking expands the sense of community beyond the realm of the human, establishing meaning for a diverse set of relations (1999:5). "Bioregionalists believe that as members of distinct communities, human beings cannot avoid interacting with and being affected by their specific location, place, and bioregion" (McGinnis 1999:2). But McGinnis emphasizes that the movement is just as much cultural as environmental, existing "wholly outside mainstream government, industry, and academic institutions" (1999:4). Bioregionalism stands opposed to globalism and industrialism, as "a response to the dramatic ecological and cultural decline that is caused by the prevailing modes of consumption and production in large-scale industrial society" (2005:189), and has attracted many radical environmentalists. Its anarchist orientation has been expressed in the writing of Gary Snyder, Peter Berg, and David Abram among others, who also tend toward pacifist intentions (Taylor 2005:1329; see also Kemmis 1999; Lynch et al. 2012).

The Catholic Worker movement can similarly be understood in terms of community-based "ecosystems" functioning outside mainstream American society. In the early twentieth century, a young agnostic socialist named Dorothy Day found her way to Catholicism (Forest 2011). Without giving up her anarchistic vigor or activist approach to life, Day began living out her beliefs through her writing, working as a journalist on the lower east side of New York. During this time she met Peter Maurin, a French intellectual. Day's journalism and Maurin's constant flow of ideas led them to start a newspaper in which they blended Catholic social teaching with socialist thought (Sicius and Day 2004). *The Catholic Worker* was first published on May Day, 1933; it was sold for a penny a copy in Union Square, and promoted union organizing and strikes as well as analysis of contemporary social issues. People began coming to their door asking for more than just words. Day and Maurin started receiving visitors who were looking for food, a bed for the night, and a place to be heard. Realizing the importance of practicing what they preached, Day made room for these visitors, expanding from a one-room shack to a couple of apartment buildings.

After much discussion with Maurin, the foundations of the Catholic Worker movement emerged, organized around the Catholic ideas of Personalism and the works of mercy. A Personalist was described by Maurin as someone who is a "go-giver not a go-getter," who "tries to give what he has instead of trying to get what the other fellow has" (Day 1963:21). This "social doctrine of the common good" sees the goodness of Christ in every person, whose value and significance transcends group identity or membership. A Christian Personalist affirms not only that are we made in the image of God, but that every individual is an embodiment of Christ. The works of mercy as articulated in Matthew 25:31–46 include feeding the hungry, giving drink to the thirsty, providing shelter for the homeless, clothing the naked, visiting the imprisoned and the sick, and burying the dead. These exhortations were taken literally by Day and Maurin, who saw them cohering with the Personalist view of individual dignity and respect, and thus formed the basis of their practice.

Implementing these concepts proved to be challenging and exciting. Day describes the faith it took to keep going in *Loaves and Fishes* (1963), relating the struggle of living daily with the gospel stories of Jesus's miraculous provision of loaves and fishes (Matt 15:34–38 and John 6:10–13). Repeatedly she would find just enough to suffice at the last minute to pay bills (Day, 1983). The fledgling Catholic Worker focused on the present, trusting that their needs would be met and drawing from the resources at hand.

Maurin spoke of three pillars of the movement: cult, culture, and cultivation. Cult referred to the importance of worship, Scripture, and tradition; he and Day drew heavily from the Bible and Catholic social teaching (see http://www.usccb.org/). Culture referred to the dominant society, which was critiqued and contested in *The Catholic Worker Newspaper* and through nonviolent civil disobedience. Cultivation referred to a return to the land, and early on, Maurin promoted the concept of the "agronomic university." This included not only working the land, but the ideal of a balanced life that incorporated both intellectual and physical labor. The notion was to create places in which people could work the land, serve others, participate in critical thought, and reflect spiritually. Although this model was not widely embraced in the movement until much later, it did spawn the first Catholic Worker farm on Staten Island (Miller 1984).

The first Catholic Worker communities received many visitors, who would pass through offering their services, causing trouble, and becoming inspired. Some were so impressed that they stayed, or started their own houses, which began opening in cities across the country. Disagreements regarding World War Two—Day was a strict pacifist—caused many community members to leave the movement to join the military or work on the home front. But after the death of Peter Maurin and the end of the war, the number of houses began to increase. Communities flourished once again in the 1960s (see McKanan 2008:71), resonating with interest in alternative lifestyles and opposition to the war in Vietnam.

Throughout these four decades Day continually visited other Worker communities, encouraging their service and promoting various social causes. Her death in 1980 did not slow the growth of the movement, however, which continued to evolve and expand, attracting both families and unmarried young people. As of 2016 there are more than 150 Catholic Worker Houses around the world; though a majority are in the U.S., there are twenty-one communities in other countries, including Belgium, Canada, Germany, Great Britain, Mexico, New Zealand, Sweden, The Netherlands, and Uganda (see http://www.catholicworker.org/communities/index.cfm; see also Kirkwood 2001; Coy and Douglas 1988; Holben 1997).

II. Catholic Worker Movement Diversity as an Expression of Bioregionalism

Dan McKanan describes the Catholic Worker movement as "an organism rather than an organization," and argues that the key to its endurance is that it "has never really tried to endure" (2008:22, 28). This organic nature leads to fluidity and even capriciousness, which has promoted growth in a variety of diverse locations and environments. Rather than instituting the same model in every location, each house or farm finds its own niche within the local region. While visiting other houses, Dorothy would counsel those new to the movement to "craft their own communities in response to local needs" (McKanan 2008:23).

McKanan notes four elements in Dorothy's advice. The first was to "identify the gifts and needs present in your neighborhood and practice the works of mercy there" (2008:35). The other three maxims follow a similar attitude of simplicity: stay small, honor your vocation, and accept mishaps and failure. Staying small counters the ideologies of globalization and industrialization; while industry crosses barriers and roams widely to impact consumers and businesses, Catholic Workers maintain small yet manageable networks of local relations, focusing on a more artisan, do-it-yourself approach to life. Pursuing vocational calling is key as well; Maurin advocated a combination of manual labor and self-reflection, and recognized the importance of living in a mindful manner, contrary to mass production culture. And because communities typically consider themselves an experiment in the making, mistakes and failures are seen as a part of the process; working with the poor, unexpected circumstances and tricky situations always arise. Soon after purchasing the Catholic Worker farm, for example, Day and Maurin discovered that the sole water source belonged to a neighbor, creating difficulty for sustaining their own crops. They overcame this by purchasing the surrounding land, which contained a reliable stream (Day, 1963:46). For Day, such challenges were to be embraced and accepted as part of the experience.

Day's four maxims are similar to principles of bioregionalism. The notion of "local action," for example, echoes the bioregionalist belief that it will take many people working in a wide range of areas in order to bring about large-scale change. As Day put it in 1938: "We must never cease emphasizing the fact that the work must be kept small. It is better to have many small places than a few big ones" (McKanan 2008:43). The movement grew in precisely this fashion. Bioregionalist McGinnis would also affirm Day and Maurin's rejection of the "ceaseless mechanization of human labor, and the general transformation of community-based economies into large-scale, formal economies, which support mass production and overconsumption" (McKanan 2008:3). And both McGinnis and Catholic Worker communities realize the importance of the goods, services, ideas, and people associated with a particular place.

As noted, anarchism informs both traditions. A Cascadia bioregionalist, for example, envisions a "secession" movement as an alternative politics (Baretich 2015). Catholic Worker communities function as independent entities, supporting themselves through monetary and material donations and other forms of "mutual aid" outside the dominant system. Most houses (though not all) follow Day's anarchistic refusal to incorporate as non-profit, tax-exempt organization, a stance that expresses opposition to larger governmental structures. This "dis-establishment" also allows for quick adaptation according to need (for example, the Gainesville Catholic Worker exceeded the meal limit placed on another local non-profit soup kitchen by local authorities). Catholic Workers have never recognized a hierarchy of authority, affirming rather the autonomy of each house while acknowledging the harm that comes from centralized structures. This allows each community to focus its efforts on the issues germane to their area.

Some brief comparisons make the point. The Los Angeles Catholic Worker, which has been serving since 1970, operates a Skid Row soup kitchen, a house of hospitality for the homeless (including hospice care), and a monthly newspaper; it also actively stands against war and injustice. Los Angeles is often called "the homeless capital of the nation," and Skid Row hosts over 10,000 homeless, poor, and marginally employed residents. So "the Hippie Kitchen" (as it is known affectionately by folks on the street) serves three days a week, averaging 1,300 meals a day (http://lacatholic-worker.org/about-the-lacw; Dietrich 2008; Morris, 2010). The Gainesville Catholic Worker, on the other hand, which operated from 2000 to 2014, also offered food to its surrounding community, but in a very different way. Recognizing the homeless in Gainesville are not calorie deficient, but rather nutrient deprived, this house focused its efforts on a weekly home-cooked vegetarian meal, incorporating fresh food that is both local and organic, in a café setting, serving an average of fifty to eighty meals each Wednesday.

Another community that focuses on food is the Mustard Seed, a Catholic Worker farm north of Ames, Iowa. They also believe in feeding the hungry, but recognize their homeless population is nowhere near that of large cities. While both the LACW and the GCW rely on outside food sources, the Mustard Seed works to grow food for those in need. Part of their harvest is donated to local shelters and soup kitchens; the other part goes toward their Community Supported Agriculture subscription service, in which people buy shares of food to help capitalize the farm. Adapting to their area, Mustard Seed provides fertile farmland instead of a soup kitchen and grounds its priorities in land stewardship. Recognizing the destructiveness of modern farming techniques, the community works to implement and promote crop rotation, cover crops, green manure, permaculture, beneficial insects, erosion control, and other organic farming methods (http://www.mustardseedfarm.org/?q=about).

St. Francis Farm in New York, located about forty miles north of Syracuse, engages more in prayerful life rooted in the gospel while connecting with the land. Created in 1976 by Father Ray McVey, the farm has been used for a variety of purposes, including as a refuge for battered women and unwed mothers, a free medical clinic, and a knitting cooperative. In the early 1980s it was turned over to a new nonprofit, and in 2001 the community adopted a mission to "live a neighborly life based on the Gospels and on the Catholic Worker principles as an alternative to the consumer culture." Since 2006, they have been sending vegetables, herbs, and goat cheese to a nearby soup kitchen, as well as to seniors, local churches, and neighbors. Their 106 wooded acres provides lumber for building, firewood, and simple wooden toys, in addition to local maple syrup (http://www.st-francisfarm.org/Home.html; see also Anglada 2013).

The mission is different for the Alderson House of Hospitality, located in Alderson, West Virginia. In 1977 they identified a need for lodging for visitors of women incarcerated at a local federal prison camp. Over the years, they have provided accommodations for over 50,000 guests who come to visit family and friends at the prison (http://www.aldersonhospitalityhouse.org/). A hospitality-based house in Silver Springs, Maryland, on the other hand, offers lodging "on a small scale to seniors and those who come to Washington, D.C. for demonstrations, lobbying, internships, and study." They have adapted to the politically active realm of the nation's capital, yet also maintain a legal clinic that offers free legal assistance in cases such as "landlord-tenant disputes, small claims, immigration, mental health, mental retardation rights, social security and disability rights, and child custody" (http://www.angelfire.com/un/cw/).

In contrast, proximity to the U.S.-Mexico border leads Casa Juan Diego to focus its efforts on immigrants and refugees in Houston, Texas (Connolly 2012; Serazio 2005; Zwick and Zwick 2010). Founded in 1980, their projects include immigrant care, English classes, a house for men new to the country, and a house primarily serving immigrant women, especially those who are pregnant, physically battered, and/or whose husbands have been deported (http://cjd.org/). In Chicago, Su Casa house serves the local Hispanic community (http://www.sucasacw.org/), while rural Montana's Bitter Root Catholic Worker Farm opens its doors as a retreat center for other Catholic Workers (Gallagher 2011). As this short but representative list indicates, understanding the work of Catholic Workers in their particular places shows how each house is able to meet needs and provide services for residents in their area directly with local resources (Riegle Troester 1993).

IV. Taking Root: Catholic Workers as "Ecological Ethnicities" and Bioregional Activists

According to anthropologist Pramod Parajuli, the "gaps between environmentalism of the global North and the global South" have been profound (2004:236). Environmentalism in the global South tends to encompass both social and environmental issues, since these two realms overlap in daily life, particularly among the poor; the same is true among "subaltern" communities in the U.S. (Pulido, 1997:191ff). Parajuli describes "ecological ethnicities" as "any group of people who derive their livelihood through day-to-day negotiation with their immediate environment," enacting justice both environmentally and socially (2004: 236). When such movements initiate "alternative modes of production, consumption, and distribution," they act as a barrier to global capital markets through resistance and political autonomy (Parajuli 2004:241, 254). Within this framework, Catholic Workers fit the model for such ecological ethnicities in how they resist mainstream culture and markets.

In 2013, New Hope Catholic Worker Farm's Eric Anglada published an article noting the new ecological path of Catholic Worker communities (2013). It focused on the fulfillment of the original Catholic Worker land ethic more than eighty years after Peter Maurin proposed it. Anglada explains how Maurin's ideas, including his dream of an "agronomic university," have been gaining speed as people are returning to local economies and homesteading projects:

> It is encouraging that today's Catholic Workers, through change in lifestyle and active protest, are confronting many of the ecological crises of our times: permanent war over distant resources, a fickle climate, technological overload, ongoing topsoil loss, rising food costs and genetically-modified organisms. It is clear that a significant "greening" of the Catholic Worker is underway.

Anglada believes this represents a sort of "return to the beginning," as Catholic Worker farms strive to achieve sustainability and justice. He, his wife and others have been practicing subsistence agriculture at New Hope

Catholic Worker Farm, using low- or no-till and seed mulching methods in their gardens. They have a strong relationship with Hope House, a Catholic Worker hospitality house in downtown Dubuque, with whom they share their harvest and host joint retreats. New Hope is one of the new breed of Catholic Worker Houses using daily practices of prayer and farming to connect ecological issues with larger social justice issues, confirming Parajuli's hypothesis.

Catholic Workers believe, as do bioregionalists, that ultimately if every region attended to its respective needs and concerns, the wider world could be healed. Yet they also realize that problems do not stop at the edge of town or bioregion in our globalized world. Insofar as they inhabit the fringes of society yet also address wider peace and justice issues, Catholic workers dwell in "ecotones"—that transitional and ecologically diverse area between bioregions (see McRay, Chapter Three). And sometimes they operate literally in borderlands, as with Casa Juan Diego. I saw this displayed also at the Gainesville Catholic Worker. The house was located in the downtown area, straddling the lower income west side with the affluent east side of town, home to the University of Florida. The location of the house bridged the gap for the diverse people we welcomed, from the mentally ill homeless and traveling Rainbow kids to professors and city commissioners. Similarly, the House was a place to question the dominant system and rethink what the future may hold; as a young adult, it provided me with a new framework and opportunities.

Catholic Workers also have a long history of "challenging the powers" on issues of social injustice (Wink 1998). Increasingly, however, they are resisting environmental destruction. For some this involves lifestyle practices, such as growing organic rather than promoting Monsanto's genetically modified food. For others it leads to active protest against the Keystone Pipeline, tar sands, and fracking. For example, in September 2013 the Rye House Catholic Worker community in Minneapolis protested an annual Frac Sands Conference held downtown. Earlier that year, house member Joe Kruse was among 24 others who were arrested for blocking trucks at a nearby frac sands facility; protests continued the following year (Klaassen 2014). During this same period, fourth generation Oklahoman and Catholic Worker Bob Waldrop locked himself to a Keystone XL machinery to protest construction of the pipeline (http://www.tarsandsblockade.org/gptsr-8th-action/). These Midwest actions indicate how Catholic Workers realize the direct connection between climate change and social injustices in their regions.

To be sure, though environmental issues are being addressed and Peter Maurin's dream of agronomic university is coming to fruition, Catholic Workers still rarely use bioregional discourse in their work. But I believe that the movement can greatly benefit from the theory and practice of bioregionalism in their growing efforts to address ecological injustices. Attention to place and emphasis on local community, service and action has always helped sustain Catholic Worker houses. The Gainesville Catholic Worker had a notable phrase displayed on the wall: "Do the best that you can in the place that you're at and be kind"—a slogan that notably resonates with the bioregionalist-informed Transition Movement (https://www. transitionnetwork.org). It is my hope that the Catholic Worker movement's style of improvisational adaptability, and local literacy and engagement, and the newer movement of bioregionalism can inform and nurture one other toward deeper sustainability as we move into a challenging future.

References

Anglada, Eric. 2013. "Taking Root: The History and New Growth of Catholic Worker Farms." *America Magazine.* May 6. (http://americamagazine.org/issue/taking-root.)

Aberley, Doug. 1999. "Interpreting Bioregionalism: A Story from Many Voices." In *Bioregionalism*, edited by Michael Vincent McGinnis, 13–42. New York: Routledge.

Baretich, Alexander. 2015. "In Regards to Political Secession and Working within Corrupt Imperial Politics." October 7. (http://freecascadia.org/in-regards-to-political-secession-and-working-within-corrupt-imperial-politics/.)

Connolly, Marshall. 2012. "Exclusive Interview: Mark and Louise Zwick of Casa Juan Diego." *Catholic Online*, December 5. (http://www.catholic.org/hf/faith/story.php?id=48734).

Coy, Patrick and Jim Douglas. 1988. *A Revolution of the Heart: Essays on the Catholic Worker.* Philadelphia: Temple University Press.

Day, Dorothy. 1983. "Another Miracle, Please, St. Joseph." In *Dorothy Day: Select Writings*, edited by Robert Ellsberg, 59–60. Maryknoll, NY: Orbis.

———. 1963. *Loaves and Fishes.* San Francisco: Harper and Row.

Dietrich, Jeff. 2008. "Los Angeles Catholic Worker: Hippie Kitchen." December 17. (http://www.youtube.com/watch?v=RpH-2OFSXcc.)

Forest, Jim. 2011. *All is Grace: A Biography of Dorothy Day.* Maryknoll, NY: Orbis.

Gallagher, Susan. 2011. "Catholic Worker Farm Encourages Simple, Sustainable Living." *Catholic Worker News*, September 16. (http://catholicworkernews.blogspot.com/2011/09/catholic-worker-farm-encourages-simple.html.)

Holben, Lawrence. 1997. *A Theological Reflection on Dorothy Day, Peter Maurin and the Catholic Worker, All the Way to Heaven.* Marion, SD: Rose Hill.

Kemmis, Daniel. 1999. "Foreword." In *Bioregionalism*, edited by Michael Vincent McGinnis, xxi–xiv. New York: Routledge.

Kirkwood, Karen. 2011. "House work: Catholic Workers of Today." *U.S. Catholic* 76 (11): 22–25. (http://www.uscatholic.org/culture/social-justice/2011/09/house-work-catholic-worker-houses-today.)

Klaassen, Elaine. 2014. "Catholic Worker House confronts local frac sand mining." *Twin Cities Daily Planet*. December 3. (http://www.tcdailyplanet.net/news/2014/12/03/opinion-catholic-worker-house-confronts-local-frac-sand-mining.)

Lynch, Tom, Cheryll Glofelty and Karla Armbruster, eds. 2012. *The Bioregional Imagination: Literature, Ecology, and Place.* Athens: University of Georgia Press.

McGinnis, Michael Vincent. 1999. "A Rehearsal to Bioregionalism." In *Bioregionalism*, edited by Michael Vincent McGinnis, 1–10 New York: Routledge.

———. 2005. "Bioregionalism." In *The Encyclopedia of Religion and Nature*, Vol. 2, edited by Bron Taylor, 1326–33. London: Continuum.

McKanan, Dan. 2008. *The Catholic Worker after Dorothy: Practicing the Works of Mercy in a New Generation.* Collegeville, MN: Liturgical.

Miller, William D. 1984. *Dorothy Day: A Biography.* San Francisco: Harper and Row.

Morris, Catherine. 2010. "Hippie Kitchen with Catherine Morris, 40th Anniversary in Skid Row." May 2. (http://www.youtube.com/watch?v=Ha5a-zyk1dM.)

Parajuli, Pramod. 2004. "Revisiting Gandhi and Zapata: Motion of Global Capital, Geographies of Difference and the Formation of Ecological Ethnicities." In *In the Way of Development: Indigenous Peoples, Life Projects and Globalization*, edited by Mario Blaser, Harvey A. Feit and Glenn McRae, 235–55. London: Zed Books Ltd.

Pulido, Laura. 1996. *Environmentalism and Economic Justice: Two Chicano Struggles in the Southwest.* 3rd ed. Tucson: University of Arizona Press.

Riegle Troester, Rosalie. 1993. *Voices from the Catholic Worker.* Philadelphia: Temple University Press.

Serazio, Michael. 2005 "The Zwicks: 'Faith People.'" *Houston Press News*, May.5. (http://www.houstonpress.com/news/the-zwicks-faith-people-6549513.)

Sicius, Francis J., and Dorothy Day. 2004. *Peter Maurin Apostle to the World.* Maryknoll, NY: Orbis.

Tar Sands Blockade. 2013. "Fourth Generation Oklahoman Catholic Worker Locks Himself to KXL Machinery." Tar Sands Blockade, May 13. (http://www.tarsandsblockade.org/gptsr-8th-action/.)

Taylor, Bron. 2005. "Radical Environmentalism." In *The Encyclopedia of Religion and Nature*, Vol. 2, edited by Bron Taylor, 1326–33. London: Continuum.

Wink, Walter. 1998. *The Powers that Be: Theology for a New Millennium.* New York: Doubleday.

Zwick, Mark and Louise Zwick. 2010. *Mercy without Borders: The Catholic Worker and Immigration.* Mahwah, NJ: Paulist.

———. 2005. *The Catholic Worker Movement, Intellectual and Spiritual Origins.* Mahwah, NJ: Paulist.

Chapter Eleven

The Carnival de Resistance
Dreams, Dance, Drums, and Disturbance

TEVYN EAST AND JAY BECK

We live in a world already turned on its head. A desolate, de-souled world, that practices the superstitious worship of machines and the idolatry of arms, an upside down world, with its left on its right, its belly-button on its backside, and its head where its feet should be. In this upside down world, children work, "development" impoverishes, the poor pay the rich, and people are bombed in order to be "liberated." In this grotesque looking glass wonderland, free speech is paid for, cars are in the streets where people should be, public servants don't serve, free trade is a monopoly, the more you have the more you get and a handful of the global population consumes a majority of the resources. If the world is upside down the way it is now, wouldn't we have to turn it over to get it to stand up straight? —Eduardo Galeano (1998:337)

By day from town to town we carry Eden in our tents and bring its wonders to the children who have lost their dream of home. —Robert Lax (2000:51)

Tevyn East and Jay Beck—*The Carnival de Resistance*

Summary: The Carnival de Resistance is an artistic, faith-rooted response to our ecological and cultural crises that exposes the world as "upside-down" in the sense expressed above by Eduardo Galeano. This experiment draws upon the legacy of Carnival, a beautiful and mixed bag of cultural traditions which express a desire of the human spirit to disrupt the dominant order. We contend that art can animate resistance efforts, but can also support cultural transformation by serving the psychological and spiritual recovery work that is critical to the paradigm shift of Watershed Discipleship.[1]

I. Carnival History as Cross-Cultural Mix

Before inviting you into our big top of incarnational dreams, let's take a tour through the tangled roots of the carnival tradition. In Catholic Christian culture, the six weeks of Lent were designated for fasting and self-examination, and thus a refrain from rich foods such as meat, dairy, or sugar. Traditionally all such perishable food and drink had to be consumed before Ash Wednesday. This "chow down" and communal celebration is thought to be the origin of carnival, which became a festive season immediately before Lent involving public celebration, parades, balls and/or street parties with masks, music and dancing.

Carnival Crew.

1. We thank our friend Stephen Landis for the substantial time he put into editing this chapter.

Like many other Christian holidays, however, carnival traditions also resemble feasts that date back to pre-Christian times. The roots of the Italian carnival, for example, drew from the Saturnalia and Bacchanalia, ancient Roman festivals of rebellion and flair, which in turn may connect to earlier Greek Dionysian festivals. During Saturnalia, all class distinctions were abolished, with slaves and their masters switching roles and laws normally governing "sensible" behavior suspended. The fusion of church celebrations and pagan festivals allowed the newly converted to retain certain subversive practices. For example, the Catholic Feast of Fools, a day for liturgical dramas that dissolved church hierarchy, celebrated becoming a "fool for Christ" (1 Cor 4:10) and enacted the Magnificat's call to turn society upside down (Luke 1:52–53). This feast day was later suppressed by European Catholic authorities, and was wholly condemned by Protestants; still, though forbidden by the Council of Basel in 1431, it lived on for centuries within medieval folk culture. Europeans eventually brought many such religious festivities to the New World under the common label "carnival."

Carnival traditions are a result of a cross-cultural exchange that started centuries ago (and continues today). But the greatest contemporary carnivals, such as those in Brazil, Trinidad, and New Orleans, reveal that the tradition flourished where Catholic European Settlers and African slaves interacted. Ancient African festivals, despite centuries of suppression in the New World, influenced unfolding carnival traditions. Through these festivals, traditional African dance, music, drum rhythms, large puppets, stick fighters, and stilt dancers began to make their appearance in the Americas. The street parties and parade routes echoed African festivals that would circle villages to call on healing spirits, bid good fortune or celebrate harvest. The wildly intricate costumes of carnival draw from African traditions of ceremonial adornment using natural objects such as bones, grasses, beads, shells, feathers, and fabric. The materials have spiritual significance and generate meaning for the community (for example, feathers were traditionally associated with flight, rebirth, rising above pain, or travel to another world). African masks were traditionally not meant to hide a person's identity (as was the case for the European carnival), but intended to bring alive an invisible truth.

For Africans in Diaspora, carnival became a tool for both emancipation and preservation of cultural memory in the midst of bondage. After slavery was abolished in Trinidad in 1838, freed Africans reappropriated carnival celebrations, which took over the streets and soon became more popular than European carnival balls. Today, schools in Trinidad sponsor carnival bands, insisting that this cultural expression is one of the best ways to teach young people about their heritage. It is important therefore for us, too, to understand the cultural heritages that influence the creative components within contemporary carnivals.

Carnival, far from being a historical relic, continues to embody deep political significance in the present. While some argue that it functions to reinforce the status quo—providing a safety valve that allows the anger and passion of the lower classes to dissipate before conformity is reinstated—we contend that oppressed people inhabit carnival in ways that "flip the script" of constructs of power, identity and social hierarchy. As the synopsis of Max Harris's important *Carnival and Other Christian Festivals: Folk Theology and Folk Performance* puts it (2003):

> That these folk celebrations, with roots reaching back to medieval times or earlier, still remain vibrant in the high-tech culture of the twenty-first century strongly suggests that they also provide an indispensable vehicle for expressing hopes, fears, and desires that people can articulate in no other way. . . Paying close attention to the signs encoded in folk performances, [Harris] finds in these festivals a folk theology of social justice that—however obscured by official rhetoric, by distracting theories of archaic origin, or by the performers' own need to mask their resistance to authority—is often in articulate and complex dialogue with the power structures that surround it.

Carnival does not, we believe, aim to promote harmony with the status quo; on the contrary, these traditions subvert the dominant reality. Inspired by this cultural heritage of resistance, we embarked on a contemporary experiment to produce our own carnival that supports movements of faith and activism.

II. The Carnival de Resistance

Imagine a band of holy fools living between worlds, weaving church into Big Top party and big band protest, creating space to: deviate from the norm; shape-shift through characters; and re-approach and reclaim old sacred stories, from the groan of creation to the earthy truth within the Gospel narratives. They are topsy-turvy tight-rope walkers straddling the worlds of faith, art and activism, dream-makers jesting on a grand scale.

Their cross-cultural and mixed-media inspirations surge at the intersection of ancient and contemporary, flesh and spirit, resounding in mythopoetic and syncretistic voices of the sacred. They present the elements, let the symbols speak, and call all to dance with the drum. Aspiring to all this is an experiment we call the Carnival de Resistance.

Its first full expression was in the fall of 2013, through two consecutive ten-day residencies on church lawns in Harrisonburg and Charlottesville, Virginia.[2] The following year we offered round-the-clock programming in a dedicated venue at the Wild Goose Festival in Holt Springs, North Carolina.[3] Our colorful presence represented both carnival world and village demonstration projects. We lived together outside, in sun and rain, gathered in circles, and shared meals, songs, stories, and games. Our crew of some twenty freaks and fools, artists and activists ran a community kitchen (the petrol-free "riff-raffateria") and erected compost toilets, sun showers, and foot pump water stations. Some of us were seasoned nomads and experienced performers, others untested seekers thirsty for something new. We became a community, immersed in a living experiment of covenant, communal effort and collaborative art. Everyone worked hard: coffee takes longer to prepare on a twig-fired rocket stove, but it requires a lot more love, too. The Carnival village experiment is our Holy Game, and we believe that when we jump in, the Holy Spirit plays along, transforming us, ripping away veils, ripening community.

To travel between our two initial residencies this young community embarked on an ambitious, glorious, mountain-crossing, 120-mile bike trip. There were bumps in the road: we got lost and incurred various forms of bike and body trouble. Underprepared, this journey was a leap of faith for many of us. But angels appeared to help with bike parts, maps, or a readiness to ride alongside. We learned how much provision we could get from water, peanut butter, and pumping hearts. Some weren't able to pedal

2. Trinity Presbyterian Church in Harrisonburg hosted our initial residency. A missional community inspired by Church of the Saviour in Washington, D.C., it was among the first Presbyterian churches to become an Earth Care Congregation. Sojourner's United Church of Christ in Charlottesville is a culturally diverse, justice-oriented, long-time open and affirming congregation.

3. The annual Wild Goose Festival (http://wildgoosefestival.org/) curates music and creative expression, hosting programs on justice, faith, and spirituality. Begun in 2011, it aspires to provide an American version of the Greenbelt Festival in England (https://www.greenbelt.org.uk/). At Wild Goose the Carnival big top operated as a school; we brought in spiritual elders and teachers who churned the theological ground for our cultural offerings.

the whole way, but many found they had a greater capacity than they knew, and we grew stronger together. We would pause to care for ourselves, lying in the sun, rejuvenating with Chi Gong, dancing in the rain, munching in the shade. By God's grace, high hopes, and genuine love we got through without major injury or trial.

At the end of those bike trips we had to immediately set about building our carnival world. On the morning of our first carnival-raising we woke with dread and doubt, wondering how we might accomplish such a feat only one day before opening. Yet later that night, with everything in place and all the lights up, we were stunned by the sight of it, trembling with excitement and exhaustion. A miracle had emerged: a carnival Big Top and midway into which we would invite the local community to experience their own transformation.

Behemoth and Skunk.

Let us draw a picture. You pass through a scrappy wooden threshold, entering a world of activity. Side-show tents, storytellers, roving performers, and a creation station encircle a broken clocktower. Small crowds gather around a dozen midway games, while children dart by chasing costumed performers. The air is full of motion, and curiosity tugs at the peripheries of your vision. You watch in wonder as a large boar-like stilt creature looms above the crowd. Barkers beckon toward the games: "Knock down the wall of oppression!" "Chase out the money-changers from the Temple!" "Spin the wheel of divine identity!" "Toss a frisbee through the eye of the needle!" "Take a whack at a corporate Goliath!" Reflecting on these symbols and stories from childhood, you find yourself drawn into the spirit of playful wonder.

Midway Game.

Emerging from the circulating crowd, a herald spouts nonsensical questions with diplomatic pomp while smashing clocks with a hammer. She teases the crowd with mechanical motions and fragmented phrases, mocking compulsive productivity before requesting those in attendance to unplug and power down. "We are leaving the tyranny of constructed *chronos* and shifting into sacred *kairos* time!" she announces. You may hesitate turning off your phone, wishing you could capture these moments on Instagram. You may feel coerced or suspicious of this unexpected requirement. Or perhaps you look forward to silencing all possible distractions. No matter which feeling, a new one quickly replaces it as you tumble through ephemeral experiences, each drawing you deeper into the immediacy of this gathering.

Midway Clock Tower.

So begins the Carnival Midway experience. Following the group power-down, guests are invited into the Big Top for our main attraction, the Carnival de Resistance Ceremonial Theater. These productions stitch together liturgical variety acts, circus arts, and a live drum and dance party. We orient our productions around the voices of the Four Elements: Earth, Water, Air, and Fire. Performances draw from many sacred rituals: Catholic mass, Protestant proclamation, creation spirituality, Native American ceremony, West African Diaspora traditions, and Joanna Macy's "Work that Reconnects."[4]

Each show journeys along a path from thanksgiving and remembering to lament and mystery, and culminates in a communally embodied ritual. We draw upon the music of oppressed, indigenous, and nomadic people groups, looking for wisdom, mystical insight, and ways to increase

4. Drawing from deep ecology, systems theory and various spiritual traditions, Macy's "Work That Reconnects" supports healing, creativity, and perseverance for those working to transition to a sustainable human culture. Macy has centered her teaching and scholarship in this pioneering, open-source body of work since 1978 (Macy and Brown, 1998).

our capacity for grief and compassion. We believe that engaging with many different cultural resistance movements and their art forms deepens our understanding of the often tricky nuances between cultural appropriation on one hand and cultural exchange and solidarity on the other. We recognize the privileged social position of many within our group, and our responsibility to address historical and current oppression. Drawing from the music and spirituality of oppressed people groups demands responsibility and accountability to those people and their struggles. We seek to apprentice to these cultural forms even as we become more anti-racist and work to end white supremacy.

At the heart of each show is an original work of theater. Each component is a theopoetic handling of ancient stories, interweaving the blazing poetry of Jim Perkinson with music, masks, dancing, and ceremony.[5] Our approach is also heavily influenced by the Jewish practice of *midrash*, a millennia-old tradition that fosters creative dialogue around biblical texts. Growing out of the fertile soil of much scholarship, these pedagogical experiments are the most finely crafted portions of our Ceremonial Theater:

- "Out of the Whirlwind." The air show centers around a conversation between loud-mouthed "Raven" and mute "Dove." Raven, a trash picking trickster and prophet of doom, first enters the scene cawing "*Ruach!*"—a warning that air, breathe, and spirit are all one. He then reunites with Dove who, communicating solely through dance, melts his corvid heart. These two remember the last time the world was destroyed by flood, and their portentous roles on the Ark (Gen 8:6–12). They recount old stories in which Raven fed Elijah in the wilderness (1 Kgs 17:4–6), and Dove descended on Jesus at baptism (Matt 3:16). And they argue over the appropriate response to the destructive ways of the two-leggeds. "Let it burn," says Raven, but Dove hovers over her threatened brood, hoping for humanity's survival. This piece was influenced by Mark Wallace's scholarship on Christian Animism (2005, 2014) and Ched Myers's teaching on the theatricality of the wilderness prophetic tradition.

- "Wade Through Deep Water." The Water show, using poetry from Thomas Merton and Jewish feminist Alicia Suskin Ostriker,

5. Perkinson is a long-time activist, theologian, author, educator and performance poet from inner city Detroit, who generously spawned original poetry for the Carnival's Earth, Air, and Fire shows. In addition to the blessing of animating his remarkable words, we have been profoundly influenced by his scholarship.

introduces two prophets, Miriam and John the Baptist (*left*), whose water-logged lives kept them swimming in transformation. Miriam remembers scheming by the Nile in a conspiracy of women that saved baby Moses (Exod 2:1–10). She tells how she delivered her people through the Red Sea to freedom, but laments her fate to "die in a dry place" (Exod 15:20–21, Num 20:1–2). Miriam's drumming and bodysong speak to the dangers of privatizing water, of desertification, and of ignoring the voice of the divine feminine. Meanwhile, John the Baptist calls the audience to a "dirty baptism," because we have poisoned the wells and dammed the rivers. With fierce love, he calls for repentance, challenges us to abandon false hopes about technological saviors, and asks us to feel the pain of the water until we're drawn back to the Source. The show culminates in a water-anointing for every audience member, and a communal dance to "Gidamba," a traditional West African rhythm played at baptisms.

Water Show: Miriam and John the Baptist.

- "Blood on the Cedars." The Earth show, drawing on language and ideas from Ched Myers (2007), brings the call of the wild alive in ancient and contemporary stories of resistance. A woman shape-shifts, dances, and claims voices of the prophet, the poet, and the professor. She encounters the "Green Man," the spirit of the wild once memorialized by our European ancestors in medieval cathedrals. Together, they spout litanies that paint pictures of the prophets's connection to the earth, of various cultural expressions concerning the sacredness of trees, and of modern activists around the globe who have suffered and been killed for the sake of the forest. They tell how Hebrew prophets railed against deforestation, and indict Solomon's massive temple-building project as part of an imperial pattern conquest and ecological destruction (Zech 11:1–3; Jer 22:13–17; 2 Chr 2:1–18). The Green Man passes out green branches and the woman embodies the cedars as they rejoice in the fall of Babylon and drink in the peace of quiet and rest (Isaiah 14).

- "Clothed with the Sun." The Fire show features the voice of "the fire that burns in the bones of the prophet" (Jer 20:7–9). A fearsome talking skull wields a flaming wand and groans warnings of rage and doom to an already burning planet. He asks us to remember the stories of a God who lives in a bush that burns but is not consumed, who calls people to liberation in the wilderness. Hope is brought from the beautiful pregnant Woman Clothed in the Sun crowned with twelve stars (Rev 12:1–17). While spinning fire on stilts, her singsong tales take us to our solar origins. She dances in mystical triumph with the spirit of the Phoenix, encircled by fire dancers flaming props and fire-breathers.

Fire Dancers.

Inspired by the Word and World People's School and the Watershed Discipleship movement, the Carnival de Resistance endeavors to be more than a traveling show; we create spaces for education, formation and outreach.[6] During the weekdays of our residencies in Harrisonburg and Charlottesville, we offered in-house events like the Potlatch (a Native American gift-giving ceremony), and sent our crew out into dozens of local engagements, plugging in with allies to uplift their programs. We offered creative workshops in mask making, drumming, storytelling, and song-writing for the young and the old. At Eastern Mennonite University we taught classes, led chapels, and led a mural painting project in which dozens of students participated. In the wider community, we joined open mic venues, Bible studies, garden work parties, and worship services. And we left beautiful things in our wake, such as murals and a tree-platform.

---

6. "Word and World was created in 2001 to carve out alternative spaces for theological formation, bridging the gulf of the seminary, the sanctuary, and the street. Through schools, retreats, and mentoring, Word and World draws faith-based activists from various movements into a community of discipleship focused on social and cultural analysis, and biblical reflection for social transformation" (http://www.wordandworld.org/history.html).

Mural Painting.

In Harrisonburg we converged for a community parade and protest launched from New Community Project, an exceptionally inspirational model for faithful resistance (see McRay, Chapter Three). We brought signs, sunflowers, crazy bike sculptures, costumes, and most importantly, drums. We shouted "Power Down, Lift Up"—lifting up the mountains, rivers, people, and stories—in a colorful parade that circled downtown and landed on the stoop of City Hall for a radiant public witness. The demonstration used our pedal-powered bicycle sound system to amplify local change agents working on immigrant rights, mountain conservation, local food systems and alternative energy. And we sang songs of struggle and hope: "Deep down inside of me, I got a fire going on. Part of me, wants to sing about the light, and part of me, wants to cry, cry, cry."

III. Social and Dissident Functions of Carnival

Carnival represents a break from the dominant reality, putting life as usual on hold in a suspended space. Russian literary theorist Mikhail Bakhtin argued that carnival as a social institution utilizes humor and popular ritual to tear through dreary compliance and enliven an alternative vision (1984). Mockery, especially for the disempowered, is perhaps one of the most effective nonviolent ways to combat the status quo. Bakhtin suggests that laughter in carnival is a therapeutic and liberating force: "Laughing truth degrades power" (1984:92). Absurdity becomes transformative when it strips bare the pretense of authority.

Carnival acts as a celebratory and sensual practice that challenges Puritan fear of the flesh. Bakhtin connects the carnival to the grotesque, to the "lower bodily strata" that push against beliefs about the sinfulness of the body (1984:62). The grotesque contradicts the notion of a disembodied salvation, and asserts that the sticky space between life and death, birth and decay, is a vital source of continual metamorphosis. We are not isolated egos, but perishable bodies that eat, defecate, copulate, and give birth. The body is neither base nor sinful, but the most honest and integral expression of our earthliness. Moreover, the fact that we are bound together biologically cuts through imposed social and political constructs that separate. Carnival thus resists alienation, individualism, and hierarchical control, and absorbs people into something bigger that serves diversity and equality. It is about communal embodiment, a celebratory experience where people share symbols and stories, lift songs, and dance rhythms together. It can dissolve boundaries between performer and audience, becoming an interdependent, collective experience that is so much greater than the sum of its parts. Andrew Robinson revels at how this phenomenon persists within a recent experiment, called "Carnival against Capital," referencing "an intense feeling of immanence and unity—of being part of a historically immortal and uninterrupted process of becoming" (2011).

The emancipatory spirit that lives within carnival comes from its transgressive energy, always simultaneously moving away from one reality toward another. Alienation and forced social conventions are undone in carnival's inclusiveness. Bakhtin refers to this as "the second life of the people," a place where community is liberated from the seriousness and tragedy of "official" reality (1984:9). Once we develop this double vision for the world—of how it *is* and how it *could be*—we begin to recognize ourselves as "creatively maladjusted." Carnival can, moreover, compel people to mobilize their bodies into political action. This energy is vital, because for many "politics" evokes a somber world of talking heads, where stuffy debates are held in sterile environments far removed from the people and lands with which politicians are meddling. Even protest politics runs the risk of falling into formulaic and legalistic patterns. In "We Are Everywhere," the Notes from Nowhere Collective asks:

> How do we make rebellion enjoyable, effective, and irresistible? Who wants the tedium of traditional demonstrations and protests—the ritual marches from point A to B, the permits and police escorts, the staged acts of civil disobedience, the verbose rallies and dull speeches by leaders? Instead, why not use a form of rebellion that embodies the movement's principles of diversity, creativity, decentralization, horizontality, and direct action? These principles can be found at the heart of an ancient form of cultural expression—the carnival (2003:174).

Carnival, concludes Robinson, "is joyous in affirming that the norms, necessities and/or systems of the present are temporary, historically variable and relative, and one day will come to an end" (2011).

Unfortunately, cultural remnants of this sort of carnival are few and far between in the United States. They have survived most notably as the Shrovetide festival of Mardi Gras in Louisiana, and in the Labor Day celebration party and parade for the West Indian community of Brooklyn. However, the carnivalesque as a medium of resistance remains alive and well in many other contemporary examples as well. In London in the late 1990s, "Reclaim the Streets" combined rave party culture and public takeover, employing multiple creative tactics to direct or shut down car traffic in order to open space for street parties. From huge sand pits to staged car crashes, these convergences significantly transformed public space. The most famous event occurred in the summer of 1996, when 8,000 people assembled on a public highway. Huge stilted carnival characters in hoop skirts moved among them—and beneath the skirts, activists with jackhammers drilled holes in the street surface and planted saplings (Jordon 2012).

This bold effort caught wind on the still young Internet, and within a few years subversive street parties were happening across the world, including at the G8 Nations Summit in 1998. The following year, a "Carnival Against Capital" movement spawned actions in financial districts around the world, and six months later, the World Trade Organization summit was shut down by mass actions that filled the streets in "the battle in Seattle." These actions drew upon carnival traditions of occupying public space, embracing creative liberty, and refusing to ask for permission from authorities, manifesting a kind of rezoning effort through wild music, costumes, raised voices, and liberated bodies.

In the wake of these anti-globalization actions, a group of young activists began weaving clowning techniques into civil disobedience and nonviolent direct action. They coalesced into the Clandestine Insurgent Rebel Clown Army (CIRCA), which continues to make ripples today. Beginning in London in 2003 with an Anti-Bush "welcome" action, CIRCA demonstrations grew to be an international phenomenon. Recognizing the challenges of unrehearsed and uninitiated volunteers, CIRCA developed a methodology for training called "rebel clowning." This movement argues that embodied clowning must move beyond the act of *pretending* toward actively *being* the clown, which requires a more holistic transformation.

CIRCA employs tactics of absurdity, carnival role playing, and intelligent mischief to undermine security forces in various ways. Clowns can flip the script of typical protest dynamics, for example. An angry protester being wrestled to the ground by a cop is one thing; a jolly trickster stuck in handcuffs is quite another. While police may dismiss them as foolishly harmless, these clowns are armed with the element of surprise. In one incident, a line of armored riot troops broke ranks because they were laughing too hard (Jordon 2012). In other cases clowns have inundated police departments with unexpected commotion and added paperwork, as they stay in character throughout the arrest process, unpacking pockets full of strange items and insisting on using their Clown Army names and addresses.

IV. Carnival as Disturbance Ecology and Cultural Commons

During conversation between the contributors to this volume, Jonathan McRay noted the ties between the historical social function of carnival and the natural phenomenon of "disturbance ecology." The survival and diversity of a wide range of species is symbiotic with natural rhythms of disturbance such as fire, flooding, and windstorms. For instance, in the plains and lowlands of Lake Michigan, shade intolerant aspens or oaks, along with a host of migratory birds and butterflies that love them, rely on periodic wildfires to clear space for them to grow. Likewise, shrubby chaparral habitats in California thrive on the regeneration that follows a wildfire. Among the southeastern long leaf pine forests, fire makes space for tortoise and snake to roam. These events reduce competition, creating a "neutral" ground for diversity to thrive, a crucial element of any healthy ecosystem. But if the natural cycle of disturbance is interrupted, as is the case when we suppress wildfires, a critical imbalance can occur.

Carnival can function as disturbance events for our social ecology, clearing space for new growth and encouraging social diversity. As the wise holy fool Edward Abbey said: "Society is like a stew. If you don't stir it up every once in a while then a layer of scum floats to the top" (1989:21). We have seen the Carnival de Resistance do this in several ways. Our Ceremonial Theater, laced with social critique, songs, and stories from oppressed people groups and invocations of the divinity within nature, means to disturb the dominant paradigm in Christian theology. Our shows specifically highlight biblical encounters with animals or people whose stories were activated by an intimate relationship with creation. We give voice to and animate these often-ignored or marginalized, though not uncommon, elements in biblical narratives. Predictably we have received pushback from theological conservatives who accuse us of being heretical earth-worshippers, but we counter that we are part of an ancient Christian tradition that regards the power of creation as an active expression of who God is. Similarly, our Carnival disturbs traditional ecclesial models through alternative expressions of liturgy, ritual and community celebration. People get wet, dance in a circle of fire, and are invited to breathe and sing and tie themselves symbolically into the web of life encircling us. They are asked to participate bodily, and to dance it all out at the end—in sharp contrast to white Western models of worship, which we believe are in need of some shaking up!

The immersion experience of the Village Demonstration Project has also been a disturbance event for Carnival crew members themselves. Life as usual is interrupted with our communal effort to live another way. Most of us encounter new practices: cycling long distances, stationary cycling to generate electrical power, collecting firewood, carrying water, stoking the cooking fire, making meals for a large community, handling humanure, or dumpster diving. We establish different daily rhythms, significantly unplugging from the industries and systems we normally rely on. Granted, there are many ways in which our experiment is flawed, and at the end of the day we still rely on public utilities, industrial inputs, and legal systems. Yet our Holy Game remains a way to see what happens when we reach toward practices that reduce our carbon footprint and animate our imagination.

This disorientation resensitizes us to the darkness of our addictive dependence on ecologically and socially dysfunctional systems, a process of realization which is both a blessing and a burden. But we look at our demonstration project as an experiment in "cultural intervention." The surreal setting of a "nomadic village" and carnival big top in a modern neighborhood, astir with games, performances, and activities, represents a place where market forces and governmental rule do not dominate, and all are truly welcome. We think this radically imagined space is enough to disturb anyone's notion of what is possible. For example, our October 2013 residency coincided with a federal government shut down. National Parks closed down, and a local church paused to consider, *should the planned women's camping trip reroute and join the Carnival?*

The Carnival de Resistance has been a generative disturbance event precisely because our advocacy of and efforts toward sustainable lifeways are bathed in song, story, study, skill-sharing, and play. Our environment is composed not only of natural surroundings, but cultural surroundings as well, and the well-being of the natural commons (i.e., ecosystems, food-sheds, and watersheds) is affected by the cultural commons (i.e., art, music, myths, rituals, and customs). The sustainable lifeways of earth-based people throughout time have been shaped by a cultural commons that recognizes the interdependence of all life; listening to the wisdom of indigenous cultures is one way we are seeking to build our awareness of this reciprocal relationship.

For traditional cultures, which rely on intergenerational oral traditions, the transmission of wisdom, cultural values, and history comes not through formal education but through myths, storytelling, drama, and art. Though many of these cultural traditions are under threat, collective gratitude, celebration, and creative expression remain a widespread wellness practice among Native peoples. A healthy cultural commons sustains them and ties them collectively to the land. Derek Rasmussen tells the story of Canadian government surveyors first encounters with Gitskan people in their traditional territory (2013). The Gitskan asked, "What are you doing here?" "Surveying our land," they answered. Incredulous, the Gitksan responded: "If this is your land, where are your stories?" Anishinaabeg elder Al Hunter put it more bluntly: "Language. Music. Stories. *That's* what has sustained us—not Nongovernmental organizations!"

In contrast, our modern Western society tends to undervalue the role of art and ceremony. Art programs are often the first things cut from a public school budget, and our cultural commons has been overdetermined by a commodity culture focused on entertainment. The stories that surround us are in the form of advertisements and pop culture, and our senses are attacked relentlessly by images and messages with ulterior motives intended to manipulate consumer behavior and socialize us to follow trends. Tabloids and the "infotainment" news industry focus on the rich, powerful, and famous, and teach us a pretend game about what is valuable. And we are enveloped by imperial mythologies that have enabled exploitation and domination over the earth and Indigenous peoples. Our minds are thus warped by insidious stories that are disconnected from the land or cultural wisdom; consequently, we've forgotten how to express our deepest truths communally, whether grief or gratitude. Abraham Heschel explains a crucial difference between modern and traditional cultural commons: "To be entertained is a passive state—it is to receive pleasure afforded by an amusing act or a spectacle . . . Celebration is a confrontation, giving attention to the transcendent meaning of one's actions" (1975:152).

The dominant media reflect the stories we value; our cultural commons will either serve or undermine the natural commons. The modern cultural crisis cannot simply be shrugged off, nor can the disaffected simply wash their hands of it and commence "consuming" native cultural expressions instead. We must unmask the real meaning of the prevailing mythologies of capitalism while engaging in formative events that explore the genuinely alternative stories of wisdom traditions that lead us deeper into a new paradigm.

V. Conclusion

To understand this watershed moment and to weave ourselves back into the watershed, we must change the stories that we inhabit. As we grow in our knowledge and love of a place, we tie our own liberation to the salvation of that web to which we belong. This requires us to forge a new covenant that enjoins us to: sing new songs and embody new experiences that honor what is truly valuable; reorganize our bodies, imaginations and prayers; celebrate, dialogue with and build stories that place us in community and in relationship to the land. The carnival tradition calls us to, and can help resource, such transformation.

Into our ecological, social and cultural crisis we hear a carnival herald beckoning, "Come one, come all!" Build local cultures that remember the story of our food, land, watersheds and all their inhabitants. "Step right up!" Take your bodies into the street, the garden, the tent, the river. "Feast your eyes on such unforgettable wonders!" Live church outside the pews, gathering courage and conviction, sowing seeds of hope and resistance.

References

Abbey, Edward. 1989. *A Voice Crying in the Wilderness: Notes from a Secret Journal.* New York: St. Martin's.

Bakhtin, Mikhail. 1984. *Rabelais and His World.* Translated by Helene Iswolsky. Bloomington, IN: Indiana University Press.

Galeano, Eduardo. 1998. *Upside Down: A Primer for the Looking Glass World.* New York: Picador/Henry Holt.

Harris, Max. 2003. *Carnival and Other Christian Festivals: Folk Theology and Folk Performance.* Austin, TX: University of Texas Press.

Heschel, Abraham Joshua. 1975. *The Wisdom of Heschel.* New York: Macmillan.

Jordon, John. 2012. "Clandestine Insurgent Rebel Clown Army." In *Beautiful Trouble: A Toolbox for Revolution*, edited by Andrew Boyd, 304–7. New York: Or.

———. 2012. "Reclaim the Streets." In *Beautiful Trouble: A Toolbox for Revolution*, edited by Andrew Boyd, 350–53. New York: Or.

Lax, Robert. 2000. *Circus Days and Nights.* Woodstock, NY: Overlook.

Macy, Joanna and Molly Young Brown. 1998. *Coming Back to Life: Practices to Reconnect Our Lives, Our World.* Gabriola Island, BC: New Society.

Myers, Ched. 2007. "'The Cedar has fallen!' The Prophetic Word vs. Imperial Clear-cutting." In *Earth and the Word: Classic Sermons on Saving the Planet*, edited by David Rhoads, 211–23. New York: Continuum.

Notes from Nowhere. 2003. "Carnival: Resistance is the Secret of Joy." In *We are Everywhere: The Irresistible Rise of Global Anti-Capitalism*, edited by Notes From Nowhere, 173–83. NewYork: Verso.

Ostriker, Alicia Suskin. 1997. *The Nakedness of the Fathers: Biblical Visions and Revisions.* New Brunswick, NJ: Rutgers University Press.

Perkinson, Jim. 2013. *Messianism against Christology: Resistance Movements, Folk Arts, and Empire.* New York: Palgrave Macmillan.

Rasmussen, Dereck. 2013. "'Non-Indigenous Culture': Implications of a Historical Anomaly." *YES! Magazine*, July 11. (http://www.yesmagazine.org/peace-justice/non-indigenous-culture-implications-of-a-historical-anomaly.)

Robinson, Andrew. 2011. "Bakhtin: Carnival against Capital, Carnival against Power." *Ceasefire*, September 9. (https://ceasefiremagazine.co.uk/in-theory-bakhtin-2/).

Wallace, Mark. 2005. *Finding God in the Singing River: Christianity, Spirit, Nature.* Minneapolis: Augsburg Fortress.

———. 2014. "A Beaked and Feathered God: Rediscovering Christian Animism." *Tikkun Magazine*, July 22. (http://www.tikkun.org/nextgen/a-beaked-and-feathered-god-rediscovering-christian-animism.)

Afterword

Toward Watershed Ecclesiology
Theological, Hermeneutic, and Practical Reflections

CHED MYERS

Abram passed through the land to the place at Shechem, to the oak of Moreh . . . Then Adonai appeared to Abram, and said, "To your offspring I will give this land." So he built there an altar to Adonai, who had appeared to him (Gen 12:6–7).

Jacob came to a certain place and stayed there for the night, because the sun had set. Taking one of the stones of the place, he put it under his head and lay down in that place. And he dreamed that there was a ladder set up on the earth, the top of it reaching to heaven; and the angels of God were ascending and descending on it . . . Then Jacob woke from his sleep and said, "Surely Adonai is in this place—and I did not know it!" And he was afraid, and said, "How awesome is this place! This is none other than the house of God, and this is the gate of heaven" (Gen 28:10–12, 16–17).

You need make for Me only an altar of earth and sacrifice on it your offerings of well-being . . . If you make for Me an altar of stone, do not build it of hewn stones; for if you use a chisel upon it you profane it (Exod 20:24–25).

THESE THREE TRADITIONS, SCHOLARS agree, are among the most ancient in our scriptural corpus. Each portrays a Creator who is, in the most primal sense, encountered *in* and *through* natural elements and spaces. Abram, the first great hero in the canonical narrative of redemption, is called by the divine voice out of the imperial city of Haran to journey to the wilderness margins of Canaan. There he encounters Creator under an oak tree; the Hebrew *'elon moreh* connotes a tree that is a "teacher or oracle giver," a medium of divine revelation. Under this sacred tree Abram pitches his nomad's tent, and here he builds the first altar in the Bible. Similarly, the later patriarch Jacob has a dream of angels while sleeping in the open desert, his head on a stone. When he awakens, he confesses that *this* wilderness place is "none other than house of God, the gate of heaven"—and he, too, builds a sacred cairn in response.

These epiphanies, under tree and over rock, imply that *any* space in creation can become an *axis mundi*, because *all* spaces are alive with Spirit. This is why, according to the overlooked "eleventh commandment" of Exodus 20:24f, we need only an "unhewn stone" to commune with the God of the Bible. Since nothing was more ubiquitous in the rocky desert bioregion of biblical Palestine, the implication is that true worship can happen *everywhere*. Except, that is, where nature has been re-engineered by human technology. This statute is emphatic that no work of human hands can improve on what Creator has made. The cosmology of all three passages is captured perfectly by a fourth biblical scene, in which Joshua seals the divine Covenant with the Israelites by setting up a large *rock* under a *tree*, exclaiming: "See, this stone shall be a witness against us; for it has heard all the words of YHWH . . . " (Josh 24:27).

To the modern mind, these biblical scenarios seem bizarre, and are pejoratively dismissed as "primitive." To an indigenous worldview, however, they make perfect sense (see, e.g., Woodley 2012; Perkinson 2013). And to those aspiring to Watershed Discipleship, such texts provide a kind of primordial foundation for the journey of re-place-ment. In this spirit, this Afterword—perhaps benediction is a better description—offers some final reflections to frame this volume's call to Watershed Discipleship.

Because discipleship takes place in community, it is appropriate to close this collection by considering the prospects for a "watershed ecclesiology" of reinhabitation, which I did not address in any depth in the

Introduction, and which receives only passing attention in the various chapters. So I conclude here with a few salient thoughts about two formidable tasks that obtain to this project. One is work of theological and hermeneutic *recovery* (the double entendre is pointed—uncovering ancient biblical roots and recovering from modern addictive-compulsive religion). The other is the work of *re-placing* our churchly practices. I offer just brief comments about each, confident that this conversation is only beginning.

I. Theological and Hermeneutic Recovery: Incarnation, Baptism, Scripture

The first talking point in my Introduction above argued that only a radically incarnational approach can do battle with the abstract doctrines and theological idealism so responsible for the church's complicity with our historic crisis. Placeless and docetic modern versions of Christian faith are no more able to combat current violations of human and terrestrial bodies than was nineteenth-century white piety able to contest American apartheid. Watershed Discipleship, on the other hand, is indivisibly contextual and geocentric, and beckons Christians back to our theological roots.

Our first step of recovery is to embrace unequivocally the assertions of the second Genesis creation account that the human being (Heb. *'adam*) was formed from the "topsoil" (Heb. *'adamah*, Gen 2:7), a wordplay that is preserved in the English "human/humus." Scripture is unembarrassed and straightforward in its understanding of earth as Mother, a cosmology that was characteristic of all indigenous cultures. Ironically, this view is increasingly embraced by the new biological sciences, but continues to be ignored by Christians.

Our second step of recovery is to affirm, as do the three ancient texts referred to above, that we "earth-lings" commune with Creator not through some sort of placeless, transcendent spirit-realm, but through immanent *geographies*—in the discourse of this volume, in specific watersheds. As Talmudic scholar Jon Levenson puts it: "Geography is simply a visible form of theology" (Titterington 2014). What does geography have to do with incarnation? The notion of the divine taking on flesh was as scandalous in antiquity as it is among docetic modernists today. Yet from this core New Testament conviction flows our most powerful rationale for protecting and nurturing land and life. The most famous articulation is found in John 1:14: "The Word became flesh . . . " The early Christologists insisted that the

Greek term *sarx* here was *not* meant metaphorically (which makes it ironic that later theologians should talk about incarnation in abstract terms). But we also need to recognize that John immediately grounds this flesh in *place*—because that is the only space that bodies can inhabit: ". . . and tented among us . . ." (John 1:14b).

The verb *eskēnōsen* means "made an encampment"; Clarence Jordan's venerable Cotton Patch translation rendered it "and the Word pitched a tent among us." People have lived in some sort of tent in the vast majority of the world's traditional cultures back to the dawn of human time. Tents were, in fact, the first human "built environment," but were liminal dwellings: portable and much closer to the earth and the elements than later permanent structures. Still today traditional tents are made from local materials that are appropriate to the climactic and topographic conditions of the region; for example, Tibetan nomads craft black yak hair tents from their livestock, hand-woven by women into a tough, durable material that is warm and water-resistant. Tents are, in other words, bioregionally designed abodes, as various as the watershed that birthed them, from tepees to yurts.

Indeed, John's "en-tenting" metaphor alludes to the deep history of his people: the wilderness tradition of the Exodus (tents are mentioned more than 300 times in the Hebrew Bible). This memory is important still in Judaism, celebrated in the Feast of Booths (or tents) as a ritual of remembering roots—a tradition with which Christians would do well to join! Tents appear elsewhere in the New Testament as well, but most notably at the very end of our canon.[1] At the culmination of John the Revelator's remarkable vision of a transfigured earth we find a *double* iteration of the fourth Gospel's notion of divine encampment: "See, the tent (*skēnē*) of God is among mortals. God will tent (*skēnōsei*) with them; they will be God's peoples, and God will dwell with them" (Rev 21:3). The end of the biblical story, in other words, posits a restoration of the primal beginnings of Israel (and other tribal peoples), a return to origins. The eschatological New Jerusalem (which comes down to earth, contrary to rapturistic eschatologies, 21:2, 10) is a polemical trope, representing an urban "grid" none in antiquity had ever seen (see Pritchett, Chapter Two). The gates of this walled city never

---

1. Jesus warns his disciples to practice Sabbath economics in resistance to the "Mammon economy" so that they will ultimately be welcomed into "eternal tents" (Luke 16:9)—an allusion to the old ways of the "manna economy" of wilderness Israel (see Myers 2012). We read of the "true tent" as primal ritual space, both past (Acts 7:44; Heb 8:2, 5) and future (Rev 15:5). And of course the Apostle Paul supports himself as a maker of tents (Acts 18:3)!

close (21:25), precious gems are as common as cobblestones (21:18–21, the Roman international economy of scarcity having been abolished, 18:12ff), and the River of Life runs right down Main Street, flanked by a perennial food forest of healing medicine (Rev 21:1). We might say that the Holy City has been thoroughly deconstructed and redesigned around the watershed, the desertified landscape of the biblical narrative rehabilitated and restored to fertility by re-hydration, in the tradition of Ezekiel 44 (Myers, 2014a). It has been transformed by a permaculture retrofit, and recentered around a perennial cosmic spring and divine encampment. This tent symbolizes repaired communion between Creator, people and creation: Eden 2.0.

This extraordinary notion of incarnation as en-tent-ment—that is, re-place-ment—challenges Christians in at least three ways. First, we must wean ourselves, once and for all, off theologies of salvation that posit "exit strategies" from the earth. Instead we need urgently to recover the soteriology of the Hebrew prophets, who stress repeatedly that salvation means a divine renewal (not destruction or abandonment) of bodies and ecosystems.[2] Second, incarnation implies that Creator is hunkered down with us here for the duration, sweating it out with us under climate catastrophe and social and political disaster. This God, we confess, is most assuredly en-tented among us in refugee camps and homeless squats. And third, it prohibits churches from segregating themselves in an exclusively "spiritual" realm, as if that were our niche market in a secular society (over to whom we turn the fate of the earth). If God takes flesh, we need to pay full attention to history and to the poor, to carbon and to the hydrologic cycle, to botany and to *bodies*—of all creatures great and small. And because flesh requires geography, we must seek and encounter God *en-tented in* the watershed. Only *here* will "we see God's glory" (Jn 1:14c).

My second introductory talking point affirmed that only the work of restoring our relationship with proximate biotic communities can wean us off our presumptive androcentric superiority. Watershed Discipleship thus recenters anthropology in placed creatureliness, with a vocation of symbiosis and servanthood instead of objectification and domination. According to Paul, creation is "groaning in travail," waiting for humans to embrace this work of liberation and restoration (Rom 8:19–23).[3] Our proper role

2. See, e.g., Isaiah 35. For a reading of that and other prophetic texts that envision redemption-as-renewal (in an imaginary specific to a desert bioregion) see Myers 2014a.

3. This text is widely used in ecotheology, yet it is rarely acknowledged that the verbs in Rom 8:22 (*sustenazō*, only here in the N.T.) and 8:23 (*stenazō*) likely allude to the "groan" of the Israelites under slavery (LXX *stenagmos*, Exod 2:24, 6:5, as in Rom 8:26).

is not to re-engineer creation for human benefit—an impulse eagerly embraced by industrial modernity, but biblically identified with the Fall (Myers 2013; Perkinson 2013:4ff). Rather it is to inhabit rightly our place in and responsibilities to the community of earth—in the language of Genesis 2, to "serve and preserve" (Myers 2004). The "unhewn stone" trope noted above not only affirms the intrinsic value of nature, but also problematizes the work of our hands which, especially when technologically mediated, is always potentially idolatrous (see, e.g., Isa 44:9–20). To this end, the "Sabbath economics" narratives of Scripture teach us about the cosmology of gift, reciprocity, equity, and self-limitation (Myers 2001), challenging both exploitative materialism *and* alienated spiritualism, compulsive work *and* addictive wealth accumulation and concentration.

Let me suggest three further keystone elements that a theology of Watershed Discipleship seeks to recover. First, the core narrative of the Hebrew Bible concerns a people who covenant with God (on a mountaintop!), with each other, and with *a specific geography*. Theological assertions that the New Testament abandons place-based covenanting in favor of a "heavenly home" have been disastrous. Second, the non-docetic Jesus was fully terrestrial. In the tradition of the wilderness prophets, he was intimate with his bioregion: apprenticing to an Elijah-like wildman in a river ritual; praying on mountains; traversing the sea; and highlighting wildflowers as object lessons. He consistently illustrates the "Reign of God" by referencing plants and animals, human bodies and food.[4] And pointedly, Jesus is executed on a "hewn" tree, raised up in a real body, in which according to eschatological faith he will return *to earth*.[5] Three Gospel moments of "conversation between heaven and earth"—baptism (Mark 1:10f), Transfiguration (Mark 9:2–7), and ascension (Luke 24:51, Acts 1:9–11)—suggest that Jesus embodies the ultimate *axis mundi*. This is why our Christology must refuse all attempts to sever flesh from spirit and earth from heaven.

This groan captured Creator's attention and animated the Exodus resistance movement, which was assisted by ecological revolt against Pharaoh (see Perkinson 2013). This semantic connection is another example of how the biblical cosmology, like indigenous ones, interrelates ecological and social degradation or liberation.

4. For example, in Matthew's Gospel alone Jesus invokes seeds (13:24, 31), fields (13:44, 20:1), fish (13:47), healed bodies (9:35), children (18:3), yeast (13:33), pearls (13:45), and wine (26:29) as expressions of God's Reign. See my exegesis of Luke 12 for an important core sample (2009).

5. For classic and important discussions of why a corporeal resurrection is crucial to the N.T. witness—and I would add, to a theology of Watershed Discipleship—see Cullman 1964 and Lorenzen 1995.

For the same reason, thirdly, we need to recover the Revelator's apocalyptic teleology: metropolis redesigned back to garden. From Noah to the New Jerusalem, the biblical tradition insists that the earth and her inhabitants matter enough to be healed and ultimately liberated *in* their terrestrial and somatic corporeality.

My third talking point asserted that only the long-term project of living sustainability some*where* can wean us off our disastrous human quest for autonomous infinitude. This involves resisting the ways industrial civilization keeps us mobile (following economic booms and busts until we are placeless), and practicing reinhabitation and solidarity with degraded places and people. We have called this the art of becoming disciples *of* our watersheds. Perhaps the most powerful biblical symbol that animates this vocation is that of baptism, both as a generative gospel story and as a central sacramental practice of the church.

In Mark's baptism narrative (1:9–12) we find a similar prepositional awkwardness to Gary Snyder's call to "come *into* the watershed." Those coming out to John are baptized *in* the Jordan (Gk *en*); Jesus, however, is baptized *into* the river (Gk *eis ton Iordanēn*), a distinction with real theological and social significance (Myers 2008:129). His "total immersion" invokes the Spirit's descent in the body of a wild bird *onto* (or into?) Jesus (Gk *eis auton*). And after this epiphany, Jesus is driven by that Spirit deeper *into* the wilderness (*eis tēn eremon),* which in its longer version (Matt 4:1–11//Luke 4:1–13) implies a kind of "vision quest" to discover the roots of the historic crisis of his people (Myers 1993). While theologians usually understand Jesus's baptism as divine empowerment "from above," we could just as well argue he was being en-spirited from "below" through a deep submersion *into* his beloved homeland, grounding him in the storied Jordan watershed of his ancestors through which Creator still speaks.[6] Being initiated *into* the sacred, wild spaces of a land groaning under Roman imperialism prepared Jesus for his campaign to liberate and heal his people *and place* (hence the allusion in Mark 1:10 to Isaiah 64:1f).

In our work of popular education we often invite groups to recontextualize Mark's prologue (1:1–20) by renarrating it in their own bioregions. Which places in your watershed might be analogous to Mark's wilderness, we ask, or to the Jordan River? What dynamics of power and social crisis

---

6. The Jordan River was of course the backbone of the narrative of early Israel, where Jacob wrestled with angels (Gen 32), Joshua drew twelve stones to announce the insurgent Israelite tribal confederacy (Joshua 3–4), Elijah was taken into the clouds (2 Kgs 1), and Elisha healed an enemy general (2 Kgs 5; see McRay, Chapter Three).

in your context might resemble Mark's geopolitical and historic specific-ity, in which people suffering foreign domination were drawn from ur-ban centers out to the margins to encounter a wilderness prophet? Who in your local history might resemble John (a notorious prophet arrested by the authorities), or the marginalized peasant fishermen Jesus called to join his movement (see Myers and Enns 2009:22–30)? This exercise builds literacy not only in the Gospel narrative, its dynamics and literary anteced-ents, but also in our own bioregions, including topography, spiritual and storied traditions, political history, and social matrices. Participants report that both ancient text and present context spring to life through such ana-logical imagination. Such exercises have strongly confirmed my hypothesis twenty years ago that "the task of re-placed theology is to reclaim symbols of redemption which are indigenous to the bioregion in which the church dwells, to remember the stories of the peoples of the place, and to sing anew the old songs of the land. These traditions can be woven together with the symbols, stories and songs of biblical radicalism. This will necessarily be a local, contextual and often deeply personal project" (1994:369).

Tellingly, ecoBuddhist Snyder resorts to the venerable language of baptism to describe the kind of deep conversion required if we Settlers are to reinhabit our bioregions today: "For the non-Native American to be-come at home on this continent, he or she must be born again in this hemi-sphere, on this continent, properly called Turtle Island" (1990:43). Baptism is the only remaining universal sacrament across the ecumenical spectrum of our churches; how might it be recovered and re-placed by Watershed Discipleship? Here I want to commend my adopted Anabaptist tradition of re-baptism as a liturgical "sign" of both resistance and renewal. In the sixteenth century, infant baptism by ecclesial authorities into the State Church doubled as enrollment into citizenship, which eventually for young men meant conscription. Radical Reformers re-placed baptism as adult re-identification with the Way of Jesus, a protest that symbolized, among other things, their refusal to fight or to rule. This ritual rejection of civil religion earned Anabaptist the ire of the Christian state—both Catholic and Protestant!—and the dissidents were often publicly drowned in rivers in order to ridicule and terrorize their re-baptizing movement.[7] For them,

7. There is little evidence of *where* Radical Reformers performed their baptisms after they had been banished from the State church; they would have been public professions necessarily done in secret. Elaine and I have visited the famous Tauferhole cave high in a rural Switzerland watershed, where early Anabaptists lived in hiding; the waterfall that cascades over the spacious cave suggests many baptisms would have performed right

Paul's reminder that "all of us who have been baptized into Christ Jesus were baptized into his death" (Rom 6:3) was all too real.

The Anabaptists lost their Reformation battle to separate church and state, but in the postmodern West, that war has long been won. Unfortunately, the theology and liturgy of baptism remain largely domesticated in our churches, with infant baptism often reduced to a cultural ceremony. Yet the ancient litany calls on us to "renounce Satan and all his works, and sin, so as to live in the freedom of the children of God." Watershed Discipleship affirms this sobering language, understanding it in terms of our struggle with the demonic personal and political pathologies that have brought us to the crisis of the Anthropocene (see Wylie-Kellermann, Chapter Four). What would it mean to experiment with the old radical practice of re-baptizing? Such a controversial practice would, on one hand, reaffirm the traditional discipleship notion of committing to the Way of Jesus; on the other, it would represent a protest of placelessness, inviting disciples to immerse ourselves, as did Jesus, into our watersheds. We would thus recover baptism as a *double* sign of renewed commitment to Creator and Christ, and to creation and Covenant—geographically defined!

Whether we are baptizing or re-baptizing, however, we ought at least rescue its captivity to indoor sprinkling rituals, and recover it as an *outdoor* sacrament. As the old gospel hymn puts it: "I went down to the river to pray, studyin' about that good Old Way . . ." In the practical logistics of re-placing this ritual in nature, church members first have to locate a suitable local watercourse, which can be something of a challenge, especially for urban dwellers. They then must confront the realities of degraded waters that are often unfit for human immersion—perhaps becoming motivated in the process to organize for the restoration of the local stream, pond, lake or beach to health (see Thompson, Chapter Six). If for mobility (or weather) reasons it is impossible to move baptism outside, we can bring local waters into the sanctuary—indeed, gathering such can be part of the ritual and pedagogy. Baptism thus intrinsically, and appropriately, demands engagement with our watershed. This is just one way in which the church's symbolic and civic life can be rebooted by disciplines of re-place-ment. Before I suggest other ways, however, let me note that my brief reflections on themes for a biblical theology of Watershed Discipleship simply mean to underline the importance of, and potential for, rereading our sacred texts with a bioregional hermeneutic. ⸙

---

there (see Wenger 2007).

Ecological readings of Scripture have broadened and deepened over the past two decades.[8] Yet many more are possible and necessary, as the efforts in this volume demonstrate.[9] At a 2014 permaculture design course we hosted here in our watershed, we redubbed this task "permeneutics," suggesting seven principles and practices for reading the Bible with a permacultural sensibility:

1. Pay attention to bioregional context, both that of the text and from where we are reading.

2. Practice thoughtful and protracted observation of the text and its terrain (surface and subsurface, synchronic design patterns and diachronic dynamics) before moving to interpretation, as a permaculture designer would with a landscape.

3. Respect each text as part of a larger, living story that we are invited to inhabit, serve and preserve, rather than extract, commodify, or exploit.

4. Look for earth-patterns and agrarian aspects of Scripture that have been ignored or under-valued in traditional approaches; they are everywhere!

5. Re-place biblical stories in their real-world social and geographic settings, and comprehend them as intrinsic to their meanings. Experiment with analogies between their historical contexts and ecological landscapes and our own (as in my example of Mark's prologue above).

6. Be sensitive to the "invisible webs" and "sub-surface complexities" that run throughout and interrelate the texture of Scripture, learning to appreciate the ecology of these ancient narratives.

7. Above all, understand that we are working on terrain that has long been disturbed and degraded. These texts were the product of

8. This includes the work of Norman Habel and colleagues at the Earth Bible Project (www.flinders.edu.au/ehl/theology/ctsc/projects/earthbible/), the Seasons of Creation Lectionary (http://seasonofcreation.com/), and the agrarian readings of Davis (2009) and Hiebert (1996); see also www.bibleandecology.org/.

9. See Friesen's watershed take on Matthew's Great Commission (Chapter One); Pritchett's reading of Daniel (Chapter Two); McRay's exposition of Jesus's Nazareth sermon and the Elisha/Naaman story (Chapter Three); Humphrey's treatment of the warning tale of Naboth's vineyard (Chapter Seven); and Adkins's riff on Psalm 118:22 (Chapter Nine). See also my explorations of the prophetic protest of deforestation (2007) and of Jesus's so-called cursing of the fig tree (2014b).

imperfect and conflicted communities of the past, and have also survived a long history of interpretive abuse (from clearcutting exegesis to monocropped meanings). Moreover, as modern readers we are not native to the cultures of these texts, and must beware of our "invasive" preconceptions, ideologies, and practices.

The Bible is an ally, not an adversary, of Watershed Discipleship. Indeed, the ancient prophetic traditions of both testaments may alone be capable of rousing us from our ecocidal slumber to a regenerative imagination.

II. Watershed Ecclesiology

Obviously, understanding Christian discipleship fundamentally in terms of a commitment to heal the world by restoring the social and ecological health of our watersheds is still marginal in our North American churches. However, our shared conviction in this volume is that ecclesial communities of place *could* make an enormous contribution to the wider struggle to reverse the catastrophe of the Anthropocene—and in the process recover the soul of their faith tradition. Christian tradition is deeply culpable in the present crisis, but these essays demonstrate that it also offers ancient resources for the deep shifts needed. It may require as many generations to reclaim our sense of rootedness in place in North America as it did to destroy it. But in the Anthropocene we have no alternative, and the process of "energy descent and identity reclamation" must proceed with urgency.

In so many ways local congregations are ideally situated to become centers for learning to know and love our places enough to defend and restore them. But we must first reinhabit our watersheds *as church*, allowing the natural and social landscapes to shape our symbolic life, mission engagements, and material habits. In some traditions, the older model of parish-as-*placed*-community still survives—though atrophied by market-driven member transiency and commuter mobility—and can be nurtured back into vibrancy. Some congregations retain a robust sense of local or regional identity, and a few are named after an ecological feature of the watershed; in such cases the task is to foreground what is likely taken for granted. Developing a watershed ecclesiology simply involves consciously rethinking our collective habits, large and small, inwardly or outwardly oriented.

As noted in the discussion of baptism above, the sacraments offer crucial opportunities to connect with the bioregion. The Abundant Table (see Chapter Eight) developed a campaign challenging Episcopalians to "localize the liturgy" by learning from what and where communion bread and wine, candles and tapestries are made, who made them and under what conditions. Even the tradition of fresh flowers in the sanctuary presents an occasion to learn and deploy native plants, using them as conversation pieces about bioregional flora. Apprehending the materiality of worship stimulates conversation about local economy and ecology, and this careful attention in turn deepens an appreciation for our symbols. How poignant was it, for example, that gallon jugs of water, brought by international caravans to Detroit to combat water shut-offs to the poor, were gathered under the altar at a local Episcopal church to be "blessed and distributed" (see Wylie-Kellermann, Chapter Four and Fahey, Chapter Five)?

A best practice would be, of course, to establish regular congregational rhythms of worshipping outside, in places that can teach us about the social and ecological character of the watershed.[10] While this is controversial in most congregations, the few existing outdoor traditions (Palm Sunday parades, Easter sunrise services, mid-summer church picnics) provide entrees upon which we can build new traditions. Why not celebrate the Feast of the Transfiguration on a local hilltop, Pentecost around a fire pit, or Christmas in a local barn? Meanwhile, parish artists can imagine ways to bring bioregional symbols into conventional worship spaces, imaging the mountain peaks or offshore islands that define the horizon, or the tumbling waterfalls or braided rivers that shape local valleys. Saguaro cactus or giant Sequoia, wild berries or migratory birds can all be celebrated in the sanctuary, stimulating bioregional theology and spirituality. Creative representations of a watershed map (quilted or collaged, painted or sculpted) are particularly important to display prominently both at church and in our homes, since we are trying to learn its design even as we wean ourselves off the abstractions of political cartography. Medieval cathedrals were literally wallpapered with iconography that functioned to teach the illiterate about the sacred traditions; given our ecological illiteracy today, such prompting and pedagogy is just as necessary. How can our music and litanies, altars

10. In our watershed, for example, we have established a tradition at our home demonstration site of celebrating every Solstice and Equinox around a bonfire with an explicitly Christian liturgy (which requires some eclectic creativity!). We are joined in this by several local house churches, including "Farm Church" (http://theabundanttable. org/farm-to-faith/farmchurch/).

and furniture, windows and statuary help (and prod) parishioners to learn about *this* place where the body of Christ is incarnated? And why would we not appropriate and indigenize for our places the venerable old (and subversive) European artistic traditions of the "Green Man" (see Anderson and Hicks 1990, Basford 1978)?

When it comes to mission, our North American churches typically struggle to get members to move from spectating to engagement. A watershed orientation can help (see Katerina Friesen's discussion of "home mission" in Chapter One). Parish hikers can organize to lure congregants out into the bioregion; so too can avid gardeners and local farmers (Sutterfield 2013). Individual or church retreats can become times to learn watershed literacy; to encourage personal healing around displacement and solastalgia; to pray outdoors, learning to be still and observe; to explore the many Christian traditions of nature mysticism; and to engage in recovery work around toxic personal patterns that feed the ecological crisis, such as compulsive consumption or work addiction. As disciples *of* our watersheds, we activists certainly have much to learn from biotic communities about interdependent diversity and long-suffering resilience.

Mission trips are ideal for investigating and responding to local social disparities, especially regarding environmental racism and the unequal impacts of climate change on the poor. Sister church relationships can be developed across watersheds, with pastoral exchanges allowing us to compare notes and cross-train. The young adult group can sojourn into the backcountry or the local wilderness park to pick up micro-trash; visit neighborhoods where they can encounter the stories of environmental refugees (who are now everywhere) or local Native people; or even venture a road trip to protest a pipeline project or local fracking site. Indeed, if our churches would help the rising generation prepare better for a difficult future that will be marked by resource wars and increasing calls for natural and social disaster relief, perhaps youth would inhabit our congregations with greater frequency!

Those of us who identify with the Peace Church tradition must make sure our work and witness are rooted in our specific basins of relations, and not just hypermetropically focusing on distant concerns (see Myers, 1994:220–33). We must discern the new shape of conscientious objection, nonviolent resistance, and restorative justice in the context of industrial culture's continuing war on the poor and escalating war on the biosphere, from mountain-top removal to deep-sea drilling. As Naomi Klein (2014) has argued, climate crisis is the ultimate expression of white supremacy; vulnerable persons of color are being as threatened by global warming as much as by racist violence, both at home and abroad.[11] To come full circle from the Foreword to this volume, we would do well to journey alongside native Water Walkers as part of our spiritual disciplines of solidarity. And as noted in the Introduction, there are other resources from within our own local histories and cultures from which to draw, such as the long tradition of agrarian adaptation among Amish, Mennonite, and other historically rural subcultures, which have so much to teach us about "more with less" modesty, practices of mutual aid and sustainable farming.

No part of the church's local life is irrelevant to Watershed Discipleship. Potluck meals become times to discuss household Sabbath economics covenanting around thorny issues like money, ecological footprints, and solidarity with the marginalized—frank talk made more possible because food is friendly (Colwell 2008; Bahnson 2013). The midweek Bible study or Sunday adult education hour can explore the rich and growing literature on ecotheology. While recognizing the need for systemic change and policy advocacy, these everyday practices represent the concrete intersection between "big" issues (such as economic justice or climate change) and our individual lives. Exploring how the personal is political (and vice versa) combats temptations to paralysis or exoneration; informed, empowered, and engaged individuals are far more likely to take collective political action. And it all has to be fun; why not recover a robust Mardis Gras tradition with a carnivalesque ecofestival, such as that narrated in Chapter Eleven?

Congregational brick and mortar could not be more crucial to these efforts. Church buildings represent some of the last local community spaces left in capitalist society. Most need, of course, to be audited and retrofitted for greater environmental resiliency, from water catchment to energy use. That can be expensive—but it can also give opportunities for volunteer labor and community work bees that double as workshops on green building. But this is only the first step; the more important challenge is reinhabiting those buildings with strategic organizing and community building. The fellowship hall can host neighborhood gatherings to improve the ecological and social health of the watershed; after all, public meeting space is in desperately short supply in the privatized urban grid. Church kitchens are

11. See the exemplary intersectional organizing around environmental racism of Gulf South Rising (http://www.gulfsouthrising.org/) and the Ecotone Project's community garden to table work in Houston (http://www.ecotoneworld.com/).

a huge asset—*if* they can become venues through the week for re-skilling around cooking with local foods and medicines, as well as fermenting, canning, and preserving. Here under-deployed congregational elders can teach young adults the older arts of home economics—especially the twenty- and thirty-somethings who are looking earnestly for places to learn such skills. Outside, significant parts of the lawn or parking lot can (and should) be repurposed for community vegetable and herb gardening and native plant propagation, and for natural building workshops and permaculture classes.

Reimagining and redesigning how we use church buildings and grounds will signal a new era of "demonstration-project evangelism"—because in our critical times, the gospel must be *shown*, not just told. Such observable projects can inspire church members, other congregations, the neighborhood, and even local authorities to replicate exemplary practices. A notable example of a "bioregional remodel" is Southside Presbyterian Church in Tucson, a congregation that was key during the Sanctuary movement of the 1980s, and still active today in immigrant rights organizing. Members reconfigured their sanctuary into the round, slightly recessing it below floor level to resemble a *kiva* (ceremonial space of the nearby Pueblo Indians), and incorporated the Catholic tradition of saints with various *nichos* around the perimeter. Native landscaping now surrounds the building, including a living ocotillo cactus fence (see www.southsidepresbyterian.org). In architecture and design, the medium is the message—and for non-docetic churches, intrinsic to our witness.

These sorts of church practices do not *require* our parishioners to embrace a dire analysis of the social and ecological crisis of the Anthropocene; they are good liturgical, stewardship, mission, and evangelism expressions in themselves. Yet pursuing them can and should open up deeper conversation and consciousness—because we *are* at a critical crossroad. Advocating for and experimenting with models of watershed ecclesiology might seem unrealistic amidst the super-concentrations of political and economic power today. But we should remember that throughout history, faith-driven visionary movements were labeled heretics before their basic insights eventually became conventional wisdom. We will have to find the spiritual resources, fierce patience, and communal stamina for the long-term prospect of living and working against mainstream culture, while stubbornly incubating radical alternatives that may only germinate in the long term. Yet if the Third Great Awakening brought us the Social Gospel movement in the nineteenth century, then surely a Fourth Great Awakening can mobilize us into a Transition church of Watershed Discipleship in the twenty-first century—so it won't be our last.

The good news is that Watershed Discipleship communities are percolating around North America.[12] In addition to those reflected in this collection, I would include the following friends as a further representative cross-section across the ecumenical spectrum:

1. Anglican activists in Vancouver, B.C. have launched the "Salal and Cedar Watershed Discipleship Community," focusing on spiritual renewal, ecologically literate liturgy and solidarity with First Nations (https://www.facebook.com/salalandcedar/);

2. The Kairos Canadian Ecumenical Justice Initiatives Network of Canada launched a "Reconciliation in the Watershed" program nationally (http://www.kairoscanada.org/what-we-do/ecological-justice/reconciliation-in-the-watershed/);

3. The Creation Care Network of Mennonite Church USA has adopted the Watershed Discipleship framework; one denominational conference has licensed a minister to promote this work (http://mennocreationcare.org/blog/walk-watershed-way-launches-mountain-states), and a seminary now hosts an annual colloquium on this theme;

4. Presbyterian churches in urban Minnesota, suburban New York and rural North Carolina are spearheading local education and skill-building efforts (see e.g. http://www.watershednownc.com/);

5. Lutherans in Portland, Oregon and Minneapolis are embodying local expressions of ecojustice pedagogy and Watershed Discipleship practice (see e.g. http://www.wildernesswaypdx.org/);

6. White Baptists in Texas and Black Baptists in Chicago are embracing this paradigm theologically, pastorally and politically (see e.g. http://www.faithinplace.org/);

7. Reformed Church colleagues in Ontario, Canada and Michigan are embodying and promoting reinhabitation through demonstration projects (http://www.russethousefarm.ca/) and publications (http://www.cultureisnotoptional.com/publishing/topology-magazine);

12. To track this movement visit our website (http://watersheddiscipleship.org/) and Facebook group page (https://www.facebook.com/groups/watersheddiscipleship/).

8. Quakers in Arizona are pioneering an extraordinary experiment in land covenanting inspired by Jim Corbett (http://www.saguaro-juniper.com/); and

9. The Chesapeake Interfaith Environmental Group hosts cutting edge watershed immersion experiences and education (http://www.chesapeakeieg.com/).

These are just some of the seeds of the future being planted in the hard soil of our times.

Only by "taking root downward," the old prophet Isaiah said, "can the surviving remnant . . . again bear fruit upward" (Isa 37:31). It is the collective prayer of the contributors to this volume that our churches might embrace the vision and potential of Watershed Discipleship. Because God is tented among us, right here.

References

Anderson, William and Clive Hicks. 1990. *Green Man: The Archetype of Our Oneness with the Earth*. London: HarperCollins.

Bahnson, Fred. 2013. *Soil and Sacrament: A Spiritual Memoir of Food and Faith*. New York: Simon and Schuster.

Basford, Kathleen. 1978. *The Green Man*. Cambridge: D. S. Brewer.

Colwell, Matthew. 2008. *Sabbath Economics: Household Practices*. Washington, DC: Tell the Word.

Cullman, Oscar. 1964. *Immortality of the Soul or Resurrection of the Dead? The Witness of the New Testament*. New York: Macmillan.

Davis, Ellen. 2009. *Scripture, Culture, and Agriculture: An Agrarian Reading of the Bible*. New York: Cambridge University Press.

Hiebert, Theodore. 1996. *The Yahwists's Landscape: Nature and Religion in Early Israel*. New York: Oxford University Press.

Klein, Naomi. 2014. "Why #BlackLivesMatter Should Transform the Climate Debate." *The Nation* online, December 12. (http://www.thenation.com/article/what-does-blacklivesmatter-have-do-climate-change/.)

Lorenzen, Thorwald. 1995. *Resurrection and Discipleship: Interpretive Models, Biblical Reflections, Theological Consequences*. Maryknoll, NY: Orbis.

Myers, Ched. 1993. "The Wilderness Temptations and the American Journey." In *Richard Rohr: Illuminations of His Life and Work*, edited by A. Ebert and P. Brockman, 143–57. New York: Crossroads.

———. 1994. *Who Will Roll Away the Stone? Discipleship Queries for First World Christians*. Maryknoll, NY: Orbis.

———. 2001. *The Biblical Vision of Sabbath Economics*. Washington, DC: Tell the Word.

———. 2004. "'To Serve and Preserve': The Genesis Commission to Earth Stewardship." *Sojourners*, March, 28–33.

———. 2007. "'The Cedar has Fallen!' The Prophetic Word vs. Imperial Clear-cutting." In *Earth and Word: Classic Sermons on Saving the Planet,* edited by David Rhoads, 211–13. London: Continuum.

———.2008. *Binding the Strong Man: A Political Reading of Mark's Story of Jesus.* Maryknoll, NY: Orbis.

———.2009. "Pay Attention to the Birds: A Bible Study on Luke 12." *Sojourners* 38:11 (December) 29–31, 53.

———.2012. "From Capital to Community: Discipleship as Defection in Jesus' Parable about a 'Manager of Injustice' (Lk 16:1–13)." In *Radical Christian Voices & Practice: Essays in Honour of Christopher Rowland,* edited by Z. Bennett and D. Gowler, 51–68. London: Oxford University Press.

———.2013. "From Garden to Tower (Genesis 1–11): Re-Visioning Our Origins." In *Buffalo Shout, Salmon Cry: Conversations on Creation, Land Justice and Life Together,* edited by Steve Heinrichs, 109–26. Harrisburg, PA: Herald.

———.2014b. "Jesus Talks to Plants: Agrarian Wisdom and Earth Symbolism." In *A Faith Encompassing All Creation: Addressing Commonly Asked Questions about Christian Care for the Environment,* edited by Tripp York and Andy Alexis-Baker, 100–110. Eugene, OR: Cascade.

———.2014a. "Reinhabiting the River of Life (Rev 22:1–2): Rehydration, Redemption, and Watershed Discipleship." *Missio Dei: A Journal of Missional Theology and Praxis* 5 (2), August (http://missiodeijournal.com/article.php?issue=md-5-2&author=md-5-2-myers).

Myers, Ched and Elaine Enns. 2009. *Ambassadors of Reconciliation, Vol I.* Maryknoll, NY: Orbis.

Perkinson, James. 2013. *Messianism against Christology: Resistance Movement, Folk Arts, and Empire.* New York: Palgrave Macmillan.

Snyder, Gary. 1990. *The Practice of the Wild.* San Francisco: Northpoint.

Sutterfield, Ragan. 2013. *Cultivating Reality: How the Soil Might Save Us.* Eugene, OR: Cascade.

Titterington, David. 2014. " Landscape Theology." Uploaded Feb 20. (http://landscapetheology.blogspot.com/2014/02/where-are-you-from.html).

Wenger, Samuel E. 2007. *A tour of ten important Anabaptist and Reformed sites in rural Switzerland: featuring Amish and Mennonite sites in the Bernese Oberland and Schwarzenburgerland in the Canton of Bern.* Anabaptist and Reformed tour guides for Switzerland, vol. 3. Morgantown, PA: Masthof.

Woodley, Randy. 2012. *Shalom and the Community of Creation: An Indigenous Vision.* Grand Rapids: Eerdmans.

Index

Index

Index

United Nations, 3, 78, 80, 83

village, 182, 184, 196–97
violence, 3, 5, 9, 17, 31, 37, 48, 63, 77,
    85, 91–92, 102-, 104, 106, 119,
    131–34, 147, 172, 212–13

Wade in the Water, 76, 82
water harvesting, 71, 213
water shut-offs, 79–86, 92, 211
Water Walkers, xii, xiii, xv, 213
watershed
    definition of, 10–11
    mind, xiii-vix

councils, 18
discipleship (definition), 1–2
conquest, 26, 34–36, 38
ecclesiology, 210–216
Wawiatonong, 79
West Atlanta Watershed Alliance,
    107–19
works of mercy, 168, 169, 171, 173
worship, 112, 128, 129, 139–40, 171,
    196, 210, 211
Wylie-Kellermann, Jeanie, 75–77

Zechariah, book of, 190
zero waste, 164, 165

CPSIA information can be obtained
at www.ICGtesting.com
Printed in the USA
LVHW052351260423
745302LV00003B/460

9 781498 280761